501 DINOSAUR JOKE-TIVITIES

Riddles, Puzzles, Fun Facts, Cartoons, Tongue Twisters, and Other Giggles!

HIGHLIGHTS PRESS
Honesdale, Pennsylvania

SAY WHAT?!

Dinosaur names can look scary, so here's a handy pronunciation guide for all 101 real dinosaurs that are mentioned in this book.

Acrocanthosaurus (ah-kroh-KAN-tho-SAW-rus)

Albertosaurus (al-BURR-tuh-SAW-rus)

Allosaurus (AL-oh-SAW-rus)

Amazonsaurus (AM-uh-zahn-SAW-rus)

Anchiornis (an-kee-OR-nis)

Ankylosaurus (AN-kee-loh-SAW-rus)

Antrodemus (an-tro-DEE-muss)

Anzu (AHN-zoo)

Apatosaurus (uh-PAT-uh-SAW-rus)

Archaeopteryx (ARE-key-AWP-terr-icks)

Argentinosaurus (ARE-jen-TEEN-oh-SAW-rus)

Avaceratops (ay-va-SAIR-uh-tops)

Avimimus (AH-vee-MIM-mus)

Balaur (ball-OW-er)

Bambiraptor (bam-bee-RAP-tur)

Barapasaurus (BAR-rap-oh-SAW-rus)

Barosaurus (BAR-oh-SAW-rus)

Beibeilong (bay-bay-long)

Bellusaurus (bel-uh-SAW-rus)

Brachiosaurus (BRACK-ee-uh-SAW-rus)

Brachylophosaurus (BRACK-ee-lof-oh-SAW-rus)

Brontosaurus (BRON-toe-SAW-rus)

Camptosaurus (CAMP-toe-SAW-rus)

Ceratosaurus (sair-RAT-oh-SAW-rus)

Corythosaurus (kor-ITH-o-SAW-rus)

Crichtonsaurus (KRY-ten-SAW-rus)

Diabloceratops (dee-AH-bloh-SAIR-uh-tops)

Diamantinasaurus (di-ah-man-TIN-uh-SAW-rush)

Dilong (DEE-long)

Diplodocus (dih-PLAW-duh-kus)

Draconyx (drak-ON-icks)

Dracorex (DRAK-o-rex)

Dracovenator (drah-KO-ven-NAY-tuhr)

Dryosaurus (DRY-o-SAW-rus)

Edmontonia (ED-mawn-TOH-nee-uh)

Edmontosaurus (ed-MON-to-SAW-rus)

Elaphrosaurus (ee-LAUGH-roh-SAW-rus)

Fabrosaurus (FAB-ruh-SAW-rus)

Falcarius (fall-CARE-ee-us)

Fruitadens (FROO-tah-dens)

Fukuiraptor (foo-KOO-ee-RAP-tur)

Galeamopus (gail-aim-uh-puss)

Gallimimus (Gal-ih-MIME-us)

Giganotosaurus (jih-guh-NOH-toh-SAW-rus)

Gorgosaurus (GORE-goh-SAW-rus)

Gryponyx (grip-ON-icks)

Gryposaurus (grip-oh-SAW-rus)

Hadrosaurus (HAD-row-SAW-rus)

Haya (hah-yah)

Hippodraco (hip-o-DRAH-co)

Hungarosaurus (hun-GAH-ro-SAW-rus)

Iguanodon (e-GWAH-no-don)

Irritator (EAR-ih-tay-tor)

Kol (khol)

Kritosaurus (KRIT-oh-SAW-rus)

Lambeosaurus (LAM-bee-o-SAW-rus)

Lamplughsaura (LAHM-plu-SAW-ruh)

Maiasaura (MY-uh-SAW-ruh)

Maxakalisaurus (MAX-a-KAH-lee-SAW-rus)

Megalosaurus (MEG-uh-low-SAW-rus)

Scientists have found about one thousand kinds of dinosaurs. But several new kinds are being discovered every year.

That means there may be hundreds or even thousands of different dinosaur types still out there to be discovered. Maybe someday you will find some of them!

Mei (may)

Micropachycephalosaurus
(MIKE-row-PACK-ee-SEF-uh-low-SAW-rus)

Microraptor (MY-kroh-RAP-tur)

Mojoceratops (mo-jo-SAIR-uh-tops)

Nanosaurus (NAN-uh-SAW-rus)

Nanotyrannus (NAN-o-tye-RAN-us)

Ornitholestes (or-nith-oh-LESS-teez)

Oviraptor (OH-vih-RAP-tur)

Paluxysaurus (puh-LUHK-see-SAW-rus)

Parasaurolophus
(PAHR-uh-SAW-ruh-LOW-fus)

Pawpawsaurus (paw-paw-SAW-rus)

Pentaceratops (PEN-tuh-SAIR-uh-tops)

Pisanosaurus (pee-SAHN-o-SAW-rus)

Proa (pro-uh)

Rhinorex (RYE-no-REX)

Saltasaurus (SAWL-tuh-SAW-rus)

Sarahsaurus (SAH-ruh-SAW-rus)

Sauroposeidon
(SAW-roh-poh-SIGH-dun)

Serendipaceratops
(seh-ren-DIP-uh-SAIR-uh-tops)

Shaochilong (sha-chi-LONG)

Spinosaurus (SPY-nuh-SAW-rus)

Stegoceras (steg-oh-SAIR-us)

Stegosaurus (STEG-uh-SAW-rus)

Supersaurus (soo-per-SAW-rus)

Syntarsus (sin-TAR-sus)

Tawa (ta-WAH)

Thescelosaurus (THES-ke-lo-SAW-rus)

Trachodon (TRACK-oh-don)

Triceratops (try-SAIR-uh-tops)

Troodon (TROH-oh-don)

Tyrannosaurus rex
(tye-RAN-uh-SAW-rus rex)

Utahraptor (YOU-taw-RAP-tur)

Velociraptor (veh-LAW-sih-RAP-tur)

Vulcanodon (vul-CAN-uh-don)

Wannanosaurus
(wah-NAHN-uh-SAW-rus)

Wendiceratops
(WEN-dee-SAIR-uh-tops)

Yi qi (EE-chee)

Yinlong (YIN-long)

Yutyrannus (YOU-tie-RAN-us)

Zby (zee-bee)

Zuul (ZOOL)

Not-a-Dinosaur
These reptiles lived at the same time as dinosaurs:

Ichthyosaur (ick-THEE-uh-sore)

Jeholopterus (je-hol-OP-ter-us)

Mosasaur (MO-suh-sore)

Nothosaur (NO-thuh-sore)

Plesiosaur (PLEE-see-uh-sore)

Pterodactyl (tair-uh-DACK-tull)

Pterosaur (TAIR-uh-sore)

Hello, I am ?

IT'S GREEK TO ME!

The word dinosaur comes from the ancient Greek words *deinos* (terrible) and *sauros* (lizard). Even though dinosaurs aren't actually lizards, when people first found dinosaur fossils, they thought they were. Most dinosaurs are named using Greek or Latin root words, often describing the dinosaur's features. Here's what some of those root words mean.

root word = meaning

allo = different

bronto = thunder

cerato = horn

diplo = double

docus = beam

maia = good mother

micro = small

ops = face

ovi = egg

penta = five

raptor = robber

sauros = lizard

stego = roof

tri = three

tyrannos = tyrant

velox = swift

Why is the word "dinosaur" not really a misnomer?

Because dinosaurs were terrible at being lizards.

FUN FACT
· · · · · · · · · · · · · · ·
THE *BRONTOSAURUS* IS BACK!
Since 1903, scientists thought that the name "Brontosaurus" was mistakenly given to a dinosaur that had already been named *Apatosaurus*. However, a study published in 2015 suggests that the *Apatosaurus* and *Brontosaurus* fossils are different enough to each keep their own names.

Using the key on the previous page, figure out what these dinosaur names mean.

Allosaurus _____

Brontosaurus _____

Diplodocus _____

Maiasaura _____

Microraptor _____

Oviraptor _____

Pentaceratops _____

Stegosaurus _____

Triceratops _____

Tyrannosaurus _____

Velociraptor _____

Use the root words to create a new dinosaur name.

_____

DRAW

a picture of it here.

Try to say these

TONGUE TWISTERS

three times, fast.

"Please!" paleontologists pleaded.

Dr. Docker determinedly digs for dinosaur fossils.

The paleontologist proposed posing proudly in the picture.

Flossie found fifteen fossils and Fred found five.

The paleontologist's experiment exceeded expectations.

Why was the fossil so tense?

He was under a lot of pressure.

DIG THIS!

Can you help the paleontologist find her way to the fossil dig?

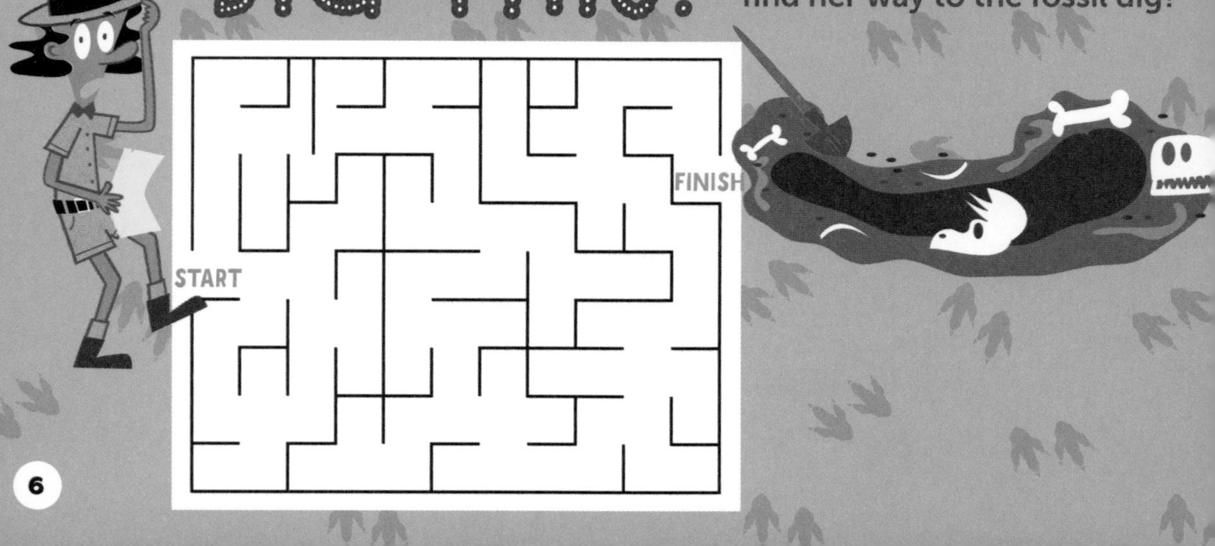

START

FINISH

Bones, grayish-yellow,
From a tall, beastly fellow,
Were found, unearthed,
And pulled from the dirt;
Then puzzled together
With wires and tethers—
Transformed from a pile
To a wide, toothy smile.

Why was the
dinosaur skeleton
so serious?
. . . .
His funny bone
was missing.

7

WHAT'S WRONG?

Which things in this picture are silly? It's up to you!

FUN FACT

Fossils are most frequently found in sedimentary rocks, like shale and limestone.

Knock, knock.
Who's there?
Shale.
Shale who?
Shale we go see the new fossil exhibit?

BBQ

HOT   SWEET

WORD FOR WORDS

At 60 feet tall, the *Sauroposeidon* is one of the largest dinosaurs ever discovered. This dino is also huge when it comes to words. The letters in **SAUROPOSEIDON** can be used to make many other words. Use the clues below to come up with some of them.

Which dinosaur loved to have its picture taken?

Sauro-POSE-idon

SAUROPOSEIDON

1. Used for cleaning   ___ ___ ___ ___

2. Water that falls from the sky   ___ ___ ___ ___

3. A dried plum   ___ ___ ___ ___ ___

4. Something a chef wears   ___ ___ ___ ___ ___

5. A curved utensil   ___ ___ ___ ___ ___

6. An instrument with a keyboard   ___ ___ ___ ___ ___ ___

7. Opposite of outdoor   ___ ___ ___ ___ ___ ___

8. An ice-cream dessert   ___ ___ ___ ___ ___ ___

9. A small creature with eight legs   ___ ___ ___ ___ ___ ___

10. Opposite of sunset   ___ ___ ___ ___ ___ ___

Can you find
22
PAINTBRUSHES
hidden in this scene?

Why did sauropods have long necks? How did they protect themselves from other dinosaurs?

No one knows for sure, but we have some reasonable ideas. *Brachiosaurus* could reach nearly five stories high. Maybe it ate leaves from high in the trees the way a giraffe does. But most plant eaters' necks were not built to reach up. *Apatosaurus* might have used its neck to save the energy needed to move its huge body. It could have stopped often to eat plants far and wide, like a huge vacuum cleaner.

The huge size of long-necked dinosaurs gave a lot of protection. Some of these big plant eaters left footprints more than three feet around—that's big enough to take a bath in!

Also, one scientist thinks that giant sauropods may have snapped their long tails like giant bullwhips. A fast snap of that giant tail might have made a booming sound by moving air even faster than the speed of sound—more than 600 miles per hour!

> What did the young *Diplodocus* think of his pop?
>
> He really looked up to him.

Did dinosaur dragons ever live?

Dragons are imaginary, and dinosaurs were real. However, dragons are "relatives" of dinosaurs in one sense. The myth of dragons might have been inspired in many cultures by the discovery of dinosaur bones, which the people who found them had trouble explaining.

In Chinese, the word for "dragon" and "dinosaur" is the same: *konglong*.

WRITE

each set of colored letters on the corresponding lines to figure out six dinosaurs whose names mean "dragon."

D H S D D R H Y R A I A C P I A O P O I V C N C E O H N
D I L O A L L O T R O N A O N N C G Y O N X R O G G

"emperor dragon" _____

"dragon claw" _____

"dragon hunter" _____

"horse dragon" _____

"shark-toothed dragon" _____

"hidden dragon" _____

LAUGH ATTACK

Why did the dinosaur cross the road?
The chicken hadn't evolved yet.

What did early dinosaurs get stuck in on the way to work?
A Triassic jam

Why can't a dinosaur ride a bicycle?
Because it doesn't have a thumb to ring the bell

Where do dinosaurs like to go on vacation?
O-claw-homa

What happened when the dinosaur took the train home?
His mom made him bring it back.

How do we know dinosaurs raced competitively?
Scientists discovered dinosaur tracks.

What was the first car Henry Fordasaurus invented?
A Model T. rex

What made the dinosaur's car stop?
A flat Tire-annosaurus

ROAD WORK AHEAD

HIGHWAY CONSTRUCTION COMPLETION: 66 million Years

HIDE AND SHRIEK

Can you find 15 differences between these two pictures?

Try to say these

TONGUE TWISTERS

three times, fast.

The thin *Triceratops* turned toward two trees.

Shirley, I'm certain that *Stegosaurus* saw us.

What do dinosaurs have that no other animals have?
Baby dinosaurs

How can you best raise a baby dinosaur?
With a crane

How do baby dinosaurs hatch?
They eggs-it.

KIDS' SCIENCE QUESTIONS

How big was a baby *T. rex*?

When we think of *Tyrannosaurus rex*, we think BIG. But the smallest *T. rex* skeleton found so far is the size of a golden retriever. Scientists think this dinosaur was two years old. A hatchling *T. rex* would have been about the size of a cat. Yet it grew into a 42-foot-long adult that weighed about 6 tons and stood over 13 feet tall. That is a lot of growing!

To figure out how fast *T. rex* grew, scientists compared the body size and age of seven *T. rex* specimens. They discovered that these dinosaurs grew fastest between the ages of 14 and 18. A teenage *T. rex* gained almost 5 pounds each day. In a year, a growing *T. rex* gained about half the weight of a Volkswagen Beetle. They reached adult size by their early twenties.

BABY DINOS

To find the answer to the riddle below, first cross out all the pairs of matching letters. Then write the remaining letters in order in the spaces beneath the riddle.

BB	EE	WH	FF	VV	GG	JJ
DD	SS	AA	EE	EN	AA	OO
LL	IT	NN	YY	RR	FF	UU
QQ	WW	HH	DR	PP	DD	NN
BB	IB	XX	MM	CC	YY	BL
GG	KK	AA	ZZ	ES	PP	TT

When is a baby dinosaur good at basketball?

___ ___ ___ ___ ___ ___ ___

___ ___ ___ ___ ___ ___ ___

TYRANNOSAURUS WHO?

Tyrannosaurus REX may be king, but what sillysaurs do
you get when you cross a dinosaur with something else?
To find out, match up these riddles with their punch lines.

What do you get when you cross a dinosaur . . .

_____ **1.** with the alphabet?

_____ **2.** with a bank?

_____ **3.** with a bodybuilder?

_____ **4.** with a chicken?

_____ **5.** with a cowboy?

_____ **6.** with an explorer?

_____ **7.** with a giraffe?

_____ **8.** with an optometrist?

_____ **9.** with a movie theater?

_____ **10.** with a wizard?

A. Tyrannosaurus checks

B. Tyrannosaurus flex

C. Tyrannosaurus hex

D. Tyrannosaurus multiplex

E. Tyrannosaurus necks

F. Tyrannosaurus pecks

G. Tyrannosaurus specs

H. Tyrannosaurus Tex

I. Tyrannosaurus treks

J. Tyrannosaurus X

LAUGH ATTACK

Knock, knock.
Who's there?
T. rex.
T. rex *who?*
**There's a *T. rex* at your
door and you want to
know its name?**

Knock, knock.
Who's there?
Adam.
Adam who?
**Adam my way, please.
There's a *T. rex* chasing me!**

Knock, knock.
Who's there?
Dinosaur go.
Dinosaur go who?
**Dinosaurs don't go who.
They go ROAR!**

Knock, knock.
Who's there?
Stan.
Stan who?
**Stan back when
a dinosaur sneezes!**

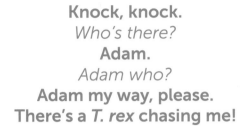

Knock, knock.
Who's there?
Dewey.
Dewey who?
**Dewey know why the
dinosaurs went extinct?**

DE
DINO

DE
TAIL

DE
END

Knock, knock.
Who's there?
Detail.
Detail who?
**De-tail of de dino
is on de end.**

A DAY AT THE MUSEUM

A natural history museum is a fun place to visit—unless you're a dinosaur!
Can you find the hidden objects in this scene?

 slice of cake

 candy corn

 battery

 ax

 muffin

 carrot

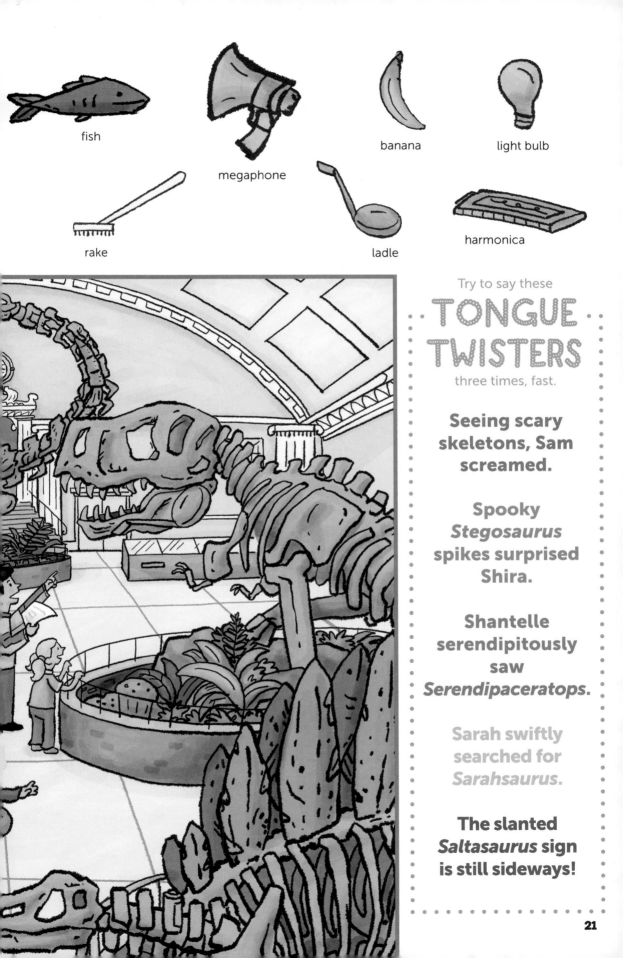

fish

megaphone

banana

light bulb

rake

ladle

harmonica

Try to say these

TONGUE TWISTERS

three times, fast.

Seeing scary skeletons, Sam screamed.

Spooky _Stegosaurus_ spikes surprised Shira.

Shantelle serendipitously saw _Serendipaceratops._

Sarah swiftly searched for _Sarahsaurus._

The slanted _Saltasaurus_ sign is still sideways!

LIVIN' LARGE

How many of these **TRUE/FALSE** statements can you answer correctly?

1. The largest meat-eating dinosaur was *Spinosaurus*, which spent most of its life in the water, possibly eating fish that were about the size of modern-day cars.

T OR F

5. *Velociraptor* was covered in feathers.

T OR F

6. Some giant dinosaurs like *Diplodocus* were longer than a basketball court.

T OR F

2. Remains of dinosaur shoes, size 54 EEE, have been discovered in Armenia.

T OR F

7. *T. rexes* invented the selfie stick because their arms were so short.

T OR F

3. The time between when *Stegosaurus* existed and when *Tyrannosaurus rex* existed is greater than the time between when *T. rex* lived and when humans appeared.

T OR F

8. Long tails helped dinosaurs keep their balance while doing ballet.

T OR F

4. Dinosaurs existed on earth longer than humans have (so far).

T OR F

TERRIFIC TOYS

Every toy but one has an exact match.
Can you find the **one toy without a match**?

Customer: How much is that *Parasaurolophus* toy?

Clerk: Ten dollars, ma'am.

Customer: I'll take it. Will you send me the bill?

Clerk: I'm sorry, ma'am. You'll have to take the whole dinosaur.

SHHHHHH!

Pssst! There are **21** words with silent letters hidden in this grid. Look for them up, down, across, and diagonally. After you've circled them all, write the leftover letters in order from left to right and top to bottom. They will spell out the answer to the riddle. We've circled the first word to get you started.

BALLET
CLIMB
COMB
DEPOT
GHOST
GNAW
HONEST
HOUR
KNEE
KNIGHT
KNOB

KNOCK
KNOT
LAMB
SWORD
THUMB
TWO
WHALE
WRIST
WRITE
WRONG

C	O	M	B	G	A	P	T	E	H
L	G	N	A	W	N	E	R	L	O
I	O	L	L	R	D	O	A	A	N
M	C	A	L	I	T	Y	R	H	E
B	L	M	E	S	B	E	C	W	S
A	U	B	T	T	S	E	R	T	T
H	K	N	O	C	K	I	E	P	I
T	H	U	M	B	T	W	O	E	S
S	S	A	L	E	O	O	E	W	W
O	A	Y	S	S	N	N	P	I	O
H	O	U	R	L	K	E	K	E	R
G	K	N	I	G	H	T	N	T	D

What is a librarian's favorite prehistoric creature?

__ _____,

_____ ____

__ ___ _____

__ __ __ __ __ __.

FIELD TRIP

What two things can't a dinosaur eat for dinner?

Breakfast and lunch

Tim's class went to the [museum]. Tim couldn't wait to see the [dinosaurs].

"Look at those sharp [teeth]!" said Tim. "They look like [knives]."

"*Allosaurus* used its sharp [teeth] to eat [meat]," said the guide.

"This dinosaur has [teeth] that look like [spoons]," said Tim.

"*Apatosaurus* used its [teeth] to eat [plants]," said the guide.

"Some [plant]-eaters also swallowed [stones] to help them grind their food."

"I'm hungry for lunch," said Tim, "but I don't want to eat [stones]!"

"Are you a [meat]-eater then?" asked the guide.

Tim looked in his [lunch box]. "Today, I'm going to be a [sandwich]-eater!"

LAUGH ATTACK

What was a herbivore's favorite type of ice cream?
Mint chocolate chip, because they only ate greens

Knock, knock.
Who's there?
Meteor.
Meteor who?
Meteor snacks are a carnivore's favorite.

A book never written:
Plant Eaters
by Herb Ivore.

Abby: There are 30 carnivores and 28 herbivores. How many didn't?
Gabby: I don't get it. How many didn't what?
Abby: Out of the 30 carnivores, 20 ate herbivores, so 10 didn't.

Why is a herbivore a bad dinner guest?
It eats, leaves.

"How many times have I told you not to play with your food?"

food?

One day, the *Rhinorex* got tired of eating plants all the time. He turned to his friend and said, "I think becoming a herbivore was a missed steak."

How does a carnivore greet a herbivore?
"Pleased to eat you."

How do dinosaurs bake a cake?
From scratch

What is a paleontologist's favorite book?

The dig-tionary

How many bones did the paleontologist need to finish the dinosaur skeleton?

Just the last one

Sue: Do you like your new job as a paleontologist?
Martha: Yes, I dig it!

What is a paleontologist's favorite period?

Lunch period

Rock #1: Why are you so upset?
Rock #2: That paleontologist was picking on me!

A book never written:
How I Found a Fossil
by Doug Deep.

PALEONTOLOGY DEPARTMENT

BACK IN 66 MILLION YEARS

KIDS' SCIENCE QUESTIONS

How do you tell the difference between a dinosaur fossil and a regular bone?

A regular bone looks and feels different from a dinosaur fossil. Newer bone is made up mostly of calcium, which makes the bone nearly white. Fresh bone is also full of tiny empty spaces, which make it light in weight. In a dinosaur fossil, minerals have filled many of the tiny spaces and have become hard, like rock. The minerals make the bone darker and heavier.

DOUBLE DIG

Can you find **14** differences between these two dig sites?

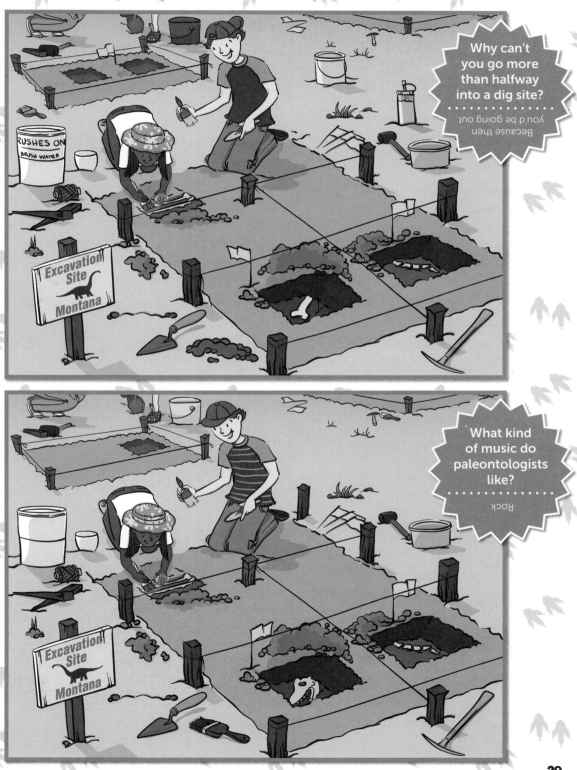

Why can't you go more than halfway into a dig site?

Because then you'd be going out

What kind of music do paleontologists like?

Rock

LAUGH ATTACK

Chloe: Want to hear a funny joke about an orthodontist dinosaur?
Amy: Sure.
Chloe: OK, brace yourself!

If a dinosaur has 24 candy bars and eats 21 of them, what does he have?
Probably a cavity

Why did the dinosaur eat the sofa, the chair, and the loveseat?
He had a suite tooth.

What do you get when a dinosaur sneezes?
Out of the way

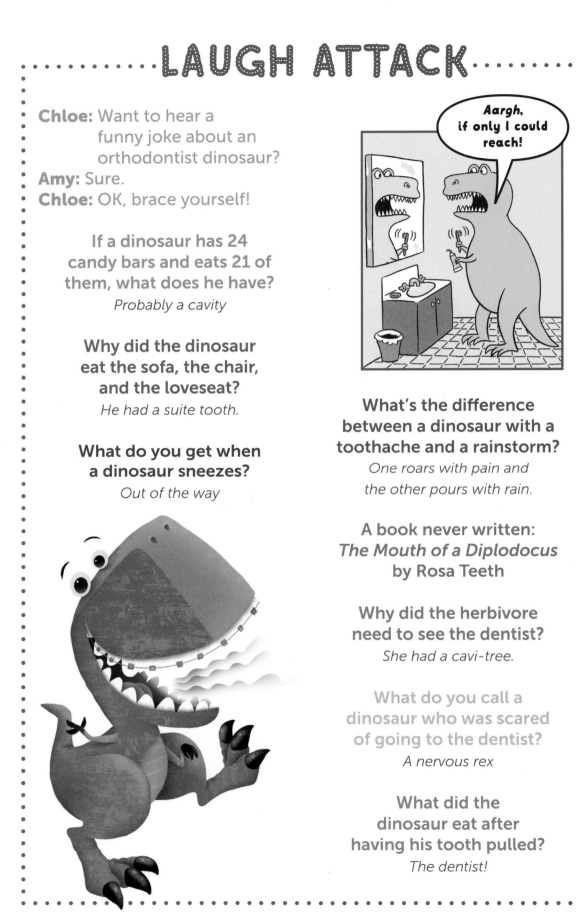

Aargh, if only I could reach!

What's the difference between a dinosaur with a toothache and a rainstorm?
One roars with pain and the other pours with rain.

A book never written:
The Mouth of a Diplodocus
by Rosa Teeth

Why did the herbivore need to see the dentist?
She had a cavi-tree.

What do you call a dinosaur who was scared of going to the dentist?
A nervous rex

What did the dinosaur eat after having his tooth pulled?
The dentist!

TOOTHBRUSH CODE

There are three jokes about dinosaurs on this page.
Use the picture code to fill in the letters and finish the jokes.

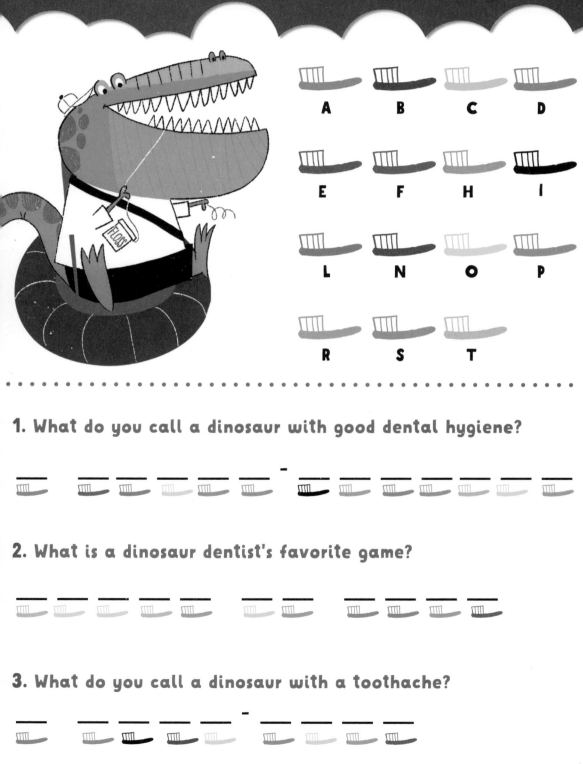

1. What do you call a dinosaur with good dental hygiene?

2. What is a dinosaur dentist's favorite game?

3. What do you call a dinosaur with a toothache?

IF I HAD A PET DINOSAUR

Pet dinosaurs never get fleas.
They don't like to chew on shoes.

They never chase cats up trees.
They read, not eat, the news.

Pet dinosaurs are good at catch.
They know all kinds of tricks.

They're always careful not to scratch.
They can count from one to six.

Pet dinosaurs aren't dangerous.
They're really tons of fun.

The problem with pet dinosaurs is—
I don't know! Can I have one?

LAUGH ATTACK

What do you call a near-sighted dinosaur's dog?

Doyouthinkhesaurus rex

Jake: I don't know what to do. I lost my pet *Iguanodon*!
Eli: Why don't you put an ad in the paper?
Jake: What good would that do? He can't read!

A book never written:
How to Pet a Dinosaur
by Bea Careful

McKayla: I wish I had enough money to buy a *Giganotosaurus*.
Augie: Why would you want a dinosaur?
McKayla: I don't. I just want that much money.

A book never written:
Bathing Your Dino
by Manny Scratches

Penny: What's your dinosaur's name?
Lucy: Ginger.
Penny: Does Ginger bite?
Lucy: No, but Ginger snaps.

Jason: Why are you crying?
Riley: Because I wanted to get a dinosaur for my baby brother.
Jason: That's no reason to cry.
Riley: Yes it is! No one would trade with me!

What do you get when you cross a dinosaur and a dog?

Jurassic Bark

"I call him Rex because he wrecks everything he sees."

DINOSAUR GAMES

Every answer in this puzzle is made up of letters from the phrase **DINOSAUR GAMES**. Roar your way to a win by filling all the answers in!

ACROSS

2. An imaginary pool of water in the desert

4. You breathe this.

5. Meat in a tube

6. A version of a magazine

7. "Goodbye" in Spanish

8. Wash your hands to get rid of these.

9. A mythical fire-breathing creature

11. This is at the bottom of the tub.

14. Done without following a plan or pattern

16. A thought or belief

18. This can be paved or unpaved.

19. Fluffy whipped dessert

20. Ingredient in 19 Across

23. Jeans are made from this material.

24. What was that strange ＿＿＿?

25. A part within a larger place

27. Order off this at 22 Down.

DOWN

1. Chairs and people have these.

3. Grandpa's wife

5. Winter, spring, summer, or fall

10. A very smart person

12. Listen to this in the car.

13. A musical instrument with sticks

15. Lion's or horse's hair

17. Someone who watches and protects something

21. "For amber waves of ＿＿＿"

22. Eat here 24 hours a day.

24. Most people have a first, middle, and last one of these.

25. How old you are

26. A long time ＿＿＿

What is a dinosaur's favorite game?

Swallow the leader

34

How did dinosaurs stay in shape?

They went to the jungle gym.

Why do *Stegosaurus* never lose games?

Because they always have the most points

SILLYSAURS

BRICKIOSAURUS

SAWASAURUS

APANASAURUS

STEGOWALRUS

SPIDERSAURUS

TYRANNOSAURUS ROCKS

FEARSOME OR PHONEY?

Six of the dinosaur names listed below are real and six are made up.
Circle the real names and then make up a few of your own.

Brachiosaurus

Trainasaurus Wrecks

Tricherrytops

Allosaurus

Apatosaurus

Whineodon

Stellaceratops

Iguanodon

Megalosaurus

Iwanasaurus

Tetrahedrasaurus

Sarahsaurus

_____

_____

_____

_____

DRAW

your own sillysaur here, then give it a name.

HOW BEASTLY!

At the Cretaceous Museum, the fossils are also code crackers. Use the list of dinosaurs to solve this puzzle. Each coded space has two numbers. The first number tells you which dinosaur to look at; the second number tells you which letter in that dinosaur to use. For example, the first coded letter is **2-3**. The 2 tells you to go to **AVACERATOPS**. Count **3** letters in, and you've got an **A**. Fill in the rest to unearth these fossil jokes.

> ### FUN FACT
> The North Carolina Museum of Natural Sciences boasts the world's most complete skeleton of an *Acrocanthosaurus*—a dinosaur known as "Terror of the South" and "Beast of the Southeast."

Dinosaurs on Display

1. ACROCANTHOSAURUS
2. AVACERATOPS
3. BAMBIRAPTOR
4. DIABLOCERATOPS
5. FALCARIUS
6. GORGOSAURUS
7. KRITOSAURUS
8. MOJOCERATOPS
9. PALUXYSAURUS
10. PAWPAWSAURUS

What do you call a 66-million-year-old dinosaur?

___   ___ ___ ___ ___ ___ ___
2-3   5-1   8-4   4-14   6-6   7-3   9-3

How do you greet a French fossil?

___ ___ ___ ___ - ___ ___ ___!"
3-1   6-2   1-7   4-8   8-3   3-10   9-9   10-10

How do fossils get their mail?

___ ___   ___ ___ ___ ___
3-1   9-6   4-4   2-9   1-7   9-6

___ ___ ___ ___ ___ ___ ___
2-5   9-5   10-4   8-7   4-8   5-9   7-11

What did the fossil say when he got angry with another fossil?

___   ___ ___ ___ ___   ___
5-7   1-9   10-5   2-2   8-6   6-7

___ ___ ___ ___   ___ ___
3-4   7-5   1-7   4-8   7-4   2-10

___ ___ ___ ___   ___ ___ ___ ___
10-1   5-7   1-2   7-1   10-6   3-5   7-4   1-9

"

___ ___ ___.
9-6   4-12   5-8

CHECK . . . AND DOUBLE CHECK

Compare these two pictures.
Can you find **18** differences?

LAUGH ATTACK

**Why does a *Brontosaurus*
have such a long neck?**

Because its feet smell

**Why are *Apatosaurus*
so slow to apologize?**

*It takes them a long time
to swallow their pride.*

A book never written:
Long Necks
by Sara Pods

Knock, knock.
Who's there?
Justin.
Justin who?
Justin case an asteroid comes,
I knitted you a sweater.

**Why should you never
ask a *Diplodocus* to
read you a story?**

*Because their tails
are so long*

TIC TAC ROW

Each of these dinos has something in common with the other
two dinos in the same row—across, down, and diagonally.
For example, in the top row across, each dinosaur has spikes.
Can you tell what's alike in each row?

When does a
dinosaur say
"quack"?

When he's trying to
learn a new language

SCRAMBLED WORDS

We've jumbled the names of 10 dino-related words. Can you unscramble each set of letters and find the words? Once you have them all, read down the column of boxes to learn the answer to this riddle:

What did dinosaurs do when it rained?

FTOOPTRIN ___ ___ ___ ___ ___ ___ ___ ___ ___

HETET ___ ___ ___ ___ ___

TEXTINC ___ ___ ___ ___ ___ ___ ___

ASCRY ___ ___ ___ ___ ___

GEG ___ ___ ___

IFLOSS ___ ___ ___ ___ ___ ___

ESKLTEON ___ ___ ___ ___ ___ ___ ___ ___

WLAC ___ ___ ___ ___

PRHISTCIORE ___ ___ ___ ___ ___ ___ ___ ___ ___ ___ ___

TPREDROA ___ ___ ___ ___ ___ ___ ___ ___

LAUGH ATTACK

How did dinosaurs tell the weather?
They looked out the window.

Ethan: The weather forecast says there is some ferocious rain outside.
William: I'll say! Forget about cats and dogs—it's raining dinosaurs!

Which dinosaur never needed rain boots?
The Dryosaurus

Did any dinosaurs get hit by lava?

Scientists have found some dinosaurs that seem to have died by being buried in volcanic ash as it fell from the sky, but it's unlikely that any were caught in the path of flowing lava.

Many bones of duck-billed dinosaurs in Montana are found in ash beds, suggesting that a volcano killed them. But for the most part, the dinosaurs weren't killed by volcanoes.

LAUGH ATTACK

Which dinosaur is full of lava?
Vulcanodon

What is a volcano?
A mountain with hiccups

What did the happy volcano say to the other volcano?
"I lava you!"

What is a volcano's favorite food?
Magma-roni and cheese

What did the angry volcano say to the other volcano?
"Stop int-erupt-ing me!"

What did the dinosaur say when he saw the volcano explode?
"What a lava-ly day!"

What did one tectonic plate say to the other when they bumped?
"Not my fault."

Where do scientists read facts about volcanoes?
In magma-zines

What do you get when you cross a volcano and a light bulb?
A lava lamp

A FORCEFUL KICK

Can you find **5** hidden books in this picture?

There once was a *T. rex* named Dwight,
Whose kick was as strong as his bite.
When he kicked the ball,
It sailed over the wall,
And flew all the way out of sight.

FUN FACT

T. rex had the strongest bite of any land animal—ever! Its maximum bite was almost 12,800 pounds of force. (A dog can bite up to 500 pounds of force.)

BOOKS NEVER WRITTEN

Check out the titles of these 10 funny books.
See how many you can match with the author.
(**HINT**: Try reading the authors' names out loud!)

__F__ 1. *How Big Are Dinosaurs?*

____ 2. *Top of the Food Chain*

____ 3. *Pterosaurs*

____ 4. *Archaeopteryx*

____ 5. *Volcanoes*

____ 6. *Chased by a Dinosaur*

____ 7. *Dinosaur Extinction*

____ 8. *Desert Weather*

____ 9. *How Far Can You Hear a Dinosaur Roar?*

____ 10. *A Triceratops's Diet*

A. Al O. Saurus

B. Anne E. Ruption

C. Aster Oid

D. Earl E. Bird

E. Fern San Palms

~~F.~~ Hugh Mongus

G. Myles A. Way

H. Ike N. Fly

I. Ronan Fast

J. Sandy Storm

What do a skeleton and a book have in common?
· · · · · · · · · · · · · · ·
Both of their spines are showing.

DINOS ON DISPLAY

Welcome to the museum's new dinosaur hall!
While everyone takes a look around, see if you can find
20 differences between these two pictures.

T. rex

Which two dinosaurs look exactly alike?

Knock, knock.
Who's there?
Annie.
Annie who?
Annie one see the new dinosaur exhibit at the museum?

Tyrannosaurus rex

How fast did *T. rex* run?

T. rex was probably faster than the animals it chased, such as ankylosaurs and duckbills. But that doesn't mean it had to be very fast, since scientists think those dinosaurs were not fast runners. Recent studies suggest that *T. rex* couldn't run at all. But some scientists think it could run at a speed of several miles an hour. No one is sure. If *T. rex* was a scavenger or ambush hunter, it might not have run much at all.

We aren't sure how fast dinosaurs ran. Scientists think some of them ran as fast as 25 miles per hour. The scientists measured the length of dinosaur steps in fossil footprints they have found. The fastest of all might have been the long-legged, ostrich-like dinosaurs.

Why did *T. rex* have short arms?

T. rex did have short arms, and perhaps that was because its weight in the front of its body was concentrated in its enormous jaws, the animal's main weapon. *T. rex*, like other two-legged dinosaurs, walked with its head almost level with its tail, like a teeter-totter that is balanced. *T. rex*'s arms couldn't touch each other because they were so short, but perhaps the arms and strong claws were used to hook into meat while the dinosaur was eating.

Why did *T. rex* never learn how to count to 10?

He only had four fingers.

MEGA MORT

Finish the poem by putting
the rhyming words in place.

Have you heard of Mega Mort?

Skating is his favorite __S__ __P__ __O__ __R__ __T__ .

Here and there and ___ ___ ___ ___ ___ ___ ___ ___ ___ ___ ,

Rolling in his trusty ___ ___ ___ ___ .

When they see that dino ___ ___ ___ ___ ,

Hear the crowd let out a ___ ___ ___ ___ !

Mort speeds along so super ___ ___ ___ ___ ,

He never, ever comes in ___ ___ ___ ___ !

He's always winning the top ___ ___ ___ ___ ___

Because, in his skates, he just ___ ___ ___ ___ ___ .

But wherever he may ___ ___ ___ ___ ,

This follows him to every ___ ___ ___ ___ ___ .

WORDLIST

EVERYWHERE
FAST
FLIES
LAST
PAIR
PLACE
PRIZE
RACE
ROAR
SOAR
SPORT

Write the highlighted letters in order
on the spaces below to solve the riddle.

What follows Mort everywhere he goes?

___ ___ ___ ___   ___ ___ ___ ___

FINISH

49

WHAT'S WRONG?

Which things in this picture are silly? It's up to you!

The post office clerk noticed a dinosaur standing in line during the holiday rush. "What are you doing at the post office?" asked the clerk, surprised. "Well," the dinosaur replied, "I have a package to mail."

LAUGH ATTACK

What is a dinosaur's least favorite reindeer?
Comet

Who delivers Christmas presents to dinosaurs?
Santa Claws

Where do dinosaurs mail their Christmas cards?
At the dead-letter office

What do dinosaurs put in their Christmas dinner?
Their teeth

What's a dinosaur's favorite Christmas carol?
"Jingle Bellusaurus"

What do you call a dinosaur at the North Pole?
Lost

Why did the dinosaur eat the Christmas lights?
Because he wanted a light snack

Where is a dinosaur when the Christmas lights turn off?
In the dark

Thanks so much! I wonder what it is?

10 TEN-TON TONGUE TWISTERS

Start out slowly if you want to last. Then say each twister three times, fast!

TEN
thirteen-ton
Triceratops

ONE
raucous
Wannanosaurus

NINE
nice
Nanotyrannus

TWO
Triassic
Tawa

EIGHT
great
Gryponyx

THREE
tricky
Troodon

SEVEN
conniving
Vulcanodon

FOUR
free
Fabrosaurus

SIX
sneaky
Spinosaurus

FIVE
irritating
Irritator

Use these clues to figure out what each of the dinosaurs above weighed. The weights range from 10 pounds to 46,000 pounds!

1. *Wannanosaurus* is the lightest, while *Spinosaurus* is the heaviest.

2. *Irritator* is one quarter the weight of *Vulcanodon,* which is 80 times heavier than *Troodon.*

3. *Gryponyx* is the same weight as *Irritator,* and 200 pounds heavier than *Nanotyrannus.*

4. *Troodon* is 11 times heavier than *Wannanosaurus.*

5. Two *Triceratops* together weigh 6,000 pounds more than one *Spinosaurus.*

6. *Fabrosaurus* is five pounds more than *Wannanosaurus* and 51 pounds less than *Tawa.*

Wannanosaurus _____

Tawa _____

Troodon _____

Fabrosaurus _____

Irritator _____

Spinosaurus _____

Vulcanodon _____

Gryponyx _____

Nanotyrannus _____

Triceratops _____

HELP THE CARTOONIST!

These cartoons are missing their captions. Write your own
punch lines, then check out the cartoonists' original gags on page 138.

A TRIO OF DINOS

Triceratops' favorite shape is a triangle!
Can you find **8** triangle-shaped hidden objects on this page?

paper airplane

safety cone

sailboat

party hat

ice-cream cone

sandwich

slice of pizza

traffic sign

Try to say these

T. REX TONGUE TWISTERS

three times, fast.

This is a *T. rex*'s X-ray.   *T. rex* tried trick-or-treating.

T. rex **tripped twice.**   **Take a trek in *T. rex*'s tracks.**

T. rex ate eight eights.   **This *T. rex* is perplexed.**

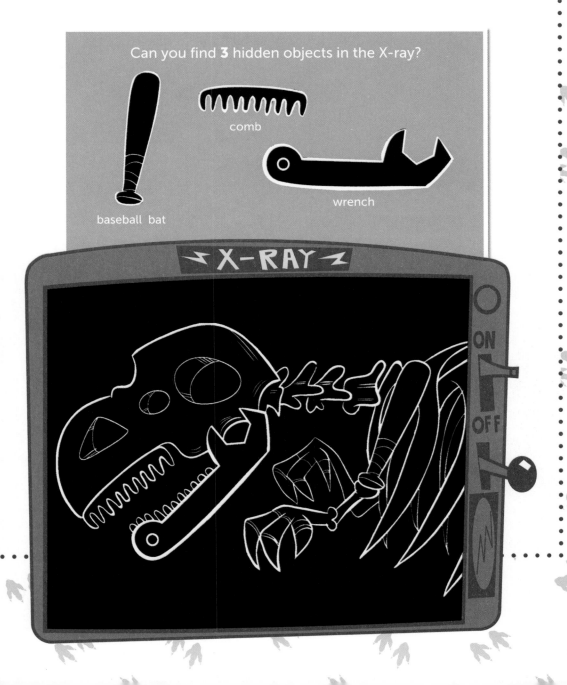

Can you find **3** hidden objects in the X-ray?

comb

wrench

baseball bat

X-RAY

ON

OFF

DINO-CHORUS

Each of these dinosaurs has a duet partner.
How many pairs of matching singers can you find?

There once was an *Apatosaurus* who was friends with a *Tyrannosaurus*. They both liked to sing, and so every spring they sang in a dinosaur chorus.

If two dinosaurs try out for choir, which one will be chosen?

The one with better scales

LAUGH ATTACK

What did the pterodactyl say when it was flying?
"I can saur!"

Who taught pterosaurs how to fly?
Nobody—they just winged it.

Why did the pterodactyl get a ticket?
It broke the law of gravity.

Why was the pterodactyl surprised after his meal?
Because he had a very big bill

How do pterodactyls fly in the rain?
They use their wing-shield wipers.

What is the difference between a pterodactyl and a parrot?
You'd know the answer if you ever let a pterodactyl sit on your shoulder.

Knock, knock.
Who's there?
Tara.
Tara who?
Tara-dactyls weren't dinosaurs. They were flying reptiles!

KIDS' SCIENCE QUESTIONS

Did pterodactyls fly or glide?

"How can we fly in a V formation? That letter hasn't been invented yet!"

Pterodactyls could fly AND glide. Gliding saves energy, but at some point, pterodactyls needed to flap their wings to stay in the air. Pterodactyls were actually reptiles, not dinosaurs. Some of them were quite large, with a wingspan of more than twenty feet!

REIGN OF TERROR

What was the scariest prehistoric animal? To find out, follow the directions below. Each sentence will tell you where one letter is in the grid. Once you've found it, write it in the correct space below the riddle.

1. Look above the **X** for this letter.
2. This letter is two down from the **B**.
3. This letter is between two **P**'s.
4. This letter is the only vowel in the last row.
5. This is the first letter in the grid.
6. This is the second to last letter in the second row.
7. Look two below the **K** for this letter.
8. This letter is the first and last of its row.
9. This letter is sandwiched between two **O**'s.
10. This letter appears side by side in the same row.

A	J	H	C	Z	M	P
V	S	A	W	K	Y	B
C	P	T	P	G	U	C
A	O	R	O	H	T	L
R	X	U	E	W	I	Z
E	Q	F	S	D	D	L

What was the scariest prehistoric animal?

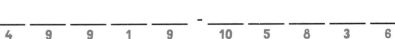

___ ___ ___
 3   7   4

___ ___ ___ ___ ___ ___ - ___ ___ ___ ___ ___ ___
 3   4   9   9   1   9   10   5   8   3   6   2

LAUGH ATTACK

Knock, knock.
Who's there?
Four eggs.
Four eggs who?
Four eggs-ample, there are only three categories of dinosaur eggs.

How did the dinosaur get off the highway?
He took the eggs-it.

Why are dinosaurs no longer around?
Because their eggs stink

WHICH EGG?

Follow the path to see which egg the dinosaur hatched from.

START

DINOSAUR EGGS

To find the answer to the riddle below, first cross out all the pairs of matching letters. Then write the remaining letters in order in the spaces beneath the riddle.

AA TT QQ SS SH EE CC
ED LL JJ VV BB ID HH
OO UU YY NT FF WW HA
EE DD NN HH PP VE RR
SS AC XX KK HA AA GG
IR MM ZZ YY II LL OO

Why did the *Iguanodon* sit on her eggs?

___ ___ ___   ___ ___ ___ ___ ___ '___

___ ___ ___ ___   ___   ___ ___ ___ ___ ___ ___.

CONSTRUCTION CREW

These workers are really raising the roof!
Can you find the hidden objects in this scene?

plunger

fly swatter

ladle

hat

drinking straw

hairbrush

pencil

flashlight

domino

wedge of orange

crown

fishhook

spoon

paper airplane

diamond

LAUGH ATTACK

What type of tool does a prehistoric reptile carpenter use?

A dino-saw

Garin: Do you want to hear a joke about dinosaur construction workers?

Eric: Sure.

Garin: Sorry, I'm still working on it!

What does a carpenter have in common with an *Ankylosaurus*?

They both have a hammer.

Two dinosaurs walked into a building. You'd think one of them would have seen it.

What do you get when you cross a dinosaur and a builder?

Tyrannosaurus decks

What time is it when a dinosaur sits on your fence?

Time to build a new fence

What dinosaur loved playing with blocks?

Lego-saurus

How do you stop a dinosaur from charging?

You unplug it.

PUNCH LINES

What do you do with a green dinosaur? To figure out the punch line, write each set of colored letters on the corresponding lines.

WURANIIPITEINTLTS

_____

_____

_____

_____ .

KIDS' SCIENCE QUESTIONS

What color were dinosaurs?

For many years, no one knew the colors of any dinosaurs. But in a few cases, dinosaur feathers were well preserved and still contain melanosomes—the tiny parts that make the colors in feathers. The shape of a melanosome shows which color it made. For example, scientists now know that *Anchiornis* was black, white, and gray with a red crest on its head. But for most dinosaurs, no one knows their colors because their skin wasn't preserved in fossils.

So anyone can use what they know about modern animals to imagine what colors they might have been. Maybe the big plant eaters were drab, like elephants, and some forest hunters might have had camouflage stripes, like tigers. Perhaps some had polka dots and purple stripes!

LAUGH ATTACK

Who makes clothes for dinosaurs?
A dino-sewer

Why did the *T. rex* put wheels on her rocking chair?
She wanted to rock and roll.

Museum Guard: Excuse me, but do you see that sign? It says "No Painting Allowed."
Triceratops: Oh, I'm not painting aloud—I'm painting very quietly.

How did the *Ankylosaurus* do in the art show?
He was a smashing success.

What did the *Stegosaurus* say when he spilled glue on his hands?
"This is a very sticky situation."

What did the dinosaur call her T-shirt business?
Try Sarah's Tops

What is a *Fukuiraptor's* favorite paper craft?
Dinos-origami

What craft do dinosaurs love?
CRAWRss stitch

Which of these two paper dinos are the same?

LAUGH ATTACK

**What has 2 tails,
4 horns, and 6 feet?**
A Triceratops with spare parts!

**What is the difference between
a car and a *Triceratops*?**
A car only has one horn.

A man was visting a museum. Pointing to a fossil, he asked the museum guide, "Why doesn't that *Triceratops* have horns? I thought *Triceratops* had three horns!"

"Well," said the museum guide, "*Triceratops* do have three horns. And that *Triceratops* is an *Apatosaurus*."

**Why is *Triceratops* such a
nuisance in traffic?**
It keeps honking its horns.

**Mom, how come every time
I blow a bubble it pops?**

KIDS' SCIENCE QUESTIONS

What did *Triceratops* do with all those horns?

Scientists think that the main use for the headgear on the *Triceratops* was probably to fight with other *Triceratops* when looking for a mate. The dinosaurs probably also used their horns and the frill to signal that they were *Triceratops*. And maybe those horns were also used to fight off a *Tyrannosaurus rex* or two. We may never know for sure.

TRY-TO-MATCH-THESE-CERATOPS

You've heard of *Triceratops*, but have you heard of these sillysaurs?
To find out which dinosaur is which,
match up these riddles with their punch lines.

Which dinosaur . . .

_____ 1. always has a friendly greeting?

_____ 2. asks a lot of questions?

_____ 3. bakes a lot?

_____ 4. doesn't like crowds?

_____ 5. knows all the secrets?

_____ 6. is always upset?

_____ 7. lives in Bangkok?

_____ 8. loves astronomy?

_____ 9. never gets wet?

_____ 10. shops a lot?

A. Buy-ceratops

B. Cry-ceratops

C. Dry-ceratops

D. Hi-ceratops

E. Pie-ceratops

F. Shy-ceratops

G. Sky-ceratops

H. Spy-ceratops

I. Thai-ceratops

J. Why-ceratops

WHAT'S WRONG?

Which things in this picture are silly? It's up to you!

What did the rock say to the dinosaur?

Nothing. Rocks can't talk!

Why do people who study dinosaurs carry buckets?

Because they are pail-eontologists

69

MEALTIME CODE

There are three food jokes on this page.
Use the picture code to fill in the letters and finish the jokes.

A   C   D   E   I   M   N

O   P   R   S   T   U   Y

1. What dinosaur loves pancakes?

__ __ __ __ — __ __ __ __ __ — __ __ __ __

2. What do you get when you cross a *Stegosaurus* with a lemon?

__ __ __ __ — __ __ __ __

3. What is a dinosaur's favorite snack?

__ __ __ __ __ __ __ __   __ __ __

__ __ __ __ __

LAUGH ATTACK

What's the worst part about eating a dinosaur?

You have leftovers for weeks and weeks.

Knock, knock.
Who's there?
Doughnut.
Doughnut who?
Doughnut make you laugh when people tell dinosaur jokes?

What dinosaur are you most likely to find in the kitchen?

Hungarosaurus

How do you know if there is a dinosaur in your refrigerator?

The door won't shut.

Do you know how long dinosaurs should be fed?

Exactly the same as short dinosaurs

DINO DRAW

Follow these steps to draw a dinosaur on the next page.
Or use your imagination to draw your own dinosaur.

1.

2.

3.

4.

5.

1.

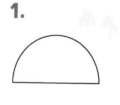

2.

3.

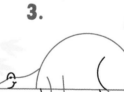

4.

5.

A teacher asked her students to draw dinosaurs eating plants. One student drew a dinosaur on the paper with no plants. The teacher asked, "Why didn't you draw any plants?" The student replied, "The dinosaur ate them! "

What side of the dinosaur has more scales?

The outside

HOW TO WALK YOUR DINOSAUR

Dinosaurs have lots of energy. If your dinosaur is acting grumpy or chewing furniture, it probably needs more exercise.

The good news is you can keep your dinosaur happy by taking it for daily walks.

Before walking, make sure your dinosaur is wearing a proper leash.

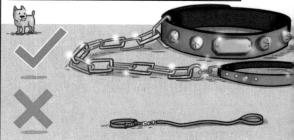

If your dinosaur starts to tug, say "Stop," "Sit," or "Stay."

To reinforce good behavior, carry plenty of treats.

Teach your dinosaur about acceptable—and unacceptable—behavior.

If your dinosaur catches cold easily, consider purchasing foul-weather gear.

Keep your dinosaur hydrated.

Luckily, dinosaurs are hard to lose. But place an ID tag around its neck just in case.

Now that you know how to walk your dinosaur, step outside and make some tracks!

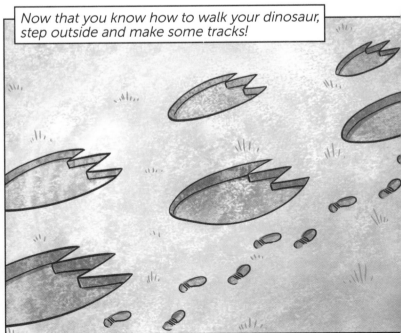

WHAT'S IN A NAME?

Each of these silly sentences is a code for some of the shortest dinosaur genus names. See if you can uncover nine names.
Hint: Look at the first letter of each word.

Who comes up with a dinosaur's name?

Their parents

Zebras bedazzled yams.

Angry newts zippered umbrellas.

Happy ants yawned absurdly.

Koalas organized lollipops.

Trendy aardvarks wiggled away.

Pandas repaired old avocados.

"Yummy invention?" queried iguanas.

Moose embroidered icicles.

Zany unicorns unplugged lamps.

PREHISTORIC GIANT BONES

This should give the fossil hunters something to think about!

FINDING FOSSILS

Paleontolgoists use grids to record where they find fossils. Use the number pairs to solve the riddle on this grid. Move to the right to the first number and then up to the second number. Write the letters you find in the correct space.

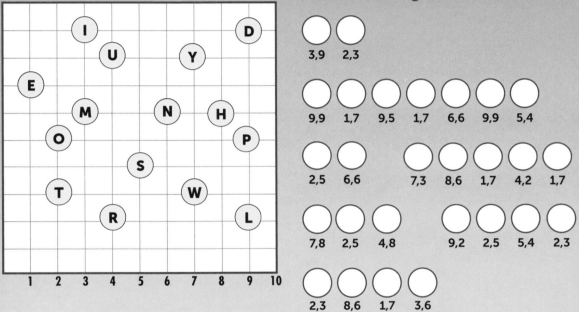

Where do you find fossils?

◯	◯
3,9	2,3

◯	◯	◯	◯	◯	◯	◯
9,9	1,7	9,5	1,7	6,6	9,9	5,4

◯	◯		◯	◯	◯	◯	◯
2,5	6,6		7,3	8,6	1,7	4,2	1,7

◯	◯	◯		◯	◯	◯	◯
7,8	2,5	4,8		9,2	2,5	5,4	2,3

◯	◯	◯	◯
2,3	8,6	1,7	3,6

WHAT'S WRONG?

Which things in this picture are silly? It's up to you!

FUN FACT

Dinosaurs roamed the earth during the Mesozoic Era, which lasted from **252 million years** ago until **66 million years** ago.

Please don't feed the dinosaurs.

Knock, knock. *Who's there?* Wendy. *Wendy who?* Wendy dinosaurs went extinct, de Mesozoic Era ended.

PLAYGROUND PALS

Finish the poem by putting the rhyming words in place.

WORDLIST

- DROP
- TOP
- TAIL
- SAIL
- PILE
- SMILE
- FUN
- ME
- ONE
- TREE

If I had a dinosaur
  as tall as a ____ ____ ____ ____,
She'd be a great playground
  for my friends and ____ ____.

We'd set up a ladder
  so no one would ____ ____ ____ ____.
Then we'd climb up her back,
  right to the ____ ____ ____.

We'd take turns sliding down
  to the end of her ____ ____ ____ ____,
Flying so fast,
  we'd practically ____ ____ ____ ____.

"Watch out!" she would say.
  "Don't land in a ____ ____ ____ ____."
"Thanks for the ride!"
  we would say with a ____ ____ ____ ____ ____.

We'd have such a blast.
  It would be so much ____ ____ ____.
I just need a dinosaur.
  Do you have ____ ____ ____?

What's a *Brontosaurus's* favorite thing at the playground?

Write the highlighted letters in the
corresponding colored spaces below to solve the riddle.

____ ____ ____ ____ ____ ____ - ____ ____ ____ - ____ ____ ____

RIDDLE SUDOKU

Fill in the squares so that the six letters appear only once in each row, column, and 2 x 3 box. Then read the yellow squares to find out the answer to the riddle.

Riddle:
What's as big as a dinosaur but weighs nothing?

Our Sudoku puzzles use letters instead of numbers.

LETTERS: **A D H O S W**

			W	D	H
			O		
				S	O
H	O				
		H			
O	S	D			

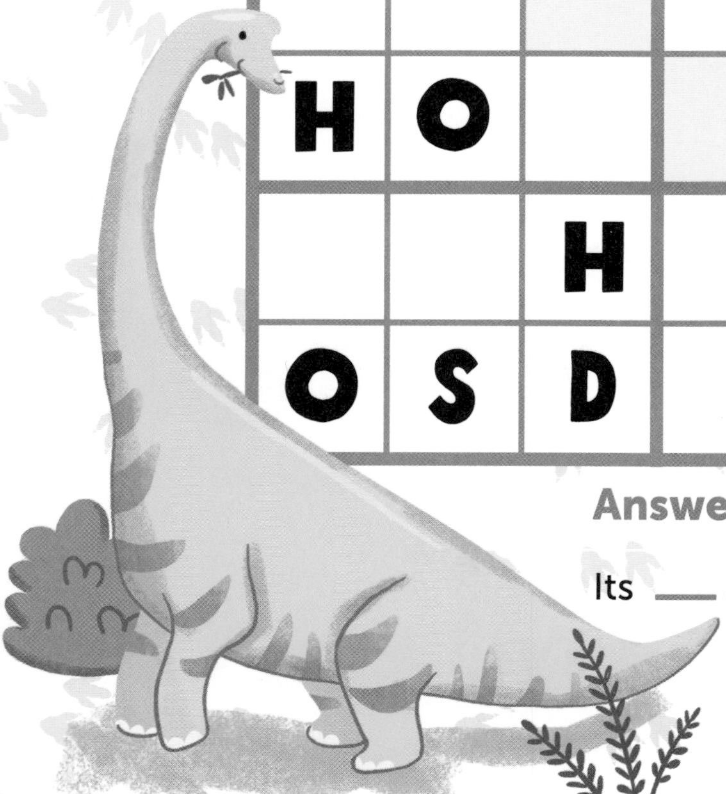

Answer:

Its ___ ___ ___ ___ ___ ___

TRICKY TRACKS

Follow each set of tracks to the dinosaur that made them.

MONTANA DINOS

People have found lots of dinosaurs in Montana. Fourteen kinds of dinosaurs whose fossils have been found there are listed below. Each will fit into the grid in only one way.

WORD LIST

9 letters
MAIASAURA

10 letters
DIPLODOCUS
EDMONTONIA
STEGOCERAS

11 letters
APATOSAURUS
AVACERATOPS
GRYPOSAURUS
HADROSAURUS
TRICERATOPS

12 letters
ANKYLOSAURUS
LAMBEOSAURUS

13 letters
ALBERTOSAURUS
TYRANNOSAURUS

14 letters
THESCELOSAURUS

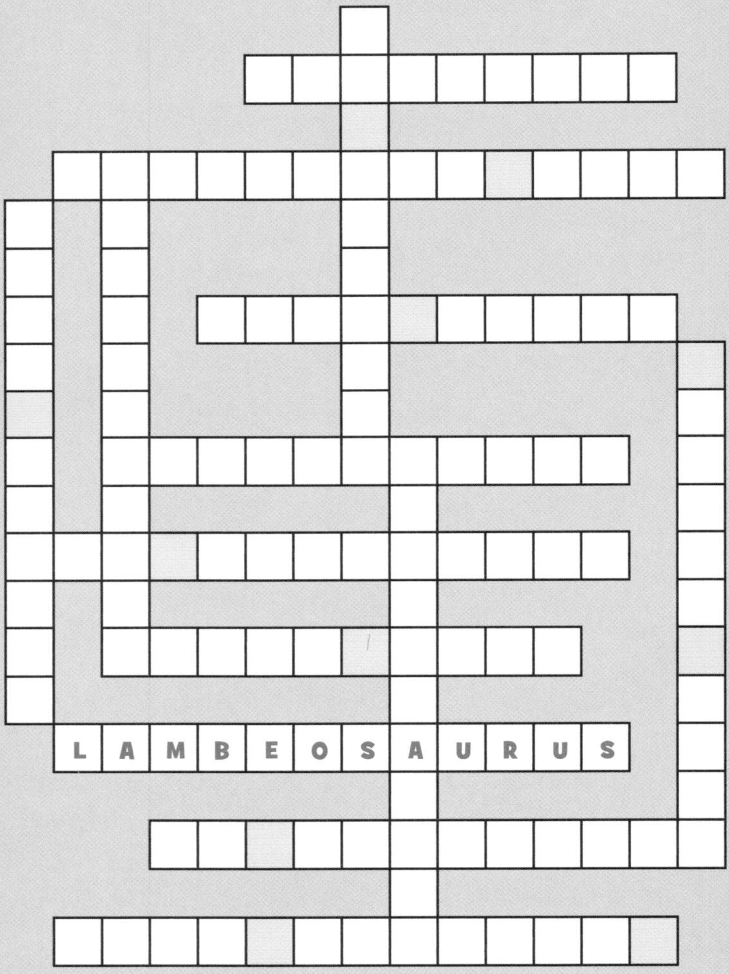

L A M B E O S A U R U S

Use the number of letters in each word as a clue to where it might fit. Once you fill them in, write the highlighted letters in from left to right and top to bottom. They will give you the answer to the riddle.

What did dinosaurs eat for breakfast?

_ _ _ _ _ _ _ - _ _ _ _ _ _

FUN FACT

When dinosaurs first appeared on the scene about 245 million years ago, all land on Earth was part of one supercontinent called **Pangea**. It started to break up about 175 million years ago.

A TRIP TO THE MUSEUM

Each blue word in the silly story is also a hidden object. After you read the story, find the objects in the big picture on the next page.

Did you know that the **EAR OF CORN**-saurus was the biggest dinosaur to ever live? I learned that on our field trip today. My class went to one of my favorite places in town, the **TABLE TENNIS PADDLE** museum. I always learn something new. Today I learned that a *T. rex*'s favorite food was a crunchy **COMB** and that *Stegosaurus* liked to sleep on a **HORSESHOE** with their head on a **BOWLING PIN**! Our tour of the museum was led by Ms. **LIGHT BULB**, the head of the **PAPER AIRPLANE** department. She was very nice and only got mad once, but that was because Billy took a purple **VASE** out of his backpack and put it on the top of a **SLICE OF BREAD** from the Jurassic Period. Silly Billy! We ate lunch in the brand new **HANGER** room, which was reserved especially for us. Then the museum director brought out a big **GOLF CLUB** with candles on it! It was ten years since the museum had opened. And we got to help celebrate. What a great **WRISTWATCH**!

MUSEUM MAZE

Help Dina get to the *T. rex* by finding a clear path from **START** to **FINISH**. Don't get lost in the crowd!

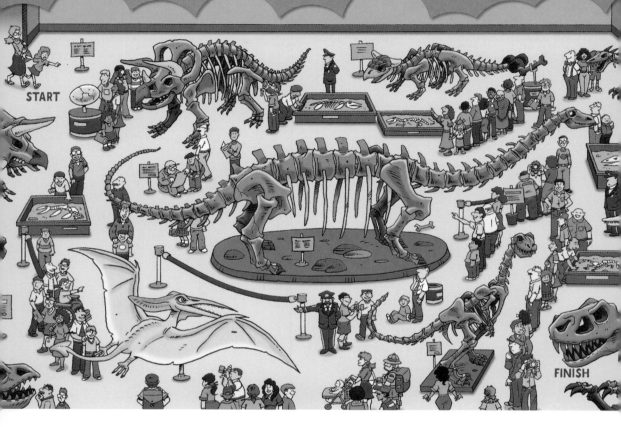

START

FINISH

Which of these two fossils are the same?

What do you call a dinosau fossil that is alw telling lies?

A bony phony

Why didn't the skeleton attack the museum visitors?

Because he had no guts

LAUGH ATTACK

What do you get if you cross a dinosaur and a football player?

A quarterback no one can tackle

What is a dinosaur's favorite racket sport?

Squash

What do you call it when a dinosaur gets a goal?

A dino-score

Why was the *Stegosaurus* such a good volleyball player?

Because she could really spike the ball

What dinosaur could jump higher than a tree?

All of them—trees can't jump.

Why couldn't dinosaurs bowl?

Their claws didn't fit in the holes.

Which long-necked dinosaur is always the first to any game?

Pronto-saurus

What is a golfer's favorite dinosaur?

Tee rex

What kind of dinosaur can you ride in a rodeo?

A Bronco-saurus

Boy, can he ever play defense!

YOU FINISH THE DINO-STORY!

What do you think will happen next? Finish the story on a separate sheet of paper or tell it to a friend.

The Dinosaur Book

Carlos scoured his bookshelf, looking for the perfect bedtime read. He grabbed his favorite biography about Barnum Brown, the paleontologist who first discovered *T. rex* bones, but then he saw a strange, dusty book tucked behind all the others. Where did that come from? he wondered. Carlos plucked the mysterious book off the shelf and hopped into bed. But before he could snuggle under his blanket, the cover burst open and . . .

BEDTIME CODE

There are three sleepy jokes on this page.
Use the picture code to fill in the letters and finish the jokes.

A	E	F	G	H	I	L	M

N	O	P	R	S	T	U

1. What do you call a sleeping dinosaur?

2. What should you do if you find a dinosaur in your bed?

3. Where do dinosaurs go at night?

HAPPY BIRTHDAY!

There are plenty of prehistoric presents at this party.
Can you find the hidden objects in this scene?

 heart

 mitten

wedge of lime

arrowhead

lollipop

adhesive bandage

 envelope

 wedge of cheese

 wishbone

artist's brush

doughnut

crown

flashlight

horn

game piece

slice of pizza

comb

magnet

toothbrush

tennis ball

seashell

tomato

LAUGH ATTACK

Why did carnivorous dinosaurs eat their meat raw?
Because they didn't know how to barbecue

What did dinosaurs use to make their hot dogs?
Jurassic Pork

How do you season a primordial soup?
With Saltandpepperasaurus

Knock, knock.
Who's there?
Steak.
Steak who?
Steak-a-saurus was a plant eater.

What do dinosaurs put on their pizza?
Tomato-saurus

What did the fossil bring to dinner?
Spare ribs

What do you get when a dinosaur lays an egg on top of a volcano?
An eggroll

LAVA HOT

Can you help the dinosaur climb to the top of the volcano to grill some grub?

START

FINISH

DINOSAUR DINNER

A very hungry dinosaur is coming here for dinner.
He hasn't had a bite in days. I think he's getting thinner!
I'll make a feast and fill him up. He loves to eat spaghetti.
If I can find a giant pot, I'll get his dinner ready!

pike, **Bertha**, **George**, and **Gertie** love to
at dinner together, but they each have a
ifferent favorite pasta. Use the clues to
gure out which of the following pastas
each dinosaur's favorite: **macaroni**,
paghetti, **ravioli**, and **tortellini**.

· · · · · · · · · · · · **CLUES:** · · · · · · · · · · · · ·

One dinosaur's name starts with the same
letter as his or her favorite pasta.
Bertha does not like tortellini.
The dinosaur who likes ravioli
is Gertie's brother.

What did
Stegosaurus
say after he
made a mess
in the kitchen?

"I'm dino-sorry!"

DINO DIG

All sorts of dinosaurs are hiding in these letters. Can you find them all? They're hidden up, down, across, backwards, and diagonally.

WORDLIST

- ALLOSAURUS
- ANKYLOSAURUS
- APATOSAURUS
- ARGENTINOSAURUS
- AVIMIMUS
- BRACHIOSAURUS
- CAMPTOSAURUS
- CORYTHOSAURUS
- DIPLODOCUS
- DRYOSAURUS
- GALLIMIMUS
- GORGOSAURUS
- IGUANODON
- LAMBEOSAURUS
- NANOSAURUS
- ORNITHOLESTES
- OVIRAPTOR
- SAUROPOSEIDON
- SPINOSAURUS
- STEGOSAURUS
- SYNTARSUS
- TRACHODON
- TRICERATOPS
- TYRANNOSAURUS REX
- UTAHRAPTOR
- VELOCIRAPTOR
- VULCANODON

FUN FACT

The person who discovers a dinosaur gets to name it! Dinosaurs are typically named for their appearance or characteristics, but they have also been named after people, places, and other creatures.

TONGUE TWISTERS

three times, fast.

Brave *Brachiosaurus* babies break branches.

***Corythosaurus,* a Cretaceous creature, carried a crest.**

```
              A N O D O H C A R T
            G A L L I M I M U S B S O P
    C S O R N I T H O L E S T E S U T W O A
  S O L U C S U R U A S O N A N R P I X M R X
  U R U A S O G E T S W U S P U K C S E H G D
  R Y U S U R U A S O T P M A C I Y P R A E I
  U T R O T P A R I V O W S I U D A I S G N P
  A H U J S B W T A G W O N N M R P N U R T R
  S O D B U G A E N E L Q O O B I U O R O I O
  O S I X R T O A R Y F G D D R G V S U T N T
  T A P D U R O R K X S J O I A U M A A P O P
  A U L R A I L N G Q A S N E C A V U S A S A
  P R O Y S C A K T O E T A S H N H R O R A R
  A U D O O E J P T X S T C O I O Q U N H U I
  R S O S E R S Q A R F A L P O D A S N A R C
    C A B A                U O S O D I A T U O
    U U M T                V R A N N O R U S L
    S R A O                A U U D S A Y K O E
    U U L P                S A R S U R T H E V
    J S D S                V S U O
                          O A S K
```

JURASSIC SKATE PARK

Find these objects hidden in the big picture.
Then use the object code and letters to solve the riddle.

What has three horns, a large head plate, and sixteen wheels?

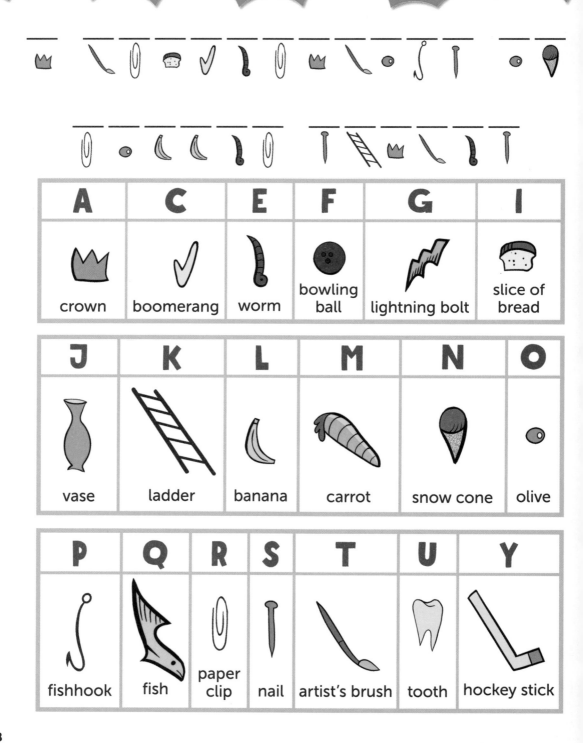

A	C	E	F	G	I
crown	boomerang	worm	bowling ball	lightning bolt	slice of bread

J	K	L	M	N	O
vase	ladder	banana	carrot	snow cone	olive

P	Q	R	S	T	U	Y
fishhook	fish	paper clip	nail	artist's brush	tooth	hockey stick

FUN FACT

Triceratops had a hooked, bird-like beak that was useful for snipping off plants.

PREHISTORIC ROAD TRIP

Scooter and Skeeter are planning a trip across the United States to visit some prehistoric sites. Show them the path from START to FINISH by answering each question correctly.

START

Ancestors of giant sequoia trees lived during the dinosaur days. What state is home to the most sequoias today?

CALIFORNIA   CONNECTICUT

Where was the first discovery of baby dinosaur bones in North America?

MONTANA   MINNESOTA

What state has a dinosaur named after it?

OHIO   UTAH

Where is the largest site of dinosaur tracks discovered in North America?

COLORADO   ARIZONA

What do maps and dinosaurs have in common?

Both have scales.

Horseshoe crabs have been around since before the dinosaurs. Which body of water is famous for having millions of horseshoe crabs?

MASSACHUSETTS BAY

DELAWARE BAY

Where was the world's first nearly complete dinosaur skeleton—a fossil of a duck-billed hadrosaur—dug up?

NEW YORK

NEW JERSEY

Welcome to New Jersey

Where was "Archie," one of the world's largest mammoth fossils, found?

NEBRASKA

OKLAHOMA

Where was the biggest, most complete fossil of a Tyrannosaurus rex found?

SOUTH DAKOTA

SOUTH CAROLINA

Which state contains the only U.S. city said to be built within a crater caused by a meterorite?

VERMONT

KENTUCKY

Which state does not have any fossils in it because it was not a landmass in the Mesozoic Era?

ALABAMA

FLORIDA

CRATER FOR SALE
Meteor Real Estate Co.

FINISH
CONGRATULATIONS!

DINOS OF ROCK

This band is jammin'! Can you find the hidden objects in this scene? You can use a highlighter to find the objects in the dark puzzle.

LAUGH ATTACK

What dinosaur liked to dance?

Disco-saurus

What kind of rock wasn't around during the age of dinosaurs?

Rock and Roll

Which dinosaur was the most musical?

The Velociraptor

What do you call a dinosaur who was up all night dancing?

My-feet-are-sore-us

What do you call a group of singing dinosaurs?

A tyranno-chorus

Why don't fossils play music in church?

They have no organs.

What's big and scaly with horns?

A Triceratops *marching band*

What is a fossil's favorite instrument?

A trombone

What happens when dinosaurs lose their beat?

They throw a tempo-tantrum.

The Four Tricera-Tops took "Battle of the Bands" a bit too literally.

PREHISTORIC PLAYTIME

Can you find **14** differences between these two pictures?

Try to say these

TONGUE TWISTERS

three times, fast.

Twelve *Tyrannosaurus* twirled twelve twigs.

A pterodactyl trio perched precariously on treetops.

How do dinosaurs check their weight?

With a scale

SILLY SIBLINGS

Hannah and Jackson love telling each other silly dinosaur jokes.
After you find all 22 dinosaurs in their room, enjoy a few of their favorite jokes.

Hannah: *Micropachycephalosaurus* is the longest dinosaur name. How do you spell it?

Jackson: M-I-C-R-O-P-A-C-H-Y-C-E-P-H-A-L-O-S-A-U-R-U-S.

Hannah: No, *it* is spelled I-T.

Jackson: A *Megalosaurus* weighs about 2,000 pounds.

Hannah: Wow! That's a ton!

Hannah: Did you hear about the race between the *Apatosaurus* and the *Diplodocus*?

Jackson: I heard it was neck and neck!

Jackson: Would you be afraid to put your head in a dinosaur's mouth?

Hannah: Yes, because I'm afraid of the dark.

SCRAMBLERS

Three punch lines are hidden in the leaves above this dino pile.
To find out what they are, first find each group of letters that matches the
color of each dinosaur. Then unscramble each group to find the punch lines.

E D B C M K H N

T E E S A U

O O R

I T

E

**What do you call a
dinosaur in a phone booth?**

_____ _____

**What did the green dinosaur
say to the purple dinosaur?**

" _____ !"

What do you call an exploding dinosaur?

- _____

DINO DIVE

These dinos were *jaws* stopping by to see if you want to go swimming. Can you find the hidden objects in this scene?

What do you call a dinosaur that swims?

Jurassic Shark

flashlight

funnel

bone

fried egg

pencil

top hat

wishbone

heart

What was the most polite prehistoric creature?
Please-iosaur

Why was the *Nothosaur* doing the backstroke?
He didn't want to swim on a full stomach.

What do you do if you find a blue *Ichthyosaur*?
Cheer him up.

Why were the *Plesiosaur* and the *Mosasaur* such good pals?
Because they got along swimmingly

"Stop holding your breath. We have air holes, remember?"

KIDS' SCIENCE QUESTIONS

Were there really dinosaurs that swam?

Some dinosaurs could swim or wade. Scientists have found footprints where dinosaurs pushed off into streams or rivers. But the big sea creatures of the time were not dinosaurs. They were sea reptiles.

Ichthyosaurs were dolphin-shaped reptiles. *Plesiosaurs* were larger water reptiles, with limbs like paddles. And *Mosasaurs* were sea lizards, with fins where most lizards have legs.

NICKNAMES

Have you ever heard of "WDC DMJ-001"? He's also known by "Jimbo."
Some dinosaurs are given nicknames in addition to their formal, scientific identifications. Jimbo is a replica skeleton at the Wyoming Dinosaur Center based on one of the largest and most complete *Supersaurus* ever found.

The nicknames of 16 dinosaur skeletons are hiding in these letters.
Can you find them all? They're hidden up, down, across, backwards, and diagonally
Only the words in CAPITAL letters are hidden. When you're done, write the leftover letters in order in the spaces below. Go from left to right and top to bottom.
They will spell out the punch line to the riddle.

WORD LIST

BABY LOUIE (*Beibeilong*)
BIG AL (*Allosaurus*)
CLIFF (*Triceratops*)
DAKOTA (*Edmontosaurus*)
DIPPY (*Diplodocus*)
ELMER (*Gorgosaurus*)
ELVIS (*Brachylophosaurus*)
FRAN (*Acrocanthosaurus*)
GORDO (*Barosaurus*)
JIMBO (*Supersaurus*)
LIZZIE (*Hadrosaur*)
MATILDA (*Diamantinasaurus*)
MAX (*Galeamopus*)
SOPHIE (*Stegosaurus*)
SUE (*Tyrannosaurus rex*)
WILLO (*Thescelosaurus*)

```
A R A N S I V L E
D Y E T W H I I J
L D N M I G U Z I
I A Y C L O O Z M
T K U W L E A I B
A O N Y O I T E O
M T B D I H F T D
L A G I B P R F R
B C E P A O A N O
T U H P E S N A G
S R Y Y O U M A X
```

Supersaurus

What do you call a *Supersaurus* wearing earmuffs if you don't know its name?

___ ___ ___ ___ ___ ___ ___ ___ ___ ___ ___ .

___ ___ ___ ___ , ___ ___ ___ ___ ___ .

ARTSY LOGIC

Stella, Enzo, Eva, and Ben entered their school's Dinosaur Art Contest. Using the clues below, can you figure out what art form each student used to create what dinosaur?

What happened when two dinosaurs had an art contest?
. . . .
It ended in a draw.

	PAPIER-MÂCHÉ	POSTER	MOSAIC	DIORAMA	STEGOSAURUS	TYRANNOSAURUS	TRICERATOPS	BRONTOSAURUS
STELLA								
ENZO								
EVA								
BEN								

Use the chart to keep track of your answers.
Put an **X** in each box that can't be true and an **O** in boxes that match.

1. Enzo used a lot of newspaper to build his dinosaur, which wasn't a *Tyrannosaurus*.

2. The *Stegosaurus* won first prize for papier-mâché art, and the *Triceratops* won second prize for diorama art.

3. Eva picked her favorite three-horned dinosaur as the subject of her creation.

4. Stella painted an herbivore for her project.

OPEN WIDE!

Time to polish those pearly whites.
Can you find the hidden objects in this scene?

Why did the dinosaur go to the doctor?

He was feeling Juras-sick.

chili pepper

ruler

mallet

mug

comb

crescent moon

drinking straw

crown

saucepan

binoculars

shoe

TRUE OR FALSE TEETH

How many of these true/false statements can you answer correctly? Go on and take a bite out of this quiz!

1. *T. rex* had teeth as sharp as steak knives and as big as bananas.

    T OR **F**

2. *Triceratops* used their scissor-like teeth for arts and crafts projects.

    T OR **F**

3. Fossils of dinosaur teeth are found so frequently because all dinosaurs could regrow teeth.

    T OR **F**

4. Duck-billed *hadrosaurs* had as many as 1,000 teeth.

    T OR **F**

5. Some dinosaurs swallowed rocks to help them grind food in their stomachs.

    T OR **F**

6. The root word *don* means "tooth," which is why many dinosaurs like *Iguanodon* and *Troodon* became orthodontists.

    T OR **F**

7. *Apatosaurus* had teeth, but they didn't chew because they wanted to save their teeth for the tooth fairy.

    T OR **F**

BRUSH 'EM

What color toothbrush does this *T. rex* use?

Why did the dinosaur give up acting?

··

He couldn't sink his teeth into the part.

LAUGH ATTACK

What do you call a dinosaur that left its armor out in the rain?

A Stegosau-rust

What is a *Stegosaurus* when it gets out of a bath?

Ex-stinked

When can a *Stegosaurus* hide under a small umbrella and not get wet?

When it's not raining!

Why won't the *Stegosaurus* invite the baseball team for dinner?

They're always stepping on his plates.

Want to play a game of leap frog?

KIDS' SCIENCE QUESTIONS

What were the plates and spikes on *Stegosaurus* for?

We think the plates on *Stegosaurus* may have been used to warm or cool off the dinosaur, depending on the weather. They were not useful for defense. But the spikes on its tail might have been used as weapons if *Stegosaurus* swung its tail at predators. Most plant-eaters, like *Stegosaurus*, had eyes at the sides of their heads so they could see danger coming from any direction.

TIME FOR A PUZZLE

The Mesozoic Era is divided into three time periods.
To figure out their names, write each set of
colored letters on the corresponding lines.

C J T U R R E R T I A A C A S E S O S S I U I C C S

252 million years ago to 201 million years ago

_____

201 million years ago to 145 million years ago

_____

145 million years ago to 66 million years ago

_____

How do you
find out a
dinosaur's age?

· · · · · · · · · · · · · · · ·

You go to its
birthday party.

LAUGH ATTACK

**Why couldn't the fossil
go to the party?**
He had nobody to go with.

Knock, knock.
Who's there?
Ice cream.
Ice cream who?
**Ice cream when I see a
dinosaur—don't you?**

Knock, knock.
Who's there?
Raptor.
Raptor who?
**Raptor not, your friend will
still love the birthday gift.**

**How do you make
a dinosaur float?**
*With two scoops of ice cream,
a bottle of root beer, and a dinosaur*

Don't worry.
No one's gonna care
what you said 66 million
years from now!

HIDDEN WORDS

Eight books in this scene are the same. Can you find all eight matching books? There are also eight synonyms hidden in this scene. Can you find **SMART**, **BRAINY**, **INTELLIGENT**, **BRILLIANT**, **WISE**, **GENIUS**, **BRIGHT**, and **CLEVER**?

What do you call a dinosaur with an extensive vocabulary?

A thesaurus

Why was the dinosaur afraid to go to the library?

His books were 66 million years overdue

TIC TAC ROW

Each of these skeletons has something in common with the other two skeletons in the same row—across, down, and diagonally. For example, in the top row across, each skeleton has velvet ropes around it. Can you tell what's alike in each row?

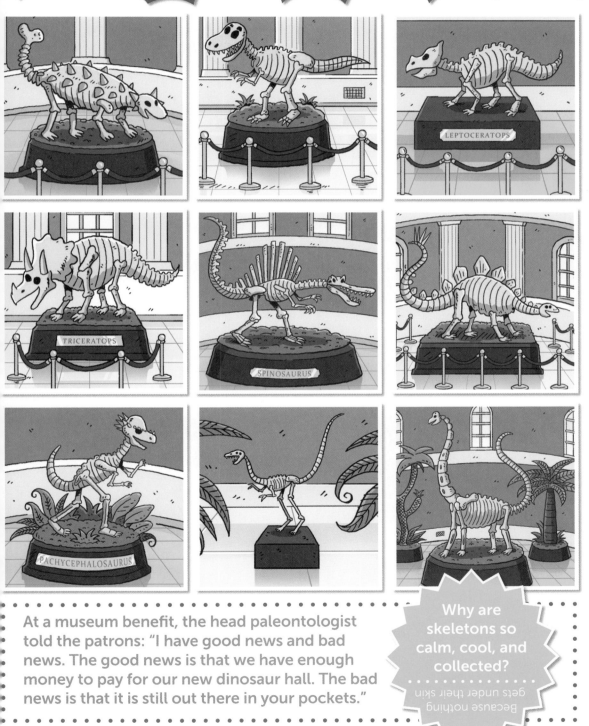

At a museum benefit, the head paleontologist told the patrons: "I have good news and bad news. The good news is that we have enough money to pay for our new dinosaur hall. The bad news is that it is still out there in your pockets."

Why are skeletons so calm, cool, and collected?

Because nothing gets under their skin

117

HUNGRY, HUNGRY HERBIVORES

These plant eaters are chowing down.
Can you find the hidden objects in this scene?

ice-cream cone

glove

bow

chili pepper

pickle

paper clip

kite

butterfly

LAUGH ATTACK

Why did the *Apatosaurus* devour the factory?

Because she was a plant eater

What did the *Triceratops* sit on?

Its Tricerabottom

What do you ask a thirsty *Tyrannosaurus*?

"Tea, Rex?"

Where does a dinosaur keep his teacup?

On a dino-saucer

Why did dinosaurs drink cold tea?

Because fire wasn't discovered yet

What is a pterosaur's least favorite tea?

Gravity

KIDS' SCIENCE QUESTIONS

What did dinosaurs eat?

Many dinosaurs ate leaves, fruits, and seeds of lots of different plants. There were plants related to pine trees, and others similar to palm trees. Dinosaurs also ate ginkgos, ferns, and flowering plants. Grass and the vegetables we have today did not exist in dinosaur times. Many big meat-eating dinosaurs ate other dinosaurs. It is likely that much of their diet was made up of plant eaters that were already dead. The smaller meat eaters might have eaten insects, little mammals, reptiles, and eggs. Plant eaters are also called herbivores, and meat eaters are also called carnivores. Dinosaurs that ate both plants and meat are called omnivores.

AROUND TOWN

Victor the *Velociraptor* lost his tail and is looking for the retail dino-store.
Use these clues to find where it is.

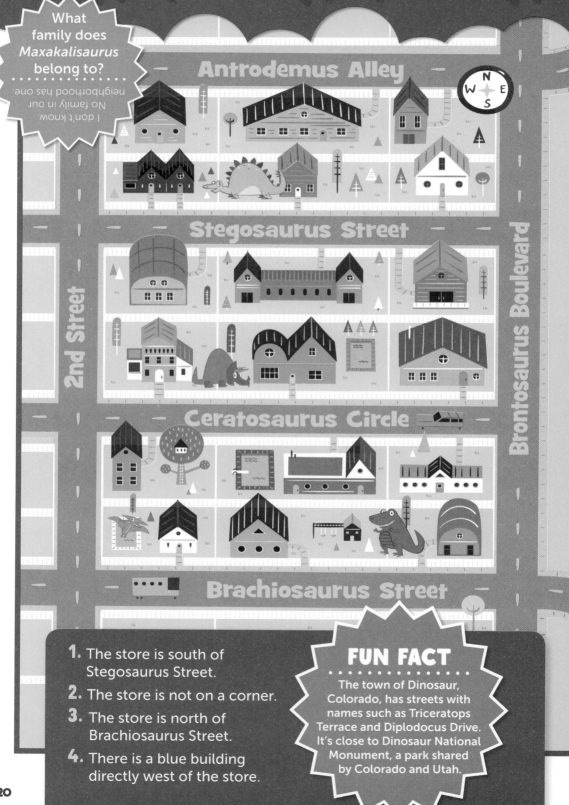

Antrodemus Alley

Stegosaurus Street

2nd Street

Ceratosaurus Circle

Brontosaurus Boulevard

Brachiosaurus Street

1. The store is south of Stegosaurus Street.
2. The store is not on a corner.
3. The store is north of Brachiosaurus Street.
4. There is a blue building directly west of the store.

FUN FACT

The town of Dinosaur, Colorado, has streets with names such as Triceratops Terrace and Diplodocus Drive. It's close to Dinosaur National Monument, a park shared by Colorado and Utah.

LAUGH ATTACK

Where did the *Supersaurus* shop for groceries?

At the supermarket

Dinosaur: I'd like to buy a pair of shorts.
Store Clerk: How long?
Dinosaur: For the whole Triassic period.

I'm afraid this is the largest size we have.

Why did the dinosaur go to the bank?

He was Broke-iosaurus.

Michelle: What's the difference between a dinosaur and a carton of milk?
Brandon: I don't know. What?
Michelle: Remind me not to send you to the grocery store!

Where do herbivores keep food?

In a pan-tree

Knock, knock.
Who's there?
Ada.
Ada who?
Ada whole tree for lunch, and now I'm really full.

KIDS' SCIENCE QUESTIONS

Were some dinosaurs happy?

It's hard to know what emotions animals have. We do know that gorillas sometimes feel sad. Some have told us so in sign language. But dinosaurs weren't as brainy as gorillas. And dinosaurs lived so long ago that it's hard to find evidence about their feelings. Maybe they felt hungry at times, or scared when a predator came close. They certainly did not smile, because they did not have lips.

121

WHAT S WRONG?

Which things in this picture are silly? It's up to you!

HAUNTED LOGIC

Atticus and his friends went as a group of dinosaurs to a Halloween party. Using the clues below, can you figure out what color costume each friend wore and what snack each brought to share?

	BLUE	RED	YELLOW	GREEN	PINK	CAKE	POPCORN	CHIPS	FRUIT SALAD	VEGGIE TRAY
ATTICUS										
LILA										
OLIVER										
LAUREL										
SOREN										

When do dinosaurs eat their Halloween candy?

On Chews-day

Use the chart to keep track of your answers.
Put an **X** in each box that can't be true and an **O** in boxes that match.

1. The girls, who wore yellow and pink, brought snacks that start with the same letter.

2. Atticus thanked the red dinosaur for bringing his favorite snack, popcorn.

3. Soren brought a snack with celery, which was the same color as his costume.

4. Lila decorated her cake with pink frosting to match her costume.

YOU'RE THE TOPS!

You've heard of *Triceratops*, but have you heard of these sillysaurs?
To find out which dinosaur is which, match up these riddles with their punch lines.

Which dinosaur . . .

_____ **1.** cleans the floor?

_____ **2.** loves to trampoline?

_____ **3.** waits at traffic lights?

_____ **4.** slices and dices food?

_____ **5.** is the best police officer?

_____ **6.** can't hold on to things?

_____ **7.** loves to buy things?

_____ **8.** gives great compliments?

_____ **9.** is a terrific grandfather?

_____ **10.** makes a big splash in a pool?

A. Tricera-chops

B. Tricera-cops

C. Tricera-drops

D. Tricera-flops

E. Tricera-hops

F. Tricera-mops

G. Tricera-pops

H. Tricera-props

I. Tricera-shops

J. Tricera-stops

LAUGH ATTACK

Why was *Barapasaurus* the smartest sauropod?

Because it has four A's and one B

Why don't dinosaurs ever forget?

Because they never knew anything in the first place

How do you spell *dinosaur* backward?

*D-I-N-O-S-A-U-R
B-A-C-K-W-A-R-D*

What is at the end of the Mesozoic Era?

The letter A

Troodon: Guess what I've had stuck in my head for a long time?
Brachiosaurus: I don't know. What?
Troodon: My brain!

Why is a volcano so smart?

It has more than 2,000 degrees!

Knock, knock.
Who's there?
Chicken.
Chicken who?
Chicken the encyclopedia— birds are related to dinosaurs.

KIDS' SCIENCE QUESTIONS

How big was a dinosaur's brain?

Scientists can tell brain size from the brain case inside a dinosaur's skull. Brain size compared to body size gives an idea of how smart an animal is (or was). Big plant eaters had small brains. *Brachiosaurus* was as big as a house, with a brain not much bigger than a lemon. It probably wasn't very smart. The smallest meat eaters had fairly big brains—bigger than the brains of any mammals of their time. *Troodon* was about as tall as an average 10-year-old, and its brain was about the size of an avocado pit. (Yours is the size of a softball.) As far as we know, it was the smartest animal in dinosaur times.

HELP THE CARTOONIST!

These cartoons are missing their captions. Write your own punch lines, then check out the cartoonists' original gags on page 143.

LAUGH ATTACK

Why was the paleontologist's head wet?
She had a brainstorm.

Which scientists don't get enough sun?
Pale-eontologists

A book never written:
One of the First Dinosaurs Discovered
by Meg A. Losaurus

How many fossils can fit in an empty box?
One. After that, the box isn't empty anymore!

Knock, knock.
Who's there?
Juicy.
Juicy who?
Juicy any fossils at the dig site?

I'm practicing to become a paleontologist!

KIDS' SCIENCE QUESTIONS

What kinds of tools do scientists use to dig up dinosaur bones?

Most often, fossils are stuck inside rock and have just been exposed by the weather. Scientists carefully dig out the fossil, using small tools such as picks and awls to chip away the rock. They leave some rock around the bone to be cleaned off with tiny tools in the laboratory.

NAME THAT DINO

How many of these true/false statements can you answer correctly? Stake your name on it!

1. The *Dracorex hogwartsia* is named after Hogwarts, the wizard school in the Harry Potter books.

    T OR **F**

2. *Pisanosaurus* was named after the Leaning Tower of Pisa.

    T OR **F**

3. *Wendiceratops* was named in honor of Canadian fossil hunter Wendy Sloboda.

    T OR **F**

4. *Fruitadens* was named after the paleontologist's favorite food.

    T OR **F**

5. *Lamplughsaura* was named because its head looks like a lampshade.

    T OR **F**

6. *Crichtonsaurus* was named after Michael Crichton, the author of *Jurassic Park*.

    T OR **F**

If a dinosaur were named after you, what would it be called?

_____

DRAW

a picture of it here.

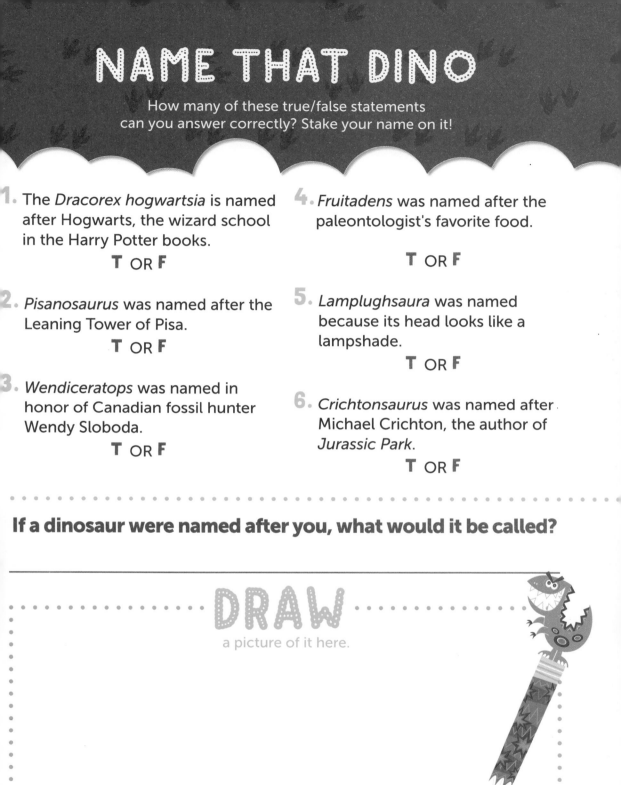

Cross out all the boxes in which the number can be evenly divided by 3. Then write the remaining letters in the spaces below to spell the answer to the riddle.

7	33	25	12	23	13	66	41	37	6	11
T	Z	H	U	E	Y	I	C	A	K	N
42	17	4	21	60	28	26	24	5	29	38
P	T	A	M	X	F	F	J	O	R	D
10	9	19	90	16	41	3	62	27	14	50
N	L	E	Q	W	O	B	N	V	E	S

Why do museums have old dinosaur bones?

___ ___ ___ ___ ___   ___ ___ ___ , ___

___ ___ ___ ___ ___ ___   ___ ___   ___ ___ ___ ___   ___ ___ ___ ___ .

Find these 15 objects hidden at the museum.

ladder

peanut

dollar bill

broccoli

mushroom

guitar

teardrop

telephone receiver

kernel of corn

baseball bat

anchor

ring

ladle

flashlight

rocket

What do you call a fossil that sleeps all the time?

Lazy bones

131

LAUGH ATTACK

What happened to the dinosaur who kept misbehaving at school?
She was egg-spelled.

Stuart: What's the first letter in *Yutyrannus*?
Ian: Y.
Stuart: Because I want to know for my dinosaur report.

How do dinosaurs pass exams?
With extinction

Phil: Can you name ten dinosaurs in ten seconds?
Christy: Sure. Eight *Iguanodons* and two *Stegosauruses*.

Where does a caveman come before a dinosaur?
In the dictionary

I've been waiting 66 million years for the bus!

I packed you a peanut butter and *Jeholopterus* sandwich.

Teacher: For homework tonight, I want you to write an essay on dinosaurs.
Seth: I'd rather write on paper.

Teacher: If you had 27 dinosaurs in one classroom and 89 in the other, what would you have?
Ann: A broken floor.

Why was school easier for dinosaurs?
There was no history to study!

Luke: Levi, do you know the first dinosaur to be discovered?
Levi: No, we were never introduced.

Why didn't the dinosaur finish his homework?
He wasn't that hungry.

AT THE ZOO

How many 3s can you find in this scene?
How many groups of three things do you see?

There once was a big, three-horned dino.
Wherever he came from, we don't know.
He showed up at the zoo
With no clue what to do.
So we made him a home with the rhino.

ZOO

DINO MITE!

333

THE LAST LAUGH

What do you call a very, very, very, very, very old dinosaur joke?
Pre-hysterical!

Why did the *Ankylosaurus* wear a suit of armor to the comedy show?
To protect himself from the punch lines

Knock, knock.
Who's there?
Noah.
Noah who?
Noah good joke about dinosaurs?

What do you call a *Stegosaurus* who tells a lot of bad jokes?
A dino-bore

Aaliyah: Want to hear a joke about the Jurassic Period?
Kaylee: Sure.
Aaliyah: Actually, never mind. It was over 145 million years ago.

What do you call a joke about dinosaurs?
Jurassic Snark

Why was *Elaphrosaurus* the funniest dinosaur?
He E-LAUGH-rosaurus-ed his head off!

Why did the dinosaur say "knock, knock"?
He was in the wrong joke.

Knock, knock.
Who's there?
Dino.
Dino who?
These jokes are dino-mite!

ANSWERS

Page 5

Allosaurus = different lizard
Brontosaurus = thunder lizard
Diplodocus = double beam
Maiasaura = good mother lizard
Microraptor = small robber

Oviraptor = egg robber
Pentaceratops = five-horned face
Stegosaurus = roof lizard
Triceratops = three-horned face
Tyrannosaurus = tyrant lizard
Velociraptor = swift robber

Page 6

Pages 10-11

1. SOAP
2. RAIN
3. PRUNE
4. APRON

5. SPOON
6. PIANO
7. INDOOR
8. SUNDAE

9. SPIDER
10. SUNRISE

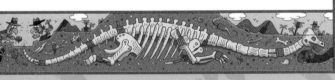

Page 12

"emperor dragon"
DILONG
"dragon claw"
DRACONYX
"dragon hunter"
DRACOVENATOR
"horse dragon"
HIPPODRACO
"shark-toothed dragon"
SHAOCHILONG
"hidden dragon"
YINLONG

Pages 14-15

Page 17

When is a baby dinosaur
good at basketball?
WHEN IT DRIBBLES

Page 18

1. J
2. A
3. B
4. F
5. H
6. I
7. E
8. G
9. D
10. C

ANSWERS

Pages 20-21

Page 22

1. T
2. F
3. T
4. T
5. T
6. T
7. F
8. F

Page 23

Pages 24-25

What is a librarian's favorite prehistoric creature?
A PTERODACTYL, BECAUSE THE *P* IS ALWAYS SILENT.

Page 29

Page 31

What do you call a dinosaur with good dental hygiene?
A FLOSS-IRAPTOR

What is a dinosaur dentist's favorite game?
TOOTH OR DARE

What do you call a dinosaur with a toothache?
A DINO-SORE

Pages 34-35

Page 37

THE SIX REAL DINOSAURS:
- *Brachiosaurus*
- *Allosaurus*
- *Apatosaurus*
- *Iguanodon*
- *Megalosaurus*
- *Sarahsaurus*

THE SIX FAKE DINOSAURS:
- Trainasaurus Wrecks
- Tricherrytops
- Whineodon
- Stellaceratops
- Iwanasaurus
- Tetrahedrasaurus

ANSWERS

Page 39

What do you call a 66-million-year-old dinosaur?
A FOSSIL

How do you greet a French fossil?
"BONE-JOUR!"

How do fossils get their mail?
BY BONY EXPRESS

What did the fossil say when he got angry with another fossil?
"I HAVE A BONE TO PICK WITH YOU."

Page 40

Page 41

All have spots. All have spikes. All are eating.	All have stripes. All have spikes	All are blue. All have spikes. **All have eggs.**
All have spots. All have sharp teeth.	All have stripes. All have sharp teeth. **All have eggs.** All are eating.	All are blue. All have sharp teeth.
All have spots. All are making a noise. **All have eggs.**	All have stripes. All are making a noise.	All are blue. All are making a noise. All are eating.

Page 42

FOOTPRINT
TEETH
EXTINCT
SCARY
EGG
FOSSIL
SKELETON
CLAW
PREHISTORIC
PREDATOR

What did dinosaurs do when it rained?
THEY GOT WET.

Page 44

Page 45

1. F
2. A
3. H
4. D
5. B
6. I
7. C
8. J
9. G
10. E

Pages 46–47

Page 49

Have you heard of Mega Mort?
Skating is his favorite **SPORT**.

Here and there and **EVERYWHERE**,
Rolling in his trusty **PAIR**.

When they see that dino **SOAR**,
Hear the crowd let out a **ROAR**!

Mort speeds along so super **FAST**,
He never, ever comes in **LAST**!

He's always winning the top **PRIZE**
Because, in his skates, he just **FLIES**.

But wherever he may **RACE**,
This follows him to every **PLACE**.

What follows Mort everywhere he goes?
HIS TAIL

ANSWERS

Page 52

Wannanosaurus = 10 lbs
Tawa = 66 lbs
Troodon = 110 lbs
Fabrosaurus = 15 lbs
Irritator = 2,200 lbs
Spinosaurus = 46,000 lbs
Vulcanodon = 8,800 lbs
Gryponyx = 2,200 lbs
Nanotyrannus = 2,000 lbs
Triceratops = 26,000 lbs

Page 53

Here are the cartoonists'
original punch lines:

1. I prefer your no-frills
   look.
2. I just grew my first plate!
3. Hey, man! Gimme two!
4. It was delicious.

Page 54

Page 55

Pages 56-57

Page 59

What was the scariest
prehistoric animal?
THE TERROR-DACTYL

Page 60

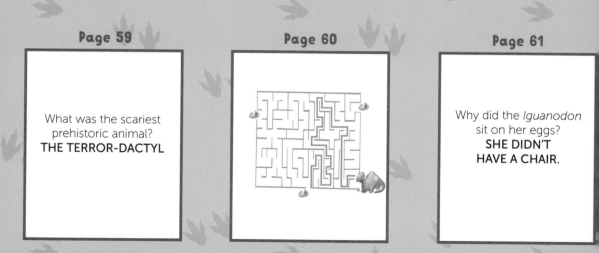

Page 61

Why did the *Iguanodon*
sit on her eggs?
**SHE DIDN'T
HAVE A CHAIR.**

ANSWERS

Page 62

Page 64

What do you do with a green dinosaur?
WAIT UNTIL IT RIPENS.

Page 65

Page 67

1. D
2. J
3. E
4. F
5. H
6. B
7. I
8. G
9. C
10. A

Page 70

What dinosaur loves pancakes?
A TRI-SYRUP-TOPS

What do you get when you cross a *Stegosaurus* with a lemon?
A DINO-SOUR

What is a dinosaur's favorite snack?
MACARONI AND TREES

Page 76

The first letter of the words in each silly sentence spells out the dinosaur name. The nine names are:

Anzu   *Yi qi*
Zby   *Kol*
Haya   *Tawa*
Proa   *Zuul*
Mei

Page 77

Where do you find fossils?
IT DEPENDS ON WHERE YOU LOST THEM

Page 80

If I had a dinosaur as tall as a **TREE**,
She'd be a great playground for my friends and **ME**.

We'd set up a ladder so no one would **DROP**.
Then we'd climb up her back, right to the **TOP**.

We'd take turns sliding down to the end of her **TAIL**,
Flying so fast, we'd practically **SAIL**.

"Watch out!" she would say. "Don't land in a **PILE**."
"Thanks for the ride!" we would say with a **SMILE**.

We'd have such a blast. It would be so much **FUN**.
I just need a dinosaur. Do you have **ONE**?

What's a *Brontosaurus's* favorite thing at the playground?
A DINO-SEE-SAUR

ANSWERS

Page 81

Page 82

LETTERS: **A D H O S W**

S	A	O	W	D	H
D	H	W	O	A	S
W	D	A	H	S	O
H	O	S	D	W	A
A	W	H	S	O	D
O	S	D	A	H	W

SHADOW

Page 83

Pages 84–85

What did dinosaurs eat for breakfast?
PANGEA-CAKES

Page 87

Page 88

Page 91

What do you call a
sleeping dinosaur?
A STEGO-SNORE-US

What should you do
if you find a dinosaur
in your bed?
SLEEP ON THE SOFA

Where do dinosaurs
go at night?
TO SLEEP

Pages 92-93

ANSWERS

Page 94

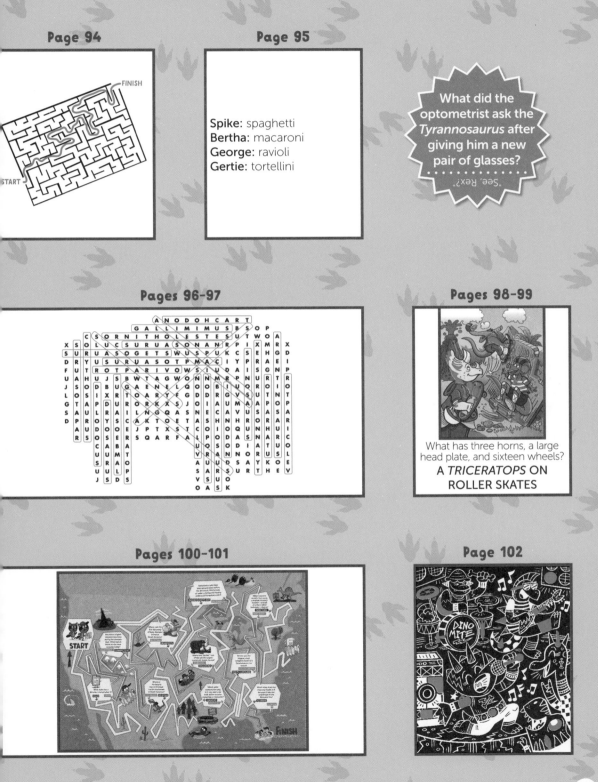

FINISH

START

Page 95

Spike: spaghetti
Bertha: macaroni
George: ravioli
Gertie: tortellini

Pages 96-97

Pages 98-99

What has three horns, a large head plate, and sixteen wheels?
A *TRICERATOPS* ON ROLLER SKATES

Pages 100-101

START

FINISH

Page 102

ANSWERS

Pages 104–105

Page 106

Page 107

What do you call a dinosaur in a phone booth?
STUCK

What did the green dinosaur say to the purple dinosaur?
"BREATHE!"

What do you call an exploding dinosaur?
DINO-MITE

Page 108

Page 110

What do you call a *Supersaurus* wearing earmuffs if you don't know its name?
ANYTHING YOU WANT. IT CAN'T HEAR YOU.

Page 111

Stella: poster;
Brontosaurus

Enzo: papier-mâché;
Stegosaurus

Eva: diorama;
Triceratops

Ben: mosaic;
Tyrannosaurus

Page 112

Page 113

1. T
2. F
3. F
4. T
5. T
6. F
7. F

Page 115

TRIASSIC
JURASSIC
CRETACEOUS

ANSWERS

Page 116

Page 117

round display pedestal velvet ropes sign naming dino horns	velvet ropes sharp teeth	velvet ropes sign naming dino four legs
windows behind horns	round display pedestal windows behind sign naming dino sharp teeth	windows behind four legs
greenery sign naming dino horns	greenery sharp teeth	round display pedestal greenery four legs

Page 118

Page 120

Page 124

Atticus: blue; fruit salad

Lila: pink; cake

Oliver: red; popcorn

Laurel: yellow; chips

Soren: green; veggie tray

Page 125

1. F
2. E
3. J
4. A
5. B
6. C
7. I
8. H
9. G
10. D

Page 127

1. That one is *Allosaurus* Centauri! That's *Tyrannosaurus* Major! That's the Big *Diplodocus*!
2. Gesundheit
3. I've never been in a bouncy house before!
4. You're not fooling me, Fred. I know who you are.

Page 129

1. T
2. F; It was named for Juan Pisano, an Argentine paleontologist.
3. T
4. F; It was named for Fruita, Colorado, where it was found.
5. F; It was named for Pamela Lamplugh, a British paleontologist.
6. T

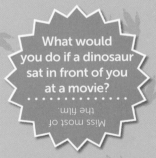

What would you do if a dinosaur sat in front of you at a movie?

Miss most of the film.

ANSWERS

Pages 130–131

Why do museums have old dinosaur bones?

THEY CAN'T AFFORD NEW ONES.

Page 133

Knock, knock.
Who's there?
Shirley.
Shirley who?
Shirley this is the last dinosaur joke.

For information about permission to reprint selections from
this book, please contact permissions@highlights.com.

Published by Highlights Press
815 Church Street
Honesdale, Pennsylvania 18431
ISBN: 978-1-68437-923-1
Manufactured in Dongguan, Guangdong, China
Mfg. 04/2020

First edition
Visit our website at Highlights.com.
10 9 8 7 6 5 4 3 2

Teach Yourself VISUALLY™

OS X® Yosemite

Paul McFedries

Visual
A Wiley Brand

Teach Yourself VISUALLY™ OS X® Yosemite

Published by
John Wiley & Sons, Inc.
10475 Crosspoint Boulevard
Indianapolis, IN 46256

www.wiley.com

Published simultaneously in Canada

Library of Congress Control Number: 2014945053

ISBN: 978-1-118-99123-7 (pbk); ISBN: 978-1-118-99127-5 (ebk); ISBN: 978-1-118-99136-7 (ebk)

Manufactured in the United States of America

10 9 8 7 6 5 4 3 2 1

Trademark Acknowledgments

Contact Us

For general information on our other products and services please contact our Customer Care Department within the U.S. at 877-762-2974, outside the U.S. at 317-572-3993 or fax 317-572-4002.

For technical support please visit www.wiley.com/techsupport.

Sales | Contact Wiley at (877) 762-2974 or fax (317) 572-4002.

Credits

Acquisitions Editor
Aaron Black

Sr. Project Editor
Sarah Hellert

Technical Editor
Galen Gruman

Copy Editor
Scott Tullis

Project Coordinator
Emily Benford

**Manager, Content Development
& Assembly**
Mary Beth Wakefield

Publisher
Jim Minatel

About the Author

Paul McFedries is a full-time technical writer. He has been authoring computer books since 1991 and has more than 85 books to his credit, including *Teach Yourself VISUALLY Windows 8.1*, *Windows 8.1 Simplified*, *Windows 8 Visual Quick Tips*, *Excel Data Analysis: Your visual blueprint for analyzing data, charts, and PivotTables*, 4th Edition, *Teach Yourself VISUALLY Excel 2013*, *Teach Yourself VISUALLY OS X Mavericks*, *The Facebook Guide for People Over 50*, *iPhone 5s and 5c Portable Genius*, and *iPad Portable Genius*, 2nd Edition, all available from Wiley. Paul's books have sold more than 4 million copies worldwide. Paul is also the proprietor of Word Spy (www.wordspy.com), a website that tracks new words and phrases as they enter the English language. Paul invites you to drop by his personal website at www.mcfedries.com, or you can follow him on Twitter @paulmcf and @wordspy.

Author's Acknowledgments

It goes without saying that writers focus on text and I certainly enjoyed focusing on the text that you will read in this book. However, this book is more than just the usual collection of words and phrases designed to educate and stimulate the mind. A quick thumb through the pages will show you that this book is also chock full of treats for the eye, including copious screen shots, meticulous layouts, and sharp fonts. Those sure make for a beautiful book and that beauty comes from a lot of hard work by an immensely talented group of designers and layout artists. I thank them for creating another gem. Of course, what you read in this book must also be accurate, logically presented, and free of errors. Ensuring all of this was an excellent group of editors that I got to work with directly, including project editor Sarah Hellert, copy editor Scott Tullis, and technical editor Galen Gruman. Thanks to all of you for your exceptional competence and hard work. Thanks, as well, to acquisitions editor Aaron Black for asking me to write this book.

How to Use This Book

Who This Book Is For

This book is for the reader who has never used this particular technology or software application. It is also for readers who want to expand their knowledge.

The Conventions in This Book

① Steps

This book uses a step-by-step format to guide you easily through each task. Numbered steps are actions you must do; bulleted steps clarify a point, step, or optional feature; and indented steps give you the result.

② Notes

Notes give additional information — special conditions that may occur during an operation, a situation that you want to avoid, or a cross reference to a related area of the book.

③ Icons and Buttons

Icons and buttons show you exactly what you need to click to perform a step.

④ Tips

Tips offer additional information, including warnings and shortcuts.

⑤ Bold

Bold type shows command names, options, and text or numbers you must type.

⑥ Italics

Italic type introduces and defines a new term.

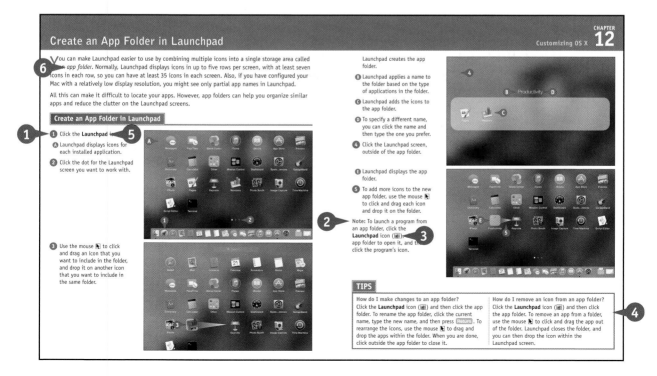

Table of Contents

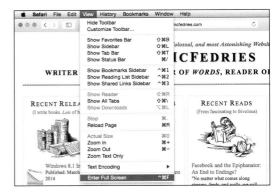

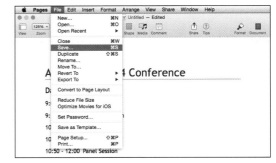

Chapter 3 Browsing the Web

Chapter 4 Communicating via Email

Table of Contents

Table of Contents

Chapter 9   Viewing and Editing Photos

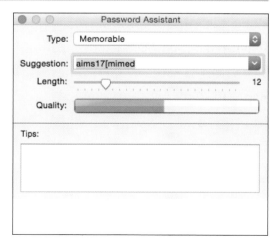

Table of Contents

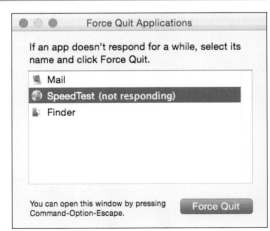

CHAPTER 1

Learning Basic Program Tasks

One of the most crucial OS X concepts is the application (also sometimes called a program), because it is via applications that you perform all other OS X tasks. Therefore, it is important to have a basic understanding of how to start and manage applications in OS X.

Explore the OS X Screen

Before you can begin to understand how the OS X operating system works, you should become familiar with the basic screen elements. These elements include the OS X menu bar, the desktop, desktop icons, and the Dock. Understanding where these elements appear on the screen and what they are used for will help you work through the rest of the tasks in this book and will help you navigate OS X and its applications on your own.

A Menu Bar

The menu bar contains the pull-down menus for OS X and most Mac software.

B Desktop

This is the OS X work area, where you work with your applications and documents.

C Mouse Pointer

When you move your mouse or move your finger on a trackpad, the pointer moves along with it.

D Desktop Icon

An icon on the desktop represents an application, a folder, a document, or a device attached to your Mac, such as a hard drive, a CD or DVD, or an iPod.

E Dock

The Dock contains several icons, each of which gives you quick access to a commonly used application.

Tour the Dock

The Dock is the strip that runs along the bottom of the Mac screen. The Dock is populated with several small images, which are called *icons*. Each icon represents a particular component of your Mac — an application, a folder, a document, and so on — and clicking the icon opens the component. This makes the Dock one of the most important and useful OS X features because it gives you one-click access to applications, folders, and documents. The icons shown here are typical, but your Mac may display a different arrangement.

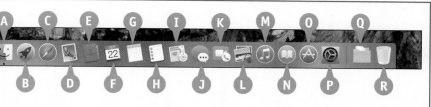

Ⓐ Finder

Work with the files on your computer.

Ⓑ Launchpad

View, organize, and start your applications.

Ⓒ Safari

Browse the World Wide Web on the Internet.

Ⓓ Mail

Send and receive email messages.

Ⓔ Contacts

Store and access people's names, addresses, and other contact information.

Ⓕ Calendar

Record upcoming appointments, birthdays, meetings, and other events.

Ⓖ Notes

Record to-do lists and other short notes.

Ⓗ Reminders

Set reminders for upcoming tasks.

Ⓘ Maps

Find and get directions to locations.

Ⓙ Messages

Send instant messages to other people.

Ⓚ FaceTime

Place video and audio calls to other FaceTime users.

Ⓛ Preview

View and work with images.

Ⓜ iTunes

Play music and other media and add media to your iPod, iPhone, or iPad.

Ⓝ iBooks

Purchase and read e-books.

Ⓞ App Store

Install new applications and upgrade existing ones.

Ⓟ System Preferences

Customize and configure your Mac.

Ⓠ Downloads

Display the contents of your Downloads folder.

Ⓡ Trash

Delete files, folders, and applications.

Start an Application

To perform tasks of any kind in OS X, you use one of the applications installed on your Mac. The application you use depends on the task you want to perform. For example, if you want to surf the World Wide Web, you use a web browser application, such as the Safari program that comes with OS X. Before you can use an application, however, you must first tell OS X what application you want to run. OS X launches the application and displays it on the desktop. You can then use the application's tools to perform your tasks.

Start an Application

1 Click the **Finder** icon (🖥️).

Note: If the application that you want to start has an icon in the Dock, you can click the icon to start the application and skip the steps in this task.

The Finder window appears.

2 Click **Applications**.

Note: You can also navigate to Applications in any Finder window by pressing **Shift**+**⌘**+**A** or by choosing **Go** and then clicking **Applications**.

The Applications window appears.

③ Double-click the icon of the application that you want to start.

Note: In some cases, double-clicking the icon just displays the contents of a folder, which is a storage area on your Mac. In this case, you then double-click the application icon.

Ⓐ The application appears on the desktop.

Ⓑ OS X adds a button for the application to the Dock.

Ⓒ The menu bar displays the menus associated with the application.

Note: Another common way to launch an application is to use Finder to locate a document you want to work with and then double-click that document.

How do I add an icon to the Dock for an application I use frequently?
To add an icon to the desktop, repeat steps 1 to 3 in this task. Right-click the application's Dock icon, click **Options**, and then click **Keep in Dock**.

How do I shut down a running application?
To shut down a running application, right-click the application's Dock icon and then click **Quit**. Alternatively, you can switch to the application and press ⌘+Q.

Start an Application Using Launchpad

You can start an application using the Launchpad feature. This is often faster than using the Applications folder, particularly for applications that do not have a Dock icon.

Launchpad is designed to mimic the Home screens of the iPhone, iPad, and iPod touch. So if you own one or more of these devices, then you are already familiar with how Launchpad works.

Start an Application Using Launchpad

1 Click the **Launchpad** icon (⬤).

The Launchpad screen appears.

2 If the application you want to start resides in a different Launchpad screen, click the dot that corresponds to the screen.

Launchpad switches to the screen and displays the applications.

③ If the application you want to start resides within a folder, click the folder.

Launchpad opens the folder.

④ Click the icon of the application you want to start.

OS X starts the application.

TIP

Is there an easier way to navigate the Launchpad screens?

Yes. OS X has designed Launchpad to work like the iPhone, iPad, and iPod touch, which you navigate by using a finger to swipe the screen right or left. With your Mac, you can also navigate the Launchpad screens by swiping. In this case, however, you must use two fingers, and you swipe right or left on either the trackpad or the surface of a Magic Mouse.

You can also use a trackpad gesture to open Launchpad: Place four fingers lightly on the trackpad and pinch them together.

To exit Launchpad without starting an application, press Esc.

Switch Between Applications

If you plan on running multiple applications at the same time, you need to know how to easily switch from one application to another. In OS X, after you start one application, you do not need to close that application before you open another one. OS X supports a feature called *multitasking*, which means running two or more applications simultaneously. This is handy if you need to use several applications throughout the day.

Switch Between Applications

1 Click the Dock icon of the application you want to switch to.

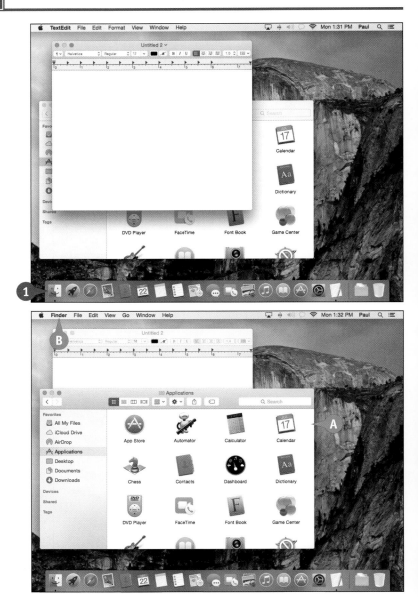

A OS X brings the application window(s) to the foreground.

B The menu bar displays the menus associated with the application.

Note: To switch between applications from the keyboard, press and hold ⌘ and repeatedly press Tab until the application that you want is highlighted in the list of running applications. Release ⌘ to switch to the application.

View Running Applications with Mission Control

The Mission Control feature makes it easier for you to navigate and locate your running applications. OS X allows you to open multiple applications simultaneously, and the only real limit to the number of open applications you can have is the amount of memory contained in your Mac. In practical terms, this means you can easily open several applications, some of which may have multiple open windows. To help locate and navigate to the window you need, use the Mission Control feature.

View Running Applications with Mission Control

1 Click the **Launchpad** icon (🚀).

2 Click the **Mission Control** icon (⬛).

Note: You can also invoke Mission Control by pressing F3 or by placing four fingers on the trackpad of your Mac and then swiping up.

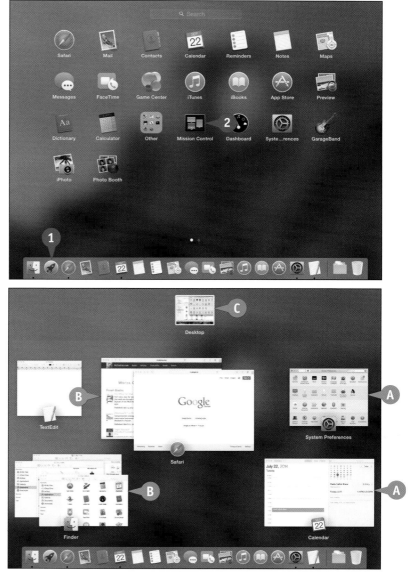

Ⓐ Mission Control displays each open window.

Ⓑ Mission Control groups windows from the same application.

To switch to a particular window, click it.

Ⓒ To close Mission Control without selecting a window, click **Desktop** or press Esc.

Tour an Application Window

When you start an application, it appears on the OS X desktop in its own window. Each application has a unique window layout, but almost all application windows have a few features in common. To get the most out of your applications and to start working quickly and efficiently in an application, you need to know what these common features are and where to find them within the application window.

A Close Button

Click the **Close** button (■) to remove the application window from the desktop, usually without exiting the application.

B Minimize Button

Click the **Minimize** button (■) to remove the window from the desktop and display an icon for the currently open document in the right side of the Dock. The window is still open, but not active.

C Zoom Button

Click the **Zoom** button (■) to display the application full screen, or to enlarge the window so that it can display either all of its content or as much of its content as can fit the screen.

D Toolbar

The toolbar contains buttons that offer easy access to common application commands and features, although not all applications have toolbars. To move the window, click and drag the toolbar.

E Vertical Scroll Bar

Click and drag the vertical scroll bar to navigate up and down in a document. In some cases, you can also click and drag the horizontal scroll bar to navigate left and right in a document.

F Resize Control

Click and drag any edge or corner of the window to make the window larger or smaller.

G Status Bar

The status bar displays information about the current state of the application or document.

Run an Application Full Screen

You can maximize the viewing and working areas of an application by running that application in full-screen mode. When you switch to full-screen mode, OS X hides the menu bar, the application's status bar, the Dock, and the top section of the application window (the section that includes the Close, Minimize, and Zoom buttons). OS X then expands the rest of the application window so that it takes up the entire screen. You must be running OS X Lion or later to use full-screen mode. Note, too, that not all programs are capable of switching to full-screen mode.

Run an Application Full Screen

1 Click **View**.

2 Click **Enter Full Screen**.

You can also press
`Control` + `⌘` + `F`

A In applications that support Full Screen, you can also click the **Zoom** button (⬜).

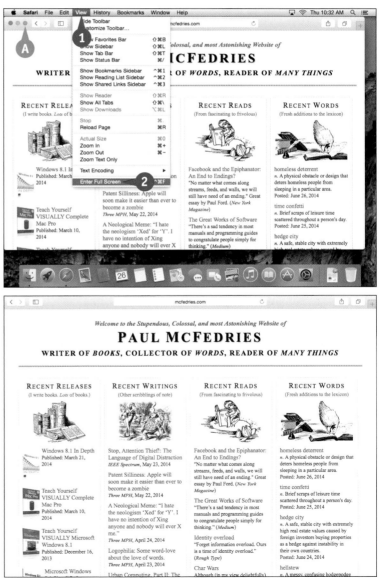

OS X expands the application window to take up the entire screen.

Note: To exit full-screen mode, move the mouse ▶ up to the top of the screen to reveal the menu bar, click **View**, and then click **Exit Full Screen**. You can also press `Esc` or `Control` + `⌘` + `F`.

Select a Command from a Pull-Down Menu

When you are working in an application, you can use the menu bar to access the application's commands and features. Each item in the menu bar represents a *pull-down menu*, a collection of commands usually related to each other in some way. For example, the File menu commands usually deal with file-related tasks such as opening and closing documents. The items in a menu are either commands that execute an action in the application, or features that you can turn on and off.

Select a Command from a Pull-Down Menu

Execute Commands

1 Click the name of the menu that you want to display.

A The application displays the menu.

2 Click the command that you want to execute.

The application executes the command.

B If a command is followed by an ellipsis (...), it means the command displays a dialog.

C If a command is followed by an arrow (▶), it means the command displays a submenu. Click the command to open the submenu and then click the command that you want to run.

Turn Features On and Off

1 Click the name of the menu that you want to display.

D The application displays the menu.

2 Click the menu item.

You may have to click for a submenu if your command is not on the main menu.

The application turns the feature either on or off.

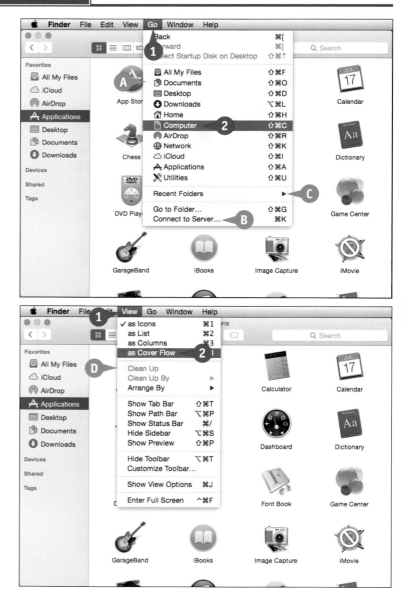

Select a Command Using a Toolbar

Yᵒu can access many application commands faster by using the toolbar. Many applications come with a toolbar, which is a collection of buttons, lists, and other controls displayed in a strip, usually across the top of the application window. Because the toolbar is always visible, you can always use it to select commands, which means that the toolbar often gives you one-click access to the application's most common features. This is faster than using the menu bar method, which often takes several clicks, depending on the command.

Select a Command Using a Toolbar

Turn Features On and Off

1 Click the toolbar button that represents the feature you want to turn on.

A The application turns the feature on and indicates this state by highlighting the toolbar button.

B When a feature is turned off, the application does not highlight the button.

Execute Commands

1 Click the toolbar button that represents the command that you want.

2 If the button displays a menu, click the command on the menu.

C The application executes the command.

Select Options with Dialog Controls

You often interact with an application by selecting options or typing text using a dialog. A *dialog* is a small window that appears when an application has information for you, or needs you to provide information. For example, when you select the File menu's Print command to print a document, you use the Print dialog to specify the number of copies that you want to print.

You provide that and other information by accessing various types of dialog controls. To provide information to an application quickly and accurately, you need to know what these dialog controls look like and how they work.

A Command Button

Clicking a command button executes the command printed on the button face. For example, you can click **OK** to apply settings that you have chosen in a dialog, or you can click **Cancel** to close the dialog without changing the settings.

B Text Box

A text box enables you to enter typed text. Press `Delete` to delete any existing characters and then type your text.

C Stepper

A stepper (⊡) appears beside some text boxes and consists of two arrows: click the upward-pointing arrow to increment the text box value; click the downward-pointing arrow to decrement the text box value.

D List Box

A list box displays a list of choices from which you select the item you want. Use the vertical scroll bar to bring the item you want into view and then click the item to select it.

E Tabs

Many dialogs offer a large number of controls, so related controls appear on different tabs, and the tab names and icons appear across the top of the dialog. Click a tab to see its controls.

F Pop-Up Menu

A pop-up menu displays a list of choices from which you select the item you want. Click the up-down arrows (⬍) to display the menu and then click the item that you want to select.

G Radio Button

Clicking a radio button turns on an application feature. Only one radio button in a group can be turned on at a time. When you click a radio button that is currently off, it changes from □ to ⬤; a radio button that is on changes from ⬤ to □.

H Check Box

Clicking a check box toggles an application feature on and off. If you are turning on a feature, the check box changes from □ to ✓; if you are turning off the feature, the check box changes from ✓ to □.

CHAPTER 2

Learning Basic Document Tasks

Much of the work you do in OS X involves documents, which are files that contain text, images, and other data. These tasks include saving, opening, printing, and editing documents, as well as copying and renaming files.

Save a Document

After you create a document and make changes to it, you can save the document to preserve your work. When you work on a document, OS X stores the changes in your computer's memory. However, OS X erases the contents of the Mac's memory each time you shut down or restart the computer. This means that the changes you make to your document are lost when you turn off or restart your Mac. However, saving the document preserves your changes on your Mac's hard drive.

Save a Document

1 Click **File**.

2 Click **Save**.

In most applications, you can also press ⌘+S.

If you have saved the document previously, your changes are now preserved, and you do not need to follow the rest of the steps in this task.

If this is a new document that you have never saved before, the Save As dialog appears.

3 Type the filename you want to use in the Save As text box.

Ⓐ To store the file in a different folder, you can click the **Where** ⊙ and then select the location that you prefer from the pop-up menu.

4 Click **Save**.

The application saves the file.

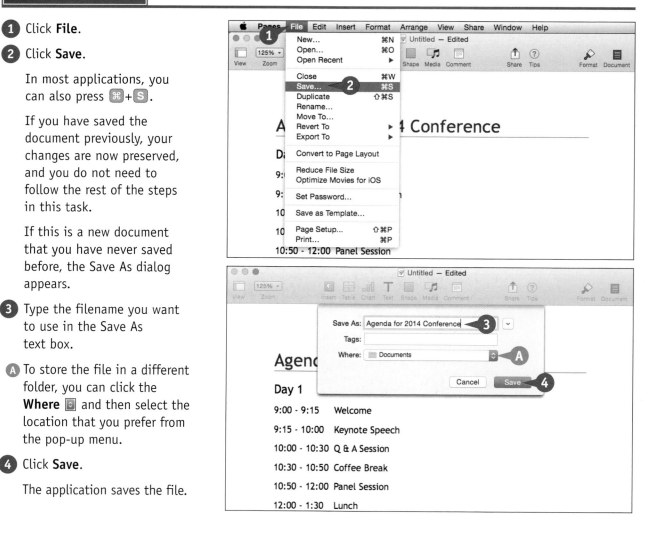

20

Open a Document

To work with a document that you have saved in the past, you can open it in the application that you used to create it. When you save a document, you save its contents to your Mac's hard drive, and those contents are stored in a separate file. When you open the document using the same application that you used to save it, OS X loads the file's contents into memory and displays the document in the application. You can then view or edit the document as needed.

Open a Document

1 Start the application you want to work with.

2 Click **File**.

3 Click **Open**.

In most applications, you can also press ⌘+O.

The Open dialog appears.

A To select a different folder from which to open a file, you can click 🔽 and then click the location that you prefer.

4 Click the document.

5 Click **Open**.

The document appears in a window on the desktop.

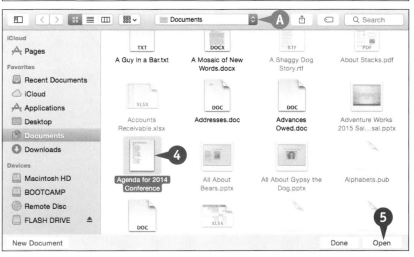

Print a Document

When you need a hard copy of your document, either for your files or to distribute to someone else, you can send the document to your printer. Most applications that deal with documents also come with a Print command. When you run this command, the Print dialog appears. You use the Print dialog to choose the printer you want, as well as to specify how many copies you want to print. Many Print dialogs also enable you to see a preview of your document before printing it.

Print a Document

1 Turn on your printer.

2 Open the document that you want to print.

2► **Agenda for 2014 Conference**

Day 1

9:00 - 9:15   Welcome

9:15 - 10:00   Keynote Speech

10:00 - 10:30 Q & A Session

10:30 - 10:50 Coffee Break

10:50 - 12:00 Panel Session

12:00 - 1:30   Lunch

3 Click **File**.

4 Click **Print**.

In many applications, you can select the Print command by pressing ⌘+P.

File menu:

New...   ⌘N
Open...   ⌘O
Open Recent   ▶

Close   ⌘W
Save   ⌘S
Duplicate   ⇧⌘S
Rename...
Move To...
Revert To   ▶
Export To   ▶

Convert to Page Layout

Reduce File Size
Optimize Movies for iOS

Set Password...

Save as Template...

Page Setup...   ⇧⌘P
Print...   **4** ⌘P

The Print dialog appears.

The layout of the Print dialog varies from application to application. The version shown here is a typical example.

5 If you have more than one printer, click the **Printer** 🔽 to select the printer that you want to use.

6 To print more than one copy, type the number of copies to print in the Copies text box.

7 Click **Print**.

Ⓐ OS X prints the document. The printer's icon appears in the Dock while the document prints.

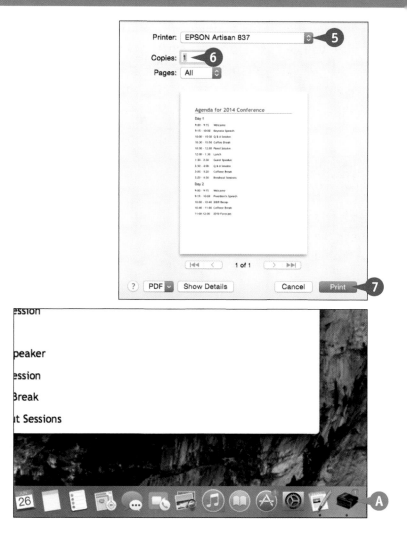

TIP

Can I print only part of my document?

Yes, you can print either a single page or a range of pages, although the steps you use to specify what you want to print vary from one application to another. In the Pages word processing application, for example, you use the Pages pop-up menu to select what you want to print: All, Single, or Range.

If you select the Single option, use the text box (or the stepper, 🔽) to specify the number of the page you want to print.

If you select the Range option, use the two text boxes (or their associated steppers, 🔽) to specify the numbers of the first and last pages you want to print.

Edit Document Text

When you work with a character-based file, such as a text or word processing document or an email message, you need to know the basic techniques for editing text. Any text you type in a document is rarely perfect the first time through. The text more than likely contains errors that require correcting, or words, sentences, or paragraphs that appear in the wrong place. To get your document text the way you want it, you need to know how to edit text, including deleting characters, selecting the text you want to work with, and copying and moving text.

Edit Document Text

Delete Characters

1 In a text document, click immediately to the right of the last character that you want to delete.

A The cursor appears after the character.

Agenda for 2014 Conference

Day 1

Morning Session
9:00 - 9:15	Welcome
9:15 - 10:00	Keynote Speech
10:00 - 10:30	Q & A Session
10:30 - 10:50	Coffee Break
10:50 - 12:00	Panel Session
12:00 - 1:30	Lunch

Afternoon Session
1:30 - 2:30	Guest Speaker
2:30 - 3:00	Q & A Session
3:00 - 3:20	Coffee Break
3:20 - 4:00	A Look at the Future of the Industry
4:00 - 5:00	Breakout Sessions

2 Press Delete until you have deleted all the characters you want.

If you make a mistake, immediately click **Edit** and then click **Undo**. You can also press ⌘+Z.

Agenda for 2014 Conference

Day 1

Morning Session
9:00 - 9:15	Welcome
9:15 - 10:00	Keynote Speech
10:00 - 10:30	Q & A Session
10:30 - 10:50	Coffee Break
10:50 - 12:00	Panel Session
12:00 - 1:30	Lunch

Afternoon Session
1:30 - 2:30	Guest Speaker
2:30 - 3:00	Q & A Session
3:00 - 3:20	Coffee Break
3:20 - 4:00	A Look at the Future
4:00 - 5:00	Breakout Sessions

Select Text for Editing

1 Click and drag across the text that you want to select.

Agenda for 2014 Conference

Day 1

Morning Session ◄ **1**

9:00 - 9:15   Welcome

9:15 - 10:00   Keynote Speech

10:00 - 10:30   Q & A Session

10:30 - 10:50   Coffee Break

10:50 - 12:00   Panel Session

12:00 - 1:30   Lunch

Afternoon Session

1:30 - 2:30   Guest Speaker

2:30 - 3:00   Q & A Session

3:00 - 3:20   Coffee Break

2 Release the mouse button.

B The application highlights the selected text.

Agenda for 2014 Conference

Day 1

2 ► Morning Session ◄ **B**

9:00 - 9:15   Welcome

9:15 - 10:00   Keynote Speech

10:00 - 10:30   Q & A Session

10:30 - 10:50   Coffee Break

10:50 - 12:00   Panel Session

12:00 - 1:30   Lunch

Afternoon Session

1:30 - 2:30   Guest Speaker

2:30 - 3:00   Q & A Session

3:00 - 3:20   Coffee Break

TIP

Are there any shortcut methods for selecting text?

Yes, most OS X applications have shortcuts you can use. Here are the most useful ones:

- Double-click a word to select it.
- Press and hold **Shift** and press ➡ or ⬅ to select entire words.
- Press and hold **Shift** and **⌘** and press ➡ to select to the end of the line, or ⬅ to select to the beginning of the line.
- Triple-click inside a paragraph to select it.
- Click **Edit** and then click **Select All**, or press **⌘**+**A** to select the entire document.

continued ►

Edit Document Text (continued)

Once you select text, you can then copy or move the text to another location in your document. Copying text is often a useful way to save work. For example, if you want to use the same passage of text elsewhere in the document, you can copy it instead of typing it from scratch. If you need a similar passage in another part of the document, copy the original and then edit the copy as needed. If you type a passage of text in the wrong position within the document, you can fix that by moving the text to the correct location.

Edit Document Text (continued)

Copy Text

1. Select the text that you want to copy.

2. Click **Edit**.

3. Click **Copy**.

   In most applications, you can also press ⌘+C.

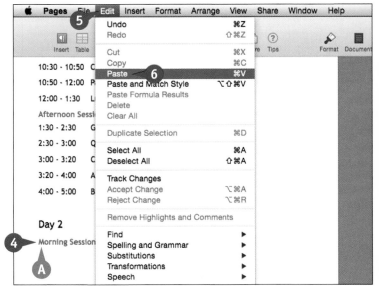

4. Click inside the document where you want the copied text to appear.

   The cursor appears in the position where you clicked.

5. Click **Edit**.

6. Click **Paste**.

   In most applications, you can also press ⌘+V.

Ⓐ The application inserts a copy of the selected text at the cursor position.

Move Text

1 Select the text that you want to move.

2 Click **Edit**.

3 Click **Cut**.

In most applications, you can also press ⌘+X.

The application removes the text from the document.

4 Click inside the document where you want to move the text.

The cursor appears at the position where you clicked.

5 Click **Edit**.

6 Click **Paste**.

In most applications, you can also press ⌘+V.

Ⓑ The application inserts the text at the cursor position.

How do I move and copy text with my mouse?

To move and copy text with your mouse, select the text that you want to move or copy. To move the selected text, position the mouse pointer over the selection and then click and drag the text to the new position within the document.

To copy the selected text, position the mouse pointer over the selection, press and hold Option, and then click and drag the text (the mouse ▲ changes to ◨) to the new position within the document.

Copy a File

You can use OS X to make an exact copy of a file. This is useful when you want to make an extra copy of an important file to use as a backup. Similarly, you might require a copy of a file if you want to send the copy on a disk to another person. Finally, copying a file is also a real timesaver if you need a new file very similar to an existing file: You copy the original file and then make the required changes to the copy. You can copy either a single file or multiple files. You can also use this technique to copy a folder.

Copy a File

1 Locate the file that you want to copy.

2 Open the folder to which you want to copy the file.

To open a second folder window, click **File** and then click **New Finder Window**, or press ⌘+N.

3 Press and hold Option, and then click and drag the file and drop it inside the destination folder.

Ⓐ The original file remains in its folder.

Ⓑ A copy of the original file appears in the destination folder.

You can also make a copy of a file in the same folder, which is useful if you want to make major changes to the file and you would like to preserve a copy of the original. Click the file, click **File**, and then click **Duplicate**, or press ⌘+D. OS X creates a copy with the word "copy" added to the filename.

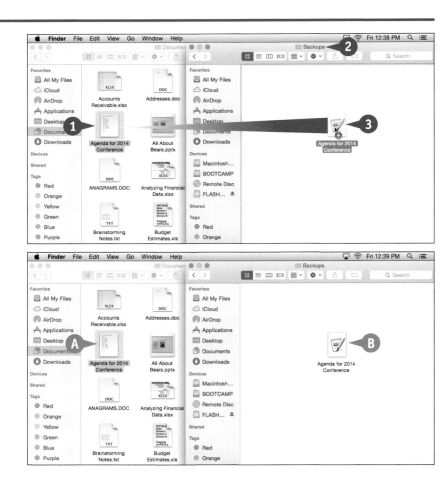

Move a File

When you need to store a file in a new location, the easiest way is to move the file from its current folder to another folder on your Mac. When you save a file for the first time, you specify a folder on your Mac's hard drive. This original location is not permanent, however. Using the technique in this task, you can move the file to another location on your Mac's hard drive. You can use this technique to move a single file, multiple files, and even a folder.

Move a File

1 Locate the file that you want to move.

2 Open the folder to which you want to move the file.

To create a new destination folder in the current folder, click **File** and then click **New Folder**, or press Shift + ⌘ + N.

3 Click and drag the file and drop it inside the destination folder.

Note: If you are moving the file to another drive, you must hold down ⌘ while you click and drag the file.

Ⓐ The file disappears from its original folder.

Ⓑ The file moves to the destination folder.

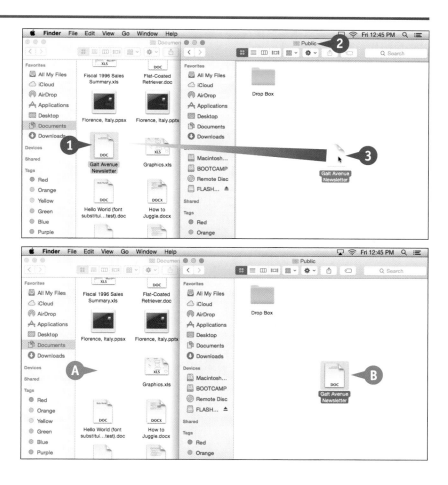

Rename a File

Y‌ou can change the name of a file, which is useful if the current filename does not accurately describe the contents of the file. Giving your document a descriptive name makes it easier to find the file later. You should rename only those documents that you have created or that have been given to you by someone else. Do not try to rename any of the OS X system files or any files associated with your applications, or your computer may behave erratically or even crash.

Rename a File

1 Open the folder containing the file that you want to rename.

2 Click the file.

3 Press Return.

A A text box appears around the filename.

You can also rename any folders that you have created.

4 Edit the existing name or type a new name that you want to use for the file.

If you decide that you do not want to rename the file after all, you can press Esc to cancel the operation.

5 Press Return or click an empty section of the folder.

B The new name appears under the file icon.

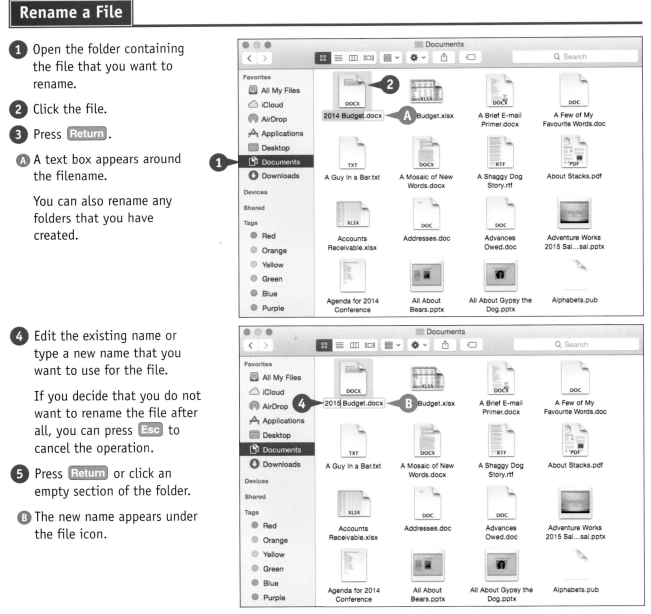

Delete a File

When you no longer need a file, you can delete it. This helps to prevent your hard drive from becoming cluttered with unnecessary files. You should ensure that you delete only those documents that you have created or that have been given to you by someone else. Do not delete any of the OS X system files or any files associated with your applications, or your computer may behave erratically or even crash.

Delete a File

1 Locate the file that you want to delete.

2 Click and drag the file and drop it on the Trash icon in the Dock.

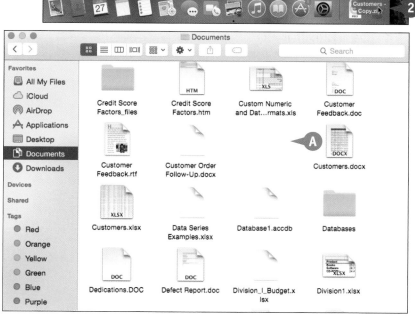

A The file disappears from the folder.

You can also delete a file by clicking it and then pressing ⌘+Delete.

If you delete a file accidentally, you can restore it. Click the Dock's Trash icon to open the Trash window. Right-click the file and then click **Put Back**.

Open a Folder in a Tab

You can make it easier to work with multiple folders simultaneously by opening each folder in its own tab within a single Finder window. As you work with your documents, you may come upon one or more folders that you want to keep available while you work with other folders. Instead of cluttering the desktop with multiple Finder windows, OS X enables you to use a single Finder window that displays each open folder in a special section of the window called a *tab*. To view the contents of any open folder, you need only click its tab.

Open a Folder in a Tab

Open a Folder in a New Tab

1 Right-click the folder you want to open.

2 Click **Open in New Tab**.

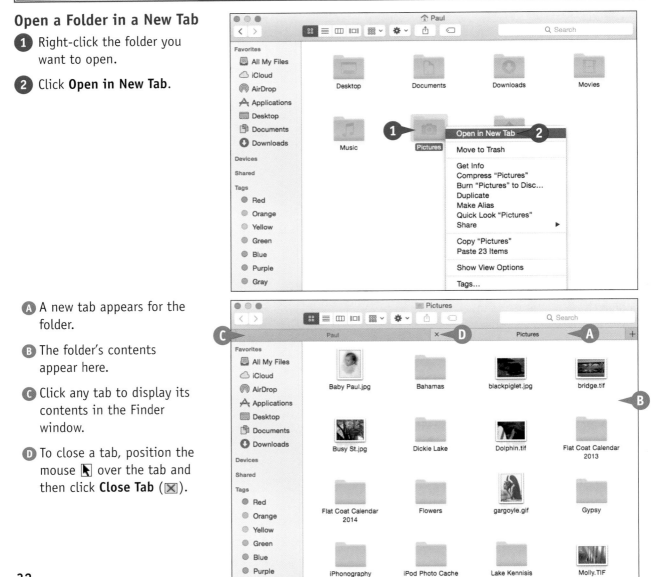

A A new tab appears for the folder.

B The folder's contents appear here.

C Click any tab to display its contents in the Finder window.

D To close a tab, position the mouse ▶ over the tab and then click **Close Tab** (✕).

Create a New Tab

1. Click **File**.

2. Click **New Tab**.

E. If you already have two or more tabs open, you can also click the **Create a new tab** icon (⊞).

   Finder creates a new tab.

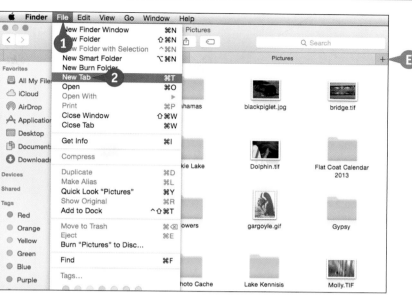

Merge Open Folder Windows into Tabs

1. Click **Window**.

2. Click **Merge All Windows**.

   Finder moves all the open folder windows into tabs in a single Finder window.

Note: To copy or move a file to a folder open in another tab, click and drag the file from its current folder and drop it on the other folder's tab.

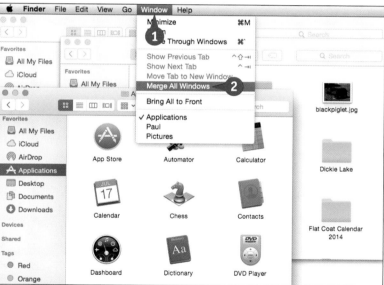

TIP

Are there any shortcuts I can use to work with folders in tabs?
Yes, here are a few useful keyboard techniques you can use:

- In a folder, press and hold ⌘ and double-click a subfolder to open it in a tab. Press and hold ⌘+**Shift** instead to open the subfolder in a tab without switching to the tab.
- In the sidebar, press and hold ⌘ (or ⌘+**Shift**) and click a folder to open it in a tab.
- Press **Shift**+⌘+**]** or **Shift**+⌘+**[** to cycle through the tabs.
- Press ⌘+**W** to close the current tab.
- Press **Option** and click **Close Tab** (⊠) to close every tab but the one you clicked.

CHAPTER 3

Browsing the Web

If your Mac is connected to the Internet, you can use the Safari browser to navigate, or *surf*, websites. Safari offers features that make it easier to browse the web. For example, you can open multiple pages in a single Safari window, and you can save your favorite sites for easier access.

Open a Link

Almost all web pages include links to other pages that contain related information. When you select a link, your web browser loads the other page. Web page links come in two forms: text and images. Text links consist of a word or phrase that usually appears underlined and in a different color from the rest of the page text. However, web page designers can control the look of their links, so text links may not always stand out in this way. Therefore, knowing what words, phrases, or images are links is not always obvious. The only way to tell for sure is to position the mouse over the text or image; if the mouse changes to a pointing finger, you know the item is a link.

Open a Link

1 In the Dock, click the **Safari** icon (▣).

2 Position the mouse ▶ over the link (▶ changes to 🖑).

3 Click the text or image.

A The status bar shows the address of the linked page.

Note: The address shown in the status bar when you point at a link may be different from the one shown when the page is downloading. This occurs when the website *redirects* the link.

Note: If you do not see the status bar, click **View** and then click **Show Status Bar**.

B The linked web page appears.

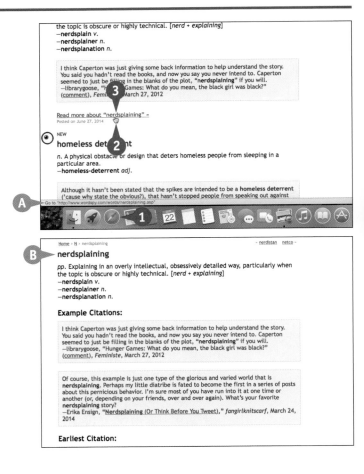

Enter a Web Page Address

Every web page is uniquely identified by an address called the Uniform Resource Locator, or URL. You can type the address into the web browser to display the page.

The URL is composed of four parts: the *transfer method* (usually HTTP, which stands for Hypertext Transfer Protocol), the *domain name*, the *directory* where the web page is located on the server, and the *filename*. The domain name suffix most often used is .com (commercial), but other common suffixes include .gov (government), .org (nonprofit organization), .edu (education), and country domains such as .ca (Canada).

Enter a Web Page Address

1 Click inside the address bar.

2 Press [Delete] to delete the existing address.

3 Type the address of the web page you want to visit.

4 Press [Return].

A You can also click the site if it appears in the list of suggested sites.

B The web page appears.

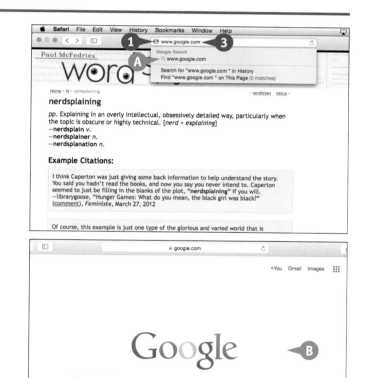

Open a Web Page in a Tab

Y ou can make it easier to work with multiple web pages and sites simultaneously by opening each page in its own tab. As you surf the web, you may come upon a page that you want to keep available while you visit other sites. Instead of leaving the page and trying to find it again when you need it, Safari lets you leave the page open in a special section of the browser window called a *tab*. You can then use a second tab to visit your other sites, and to resume viewing the first site, you need only click its tab.

Open a Web Page in a Tab

Open a Link in a New Tab

1 Right-click the link you want to open.

2 Click **Open Link in New Tab**.

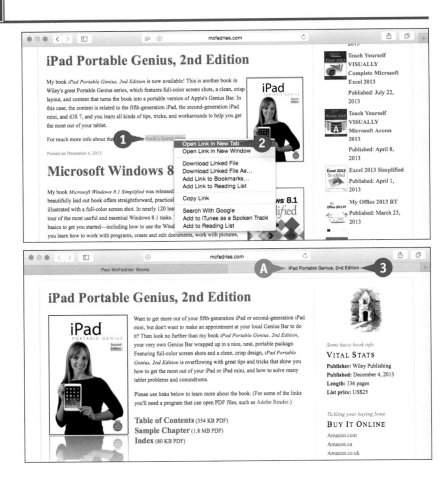

A A new tab appears with the page title.

3 Click the tab to display the page.

Create a New Tab

1 Click **File**.

2 Click **New Tab**.

B If you already have two or more tabs open, you can also click the **Create a new tab** icon (⊞).

C Safari creates a new tab and displays the Favorites pane.

After you have used Safari for a while, the Favorites pane lists the websites that you have visited most often.

3 Type the address of the page you want to load into the new tab.

4 Press **Return**.

D Safari displays the page in the tab.

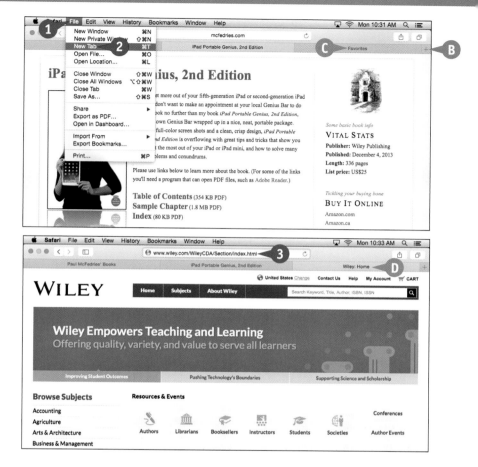

TIP

Are there any shortcuts I can use to open web pages in tabs?

Yes, here are a few useful keyboard techniques you can use:

- Press and hold ⌘ and click a link to open the page in a tab.
- Type an address and then press ⌘+**Return** to open the page in a new tab.
- Press **Shift**+⌘+**]** or **Shift**+⌘+**[** to cycle through the tabs.
- Press ⌘+**W** to close the current tab.

Navigate Web Pages

After you have visited several pages, you can return to a page you visited earlier. Instead of retyping the address or looking for the link, Safari gives you some easier methods. When you navigate from page to page, you create a kind of path through the web. Safari keeps track of this path by maintaining a list of the pages you visit. You can use that list to go back to a page you have visited. After you go back to a page you have visited, you can use the same list to go forward through the pages again.

Navigate Web Pages

Go Back One Page

1 Click the **Previous Page** icon (◁).

The previous page you visited appears.

Go Back Several Pages

1 Click and hold down the mouse ▶ on the **Previous Page** icon (◁).

Note: The list of visited pages is different for each tab that you have open. If you do not see the page you want, you may need to click a different tab.

A list of the pages you have visited appears.

2 Click the page you want to revisit.

The page appears.

Go Forward One Page

1 Click the **Next Page** icon (▷).

The next page appears.

Note: If you are at the last page viewed up to that point, the Next Page icon (▷) is not active.

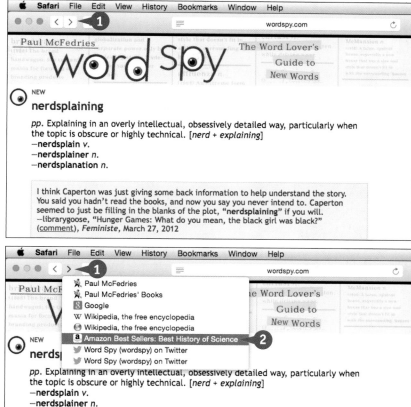

Go Forward Several Pages

1 Click and hold down on the **Next Page** icon (▷).

A list of the pages you have visited appears.

Note: The list of visited pages is different for each tab that you have open. If you do not see the page you want, you may need to click a different tab.

2 Click the page you want to revisit.

The page appears.

TIP

Are there any shortcuts I can use to navigate web pages?

Yes, a few useful keyboard shortcuts you can use are

Press ⌘+[to go back one page.

Press ⌘+] to go forward one page.

Press Shift+⌘+H to return to the Safari home page (the first page you see when you open Safari).

Navigate with the History List

The Previous Page and Next Page icons (◁ and ▷) enable you to navigate pages in the current browser session. To redisplay sites that you have visited in the past few days or weeks, you need to use the History list, which is a collection of the websites and pages you have visited over the past month.

If you visit sensitive places such as an Internet banking site or your corporate site, you can increase security by clearing the History list so that other people cannot see where you have been.

Navigate with the History List

Load a Page from the History List

1 Click **History**.

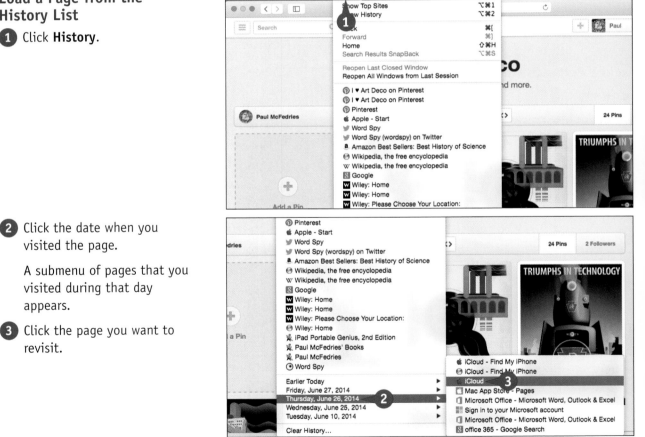

2 Click the date when you visited the page.

A submenu of pages that you visited during that day appears.

3 Click the page you want to revisit.

Ⓐ The page appears.

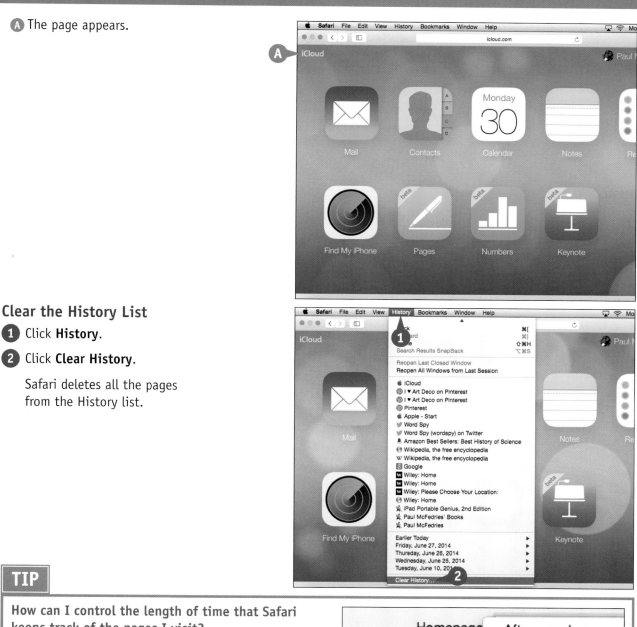

Clear the History List

1 Click **History**.

2 Click **Clear History**.

Safari deletes all the pages from the History list.

TIP

How can I control the length of time that Safari keeps track of the pages I visit?

In the menu bar, click **Safari** and then **Preferences**. The Safari preferences appear. Click the **General** tab. Click the **Remove history items** 🔽 and then select the amount of time you want Safari to track your history (Ⓐ). Click **Close** (⬛) to close the Safari preferences.

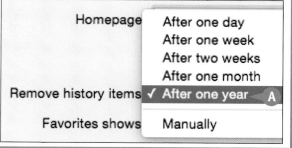

Change Your Home Page

Your home page is the web page that appears when you first start Safari. The default home page is usually the Apple.com Start page, but you can change that to any other page you want, or even to an empty page. This is useful if you do not use the Apple.com Start page, or if there is another page that you always visit at the start of your browsing session. For example, if you have your own website, it might make sense to always begin there. Safari also comes with a command that enables you to view the home page at any time during your browsing session.

Change Your Home Page

Change the Home Page

1 Display the web page that you want to use as your home page.

2 Click **Safari**.

3 Click **Preferences**.

The Safari preferences appear.

④ Click **General**.

⑤ Click **Set to Current Page**.

Ⓐ Safari inserts the address of the current page in the Homepage text box.

Note: If your Mac is not currently connected to the Internet, you can also type the new home page address manually using the Homepage text box.

⑥ Click **Close** (■).

View the Home Page

① Click **History**.

② Click **Home**.

Note: You can also display the home page by pressing
Shift + ⌘ + H.

Safari displays the home page.

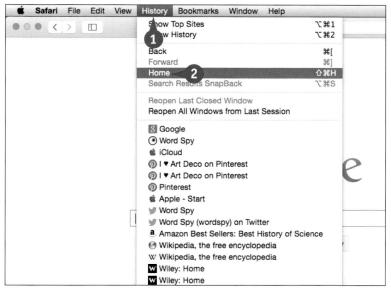

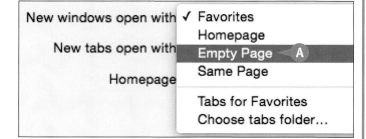

TIP

How can I get Safari to open a new window without displaying the home page?
In the menu bar, click **Safari** and then **Preferences**. The Safari preferences appear. Click the **General** tab. Click the **New windows open with** 🔽 and then select **Empty Page** (Ⓐ) from the pop-up menu. Click **Close** (■) to close the Safari preferences.

Bookmark Web Pages

If you have web pages that you visit frequently, you can save yourself time by storing those pages as bookmarks — also called favorites — within Safari. This enables you to display the pages with just a couple of mouse clicks.

The bookmark stores the name as well as the address of the page. Most bookmarks are stored on the Safari Bookmarks menu. However, Safari also offers the Favorites bar, which appears just below the address bar. You can put your favorite sites on the Favorites bar for easiest access.

Bookmark Web Pages

Bookmark a Web Page

1 Display the web page you want to save as a bookmark.

2 Click **Bookmarks**.

3 Click **Add Bookmark**.

Ⓐ You can also run the Add Bookmark command by clicking **Share** (🔗) and then clicking **Add Bookmark**.

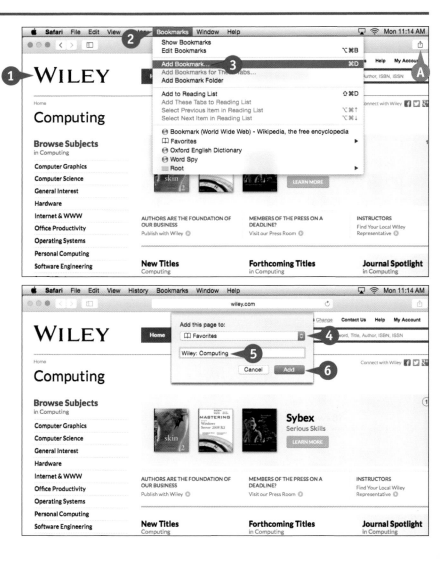

The Add Bookmark dialog appears.

Note: You can also display the Add Bookmark dialog by pressing ⌘+D.

4 Click 🔽 and then click the location where you want to store the bookmark.

5 Edit the page name, if necessary.

6 Click **Add**.

Safari adds a bookmark for the page.

Display a Bookmarked Web Page

1. Click the **Show sidebar** button (▱).

2. Click **Bookmarks** (▦).

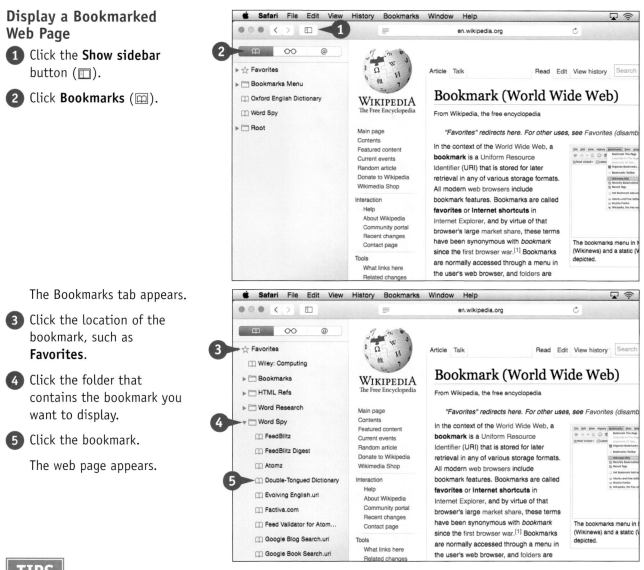

The Bookmarks tab appears.

3. Click the location of the bookmark, such as **Favorites**.

4. Click the folder that contains the bookmark you want to display.

5. Click the bookmark.

The web page appears.

TIPS

Is there an easier way to display favorite pages?

Yes. Click **View** and then click **Show Favorites Bar**. Safari assigns keyboard shortcuts to the first nine bookmarks, counting from left to right and excluding folders. Display the leftmost bookmark by pressing ⌘+1. Moving to the right, the shortcuts are ⌘+2, ⌘+3, and so on.

How do I delete a bookmark?

If the site is on the Favorites bar, right-click the bookmark and then click **Delete**, or hold down ⌘ and drag it off the bar. For all other bookmarks, click the **Show sidebar** button (▱) and then **Bookmarks** (▦) to display the Bookmarks tab. Locate the bookmark to remove, right-click the bookmark, and then click **Delete**.

Search for Sites

If you need information on a specific topic, Safari has a built-in feature that enables you to quickly search the web for sites that have the information you require. The web has a number of sites called *search engines* that enable you to find what you are looking for. By default, Safari uses the Google search site (www.google.com). Simple, one-word searches often return tens of thousands of *hits*, or matching sites. To improve your searching, type multiple search terms that define what you are looking for. To search for a phrase, enclose the words in quotation marks.

Search for Sites

1 Click in the address bar.

2 Press **Delete** to delete the address.

Ⓐ You can click an item in this list to select the search engine you prefer to use.

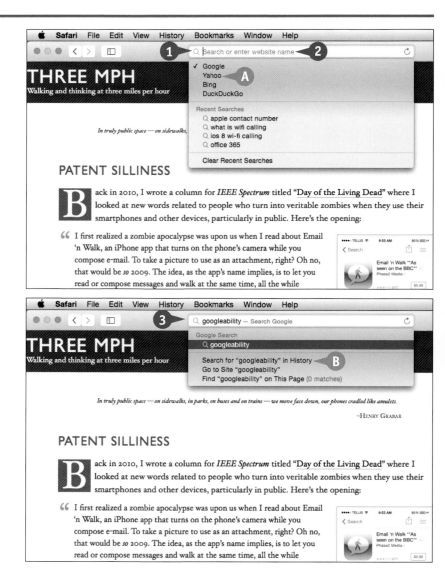

3 Type a word, phrase, or question that represents the information you want to find.

Ⓑ If you see the search text you want to use in the list of suggested searches, click the text and skip step **4**.

4 Press **Return**.

C A list of pages that matches your search text appears.

5 Click a web page.

Google googleability

Web   Maps   Shopping   Images   Videos   More ▾   Search tools

About 49,400 results (0.28 seconds)

googleability - Wiktionary
en.wiktionary.org/wiki/**googleability** ▾ Wiktionary ▾
The good news is that you can improve your **Googleability** (or ability to show up on any search engine) so that people who search for information about you on ...

Urban Dictionary: googleability
www.urbandictionary.com/define.php?...**googleability** ▾ Urban Dictionary ▾
Apr 28, 2008 - ... social networking web pages will be pages listed in the search. The **googleability** of her name makes it easy to find her My Space web pages.

SEO Tips: 5 Ways To Increase A Writer's Googleability
www.huffingtonpost.com/.../seo-tips-writers-_n_335... ▾ The Huffington Post ▾
May 29, 2013 - **Googleability**—the likelihood of being found by an Internet search engine, especially Google—is an integral part of establishing a recognizable ...

Word Spy - googleability ◄ **5**
www.wordspy.com › G ▾
Jun 4, 2007 - **googleability**. (goo.gul.uh.BIL.uh.tee) n. The ease with which information about a person can be found on an Internet search engine, particularly ...

The page appears.

wordspy.com

Paul McFedries

word spy

The Word Lover's Guide to New Words

Home › G › googleability — google   Google bombing -

googleability

(goo.gul.uh.BIL.uh.tee) *n.* The ease with which information about a person can be found on an Internet search engine, particularly Google. Also: **Googleability, googlability, google-ability**.
—**googleable** *adj.*

Example Citations:

What's your '**googleability**' quotient? No clue? Well, then check it out right away because if the world's premier search engine can't trace you in less than a second, then you are a certified also-ran; or so parents of newborns in the US feel. News reports say that '**googleability**' is now a primary baby-naming requirement, which means that parents want names for their children which will work well for web searches: an unusual name that might figure among the first top 10 search results.
—"The name of the game," *Hindustan Times*, May 14, 2007

All the Googler needs is a name, and she's off. It's worse if your name is unusual, as mine is. The difference in **Googleability** between a person with the name "Mary Smith" and a person with my name makes me wonder whether **Googleability** might one day affect how parents name their children. If Mary Smith had been named, instead, Upanishad Smith, she'd be more Googleable. Of course, that's not to guarantee she'd do anything Googleworthy. But what will future conscientious parents decide? Will

TIP

Is there an easy way that I can rerun a recent search?
Yes. Follow these steps to quickly rerun your search:

1 Click **History**.

2 Click **Search Results SnapBack**.

You can also press Option + ⌘ + S.

Safari sends the search text to Google again.

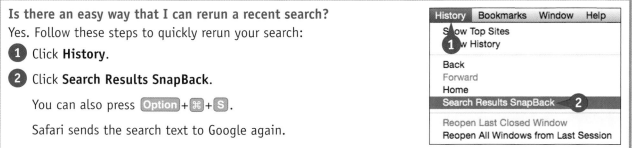

| History | Bookmarks | Window | Help |

1 ▸ Show Top Sites / Show History

Back
Forward
Home
Search Results SnapBack ◄ **2**

Reopen Last Closed Window
Reopen All Windows from Last Session

Download a File

Some websites make files available for you to open on your Mac. To use these files, you can download them to your Mac using Safari. Saving data from the Internet to your computer is called *downloading*. For certain types of files, Safari may display the content right away instead of letting you download it. This happens for files such as text documents and PDF files. In any case, to use a file from a website, you must have an application designed to work with that particular file type. For example, if the file is an Excel workbook, you need either Excel for the Mac or a compatible program.

Download a File

1 Navigate to the page that contains the link to the file.

2 Scroll down and click the link to the file.

Safari downloads the file to your Mac.

A The Show Downloads button shows the progress of the download.

3 When the download is complete, click the **Show Downloads** button (⊡).

4 Right-click the file.

B You can also double-click the icon to the left of the file.

C You can click **Show in Finder** (⊡) to view the file in the Downloads folder.

5 Click **Open**.

The file opens in Finder (in the case of a compressed Zip file, as shown here) or in the corresponding application.

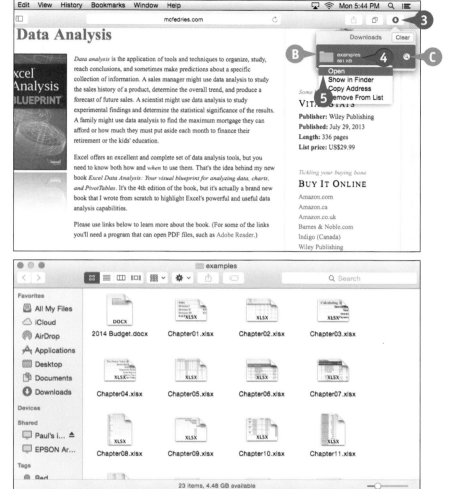

If Safari displays the file instead of downloading it, how do I save the file to my Mac?
Click **File** and then click **Save As**. Type a name for the new file, choose a folder, and then click **Save**.

Is it safe to download files from the web?
Yes, but download files only from sites you trust. If you notice that Safari is attempting to download a file without your permission, cancel the download immediately; the file likely contains a virus or other malware. If you do not trust a file that you have downloaded, use an antivirus program, such as ClamXav at www.clamxav.com, to scan the file before you open it.

View Links Shared on Social Networks

You can make your web surfing more interesting and your social networking more efficient by using Safari to directly access links shared by the people you follow. Social networks are about connecting with people, but a big part of that experience is sharing information, particularly links to interesting, useful, or entertaining web pages. You normally have to log in to the social network to see these links, but if you have used OS X to sign in to your accounts, you can use Safari to directly access links shared by your Twitter and LinkedIn connections.

View Links Shared on Social Networks

Note: For more information on signing in to your social networking accounts, see Chapter 8.

 Click the **Show sidebar** button (▢).

The Bookmarks sidebar appears.

② Click **Shared Links** (@).

Safari displays the Shared Links sidebar, which lists the most recent links shared by the people you follow on Twitter and LinkedIn.

③ Click the shared link you want to view.

Ⓐ Safari displays the linked web page.

Ⓑ For a Twitter link, if you want to retweet the link to your followers, click **Retweet**.

How can I be sure that I am seeing the most recent shared links?

Safari usually updates the Shared Links list each time you open it. However, to be sure that you are seeing the most recent links shared by people you follow on Twitter or are connected to on LinkedIn, click the **View** menu and then click **Update Shared Links**.

How do I hide the Shared Links sidebar when I do not need it?

To give yourself more horizontal screen area for viewing pages, hide the sidebar by clicking the **Show sidebar** button (▥) again. You can also toggle the Shared Links sidebar on and off by pressing Control + ⌘ + 3.

Create a Web Page Reading List

If you do not have time to read a web page now, you can add the page to your Reading List and then read the page later when you have time. You will often come upon a page with fascinating content that you want to read, but lack the time. You could bookmark the article, but bookmarks are really for pages you want to revisit often, not for those you might read only once. A better solution is to add the page to the Reading List, which is a simple list of pages you save to read later.

Create a Web Page Reading List

Add a Page to the Reading List

1. Navigate to the page you want to read later.

2. Click **Bookmarks**.

3. Click **Add to Reading List**.

   Safari adds the page to the Reading List.

Select a Page from the Reading List

1 Click the **Show sidebar** button (▭).

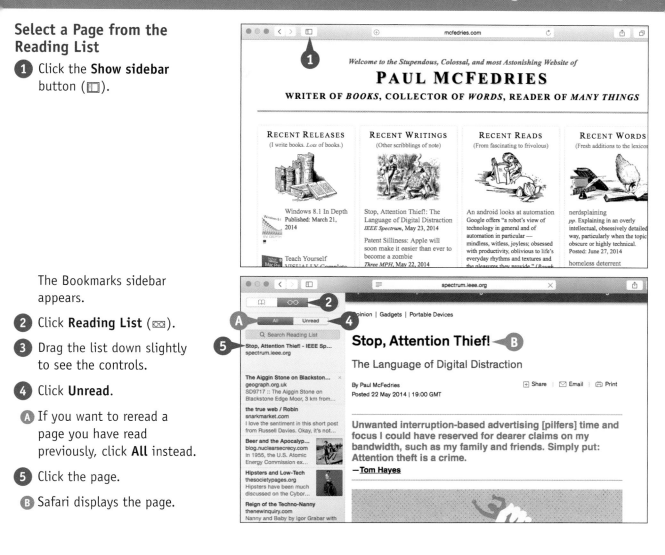

The Bookmarks sidebar appears.

2 Click **Reading List** (👓).

3 Drag the list down slightly to see the controls.

4 Click **Unread**.

Ⓐ If you want to reread a page you have read previously, click **All** instead.

5 Click the page.

Ⓑ Safari displays the page.

Subscribe to a Website Feed

You can keep up to date with a website by subscribing to its feed. A *feed* — sometimes called an *RSS feed* (where RSS stand for Real Simple Syndication) — is a special file that contains links to the latest articles that have been posted to the website. When you subscribe to a feed, Safari automatically checks for updates to the file, so you always know when the website has added new content. This saves you from having to check the site manually from time to time.

Subscribe to a Website Feed

① Navigate to the website that has the feed.

② Click the **Show sidebar** button ().

③ Click **Shared Links** ().

④ Click **Subscriptions**.

5 Click **Add Feed**.

Safari displays a list of the available feeds.

6 Click 🔹 and then click the feed you want.

7 Click **Add Feed**.

Safari adds the feed to the Subscribed Feeds section.

8 Click **Done**.

Safari will now add new content from the site's RSS feed to the Shared Links tab.

Note: To unsubscribe from a feed, repeat steps **1** to **4** to display the Subscribed Feeds list. Click the **Delete** icon (🔘) that appears to the left of the feed you no longer want to view.

Is there a more direct way to subscribe to a feed?

Yes. Most websites that offer a feed also offer a link to the feed file. When you click that link, Safari asks if you want to subscribe to the feed. Click **Subscribe in Shared Links** (🅐).

Subscribe to articles from "www.wordspy.com" in Shared Links?

You can add articles from "www.wordspy.com" to your list of Shared Links

Cancel   Subscribe in Shared Links   🅐

CHAPTER 4

Communicating via Email

OS X comes with the Apple Mail application that you can use to exchange email messages. After you type your account details into Mail, you can send email to friends, family, colleagues, and even total strangers almost anywhere in the world.

Add an Email Account

To send and receive email messages, you must add your email account to the Mail application. Your account is usually a POP (Post Office Protocol) account supplied by your Internet service provider, which should have sent you the account details. You can also use services such as Hotmail and Gmail to set up a web-based email account, which enables you to send and receive messages from any computer. If you have an Apple ID — that is, an account for use on the Apple iCloud service (www.icloud.com) — you can also set up Mail with your iCloud account details.

Add an Email Account

Get Started Adding an Account

1. In the Dock, click the **Mail** icon ( ).

2. Click **Mail**.

3. Click **Add Account**.

Note: If you are just starting Mail and the Welcome to Mail dialog is on-screen, you can skip steps **2** and **3**.

4. Click the type of account you are adding (☐ changes to ◉).

5. Click **Continue**.

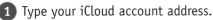

Add an iCloud Account

1. Type your iCloud account address.

2. Type your iCloud account password.

3. Click **Sign In**.

   Mail signs in to your iCloud account.

Note: Mail prompts you to choose which services you want to use with iCloud. See Chapter 14 to learn more.

4. Click **Add Account** (not shown).

   Mail adds your iCloud account.

Add a POP Account

1 Type your name.

2 Type your account address.

3 Type your account password.

4 Click **Create**.

5 Click **POP**.

6 Type the address of the account's incoming mail server.

7 Edit the User Name text as required.

8 Click **Next**.

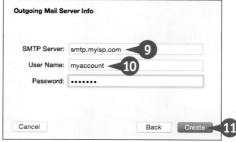

9 Type the address of the outgoing mail server, which is sometimes called the SMTP server.

10 Type the outgoing mail server username and password, if required by your ISP.

11 Click **Create**.

Note: If you see a Verify Certificate dialog, click **Connect**.

12 Click **Create** (not shown).

TIP

My email account requires me to use a nonstandard outgoing mail port. How do I set this up?
In the menu bar, click **Mail** and then **Preferences**. The Mail preferences appear. Click the **Accounts** tab. Click the **Outgoing Mail Server (SMTP)** ⊙ and then click **Edit SMTP Server List**. Click the outgoing mail server. Click the **Advanced** tab. Click **Use custom port** (☐ changes to ◉). Type the nonstandard port number. Click **OK**. Click **Close** (■). Click **Save**.

Send an Email Message

If you know the recipient's email address, you can send a message to that address. An email address is a set of characters that uniquely identifies the location of an Internet mailbox. Each address takes the form *username@domain*, where *username* is the name of the person's account with the ISP or with an organization; and *domain* is the Internet name of the company that provides the person's account. When you send a message, it travels through your ISP's outgoing mail server, which routes the message to the recipient's incoming mail server, which then stores the message in the recipient's mailbox.

Send an Email Message

1 Click **New Message** (🖉).

Note: You can also start a new message by pressing ⌘+N.

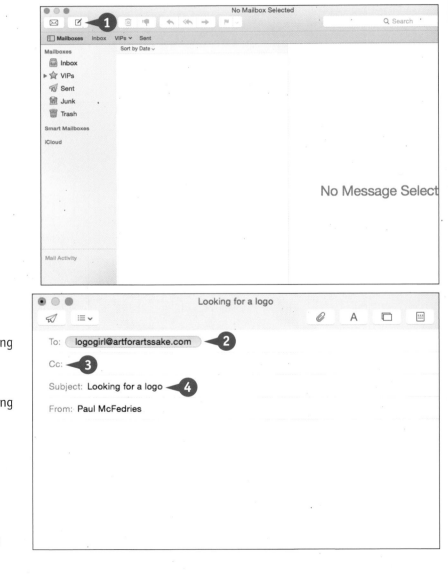

A message window appears.

2 Type the email address of the person to whom you are sending the message in the To field.

3 Type the email address of the person to whom you are sending a copy of the message in the Cc field.

Note: You can add multiple email addresses in both the To field and the Cc field by separating each address with a comma (,).

4 Type a brief description of the message in the Subject field.

5 Type the message.

A To change the message font, click **Fonts** (△) to display the Font panel.

B To change the overall look of the message, click **Show Stationery** (▤) and then click a theme.

Note: Email is a text medium, so most people would rather not receive messages with extraneous graphics. It is best to keep your messages simple and unadorned. If you want to send plain-text messages, click **Format** and then click **Make Plain Text**.

6 Click **Send** (⌦).

Mail sends your message.

Note: Mail stores a copy of your message in the Sent folder.

Looking for a logo

To: logogirl@artforartssake.com

Cc:

Subject: Looking for a logo

From: Paul McFedries

Hi Sheila,

First, let me say that I'm a big fan of your work. Your logos and designs are fresh and original and always just so. I'm hoping I can hire you to design a logo for an app I'm making. I run Word Spy (www.wordspy.com), a site that tracks new words as they enter the language, and I'm in the process of programming an app for the site. Would you have the interest and the time to help with the app's graphics? If so, let me know and I'll pass along some specifics.

Bye for now,

Paul McFedries

Looking for a logo

To: logogirl@artforartssake.com

Cc:

Subject: Looking for a logo

From: Paul McFedries

Hi Sheila,

First, let me say that I'm a big fan of your work. Your logos and designs are fresh and original and always just so. I'm hoping I can hire you to design a logo for an app I'm making. I run Word Spy (www.wordspy.com), a site that tracks new words as they enter the language, and I'm in the process of programming an app for the site. Would you have the interest and the time to help with the app's graphics? If so, let me know and I'll pass along some specifics.

Bye for now,

Paul McFedries

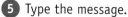

TIP

How can I compose a large number of messages offline?

You can compose your messages offline by following these steps. While disconnected from the Internet, click the **Mail** icon (▤) in the Dock to start Mail. To ensure that you are working offline, click **Mailbox**. If the Take All Accounts Offline command is enabled, click that command. Compose and send the message. Each time you click **Send** (⌦), your message is stored temporarily in the Outbox folder. When you are done, connect to the Internet. After a few moments, Mail automatically sends all the messages in the Outbox folder.

Add a File Attachment

If you have a file you want to send to another person, you can attach it to an email message. A typical message is fine for short notes, but you may have something more complex to communicate, such as budget numbers or a slideshow, or some form of media that you want to share, such as an image.

These more complex types of data come in a separate file — such as a spreadsheet, presentation file, or picture file — so you need to send that file to your recipient. You do this by attaching the file to an email message.

Add a File Attachment

1 Click **New Message** (⬚).

A message window appears.

2 Fill in the recipients, subject, and message text as described in the previous task, "Send an Email Message."

3 Press Return two or three times to move the cursor a few lines below your message.

4 Click **Attach** (⬚).

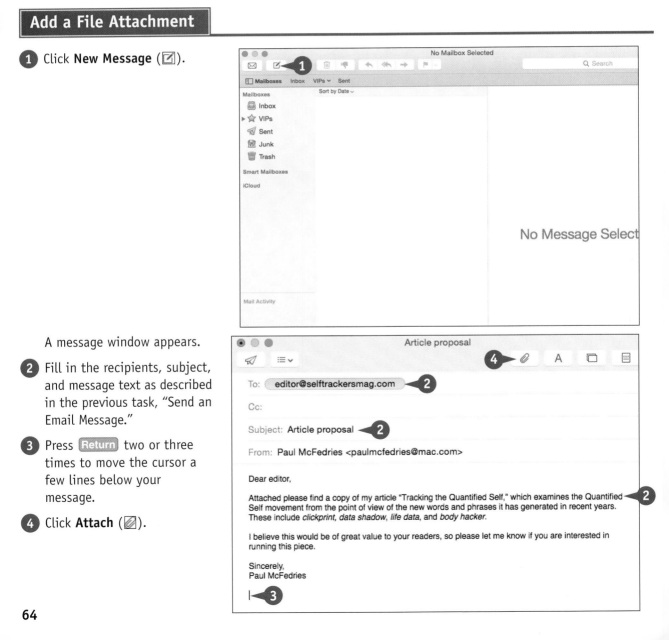

A file selection dialog appears.

5 Click the file you want to attach.

6 Click **Choose File**.

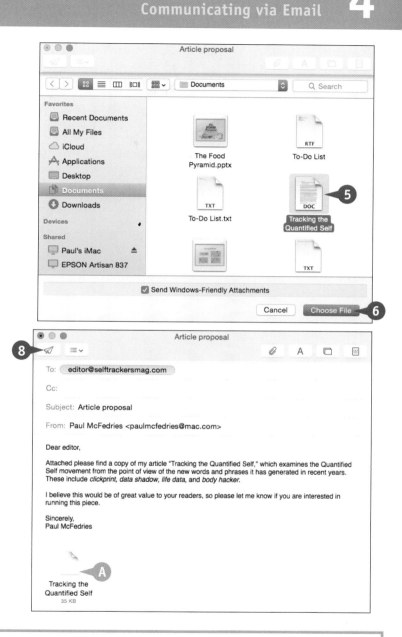

A Mail attaches the file to the message.

Note: Another way to attach a file to a message is to click and drag the file from Finder and drop it inside the message.

7 Repeat steps **4** to **6** to attach additional files to the message.

8 Click **Send** ($\boxtimes$).

Mail sends your message.

TIP

Is there a limit to the number of files I can attach to a message?

The number of files you can attach to the message has no practical limit. However, you should be careful with the total *size* of the files you send to someone. Many ISPs place a limit on the size of a message's attachments, which is usually between 2MB and 5MB. In general, use email to send only a few small files at a time.

If you have an iCloud account, when you send a large attachment Mail asks if you want to use the new Mail Drop feature, which stores the attachment in iCloud. Click **Use Mail Drop** to enable your recipient to download the attachment from iCloud.

Annotate an Attachment

You can personalize or make an attachment easier for your recipient to understand by annotating the attachment before you send it. *Annotating* an attachment means adding your own text or shapes, such as lines, arrows, or circles. These annotations — which are also called *markup* — do not alter the existing text or graphics in the attachment. Instead, they appear "on top" of the attached document in much the same way as you might write or draw on a physical document. You can add markup to images and some types of documents, including PDF files.

Annotate an Attachment

Display the Annotation Tools

1. Position the mouse  over the attachment.

2. Click **Actions** (⌄).

3. Click **Markup**.

Ⓐ Mail displays the annotation tools.

Draw a Line

1. Click **Line Options** (☰) and then click a line thickness and type.

2. Click **Color** (▣) and then click a line color.

3. Click the **Line** tool (⬚).

4. Drag the mouse on the attachment in the shape of the line you want.

Ⓑ You can also click **Shapes** (▢) to draw a shape on the attachment.

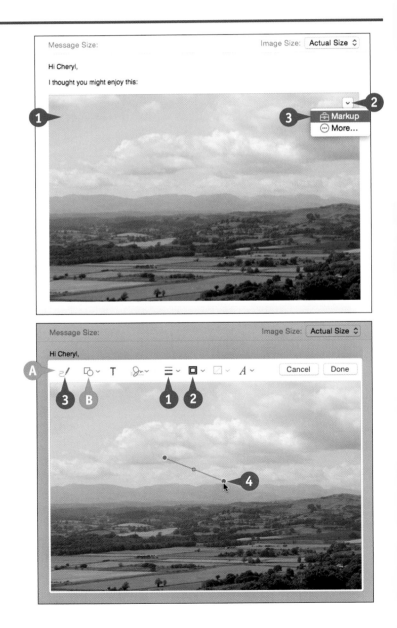

Add Text

1. Click **Font** () and then click the font options you want to use, such as the typeface and type size.

2. Click **Text** (T).

   Mail adds a text box on the attachment.

3. Click inside the text box and then type the text.

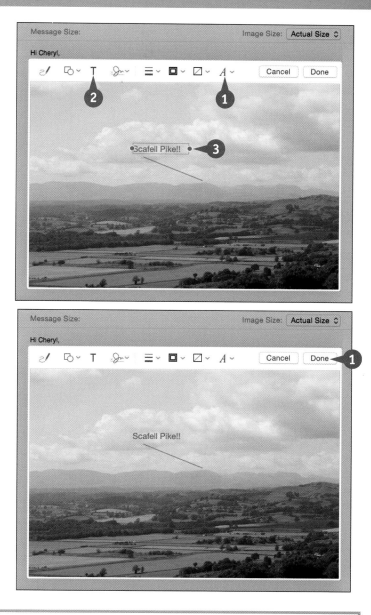

Complete the Annotation

1. Click **Done**.

   Mail saves the annotations with the attached file.

When I add a text box, I can hardly see the text. Why?
If the image you are annotating is large, Mail adds the text in proportion to the image size, so it appears small. Click **Font** (A) and then select a large font size, such as 125 or 150 points.

Can I add my written signature as an annotation?
Yes, if you have your signature on paper, and your Mac has a camera attached. In the annotation tools, click **Signature** (⌖) and then click **Camera**. Hold your signature up to the Mac's camera and align the bottom with the horizontal blue line that appears on-screen. Click **Done** and then click your signature to add it.

Add a Signature Block

A *signature block* is a small amount of text that appears at the bottom of an email message. Instead of typing this information manually, you can save the signature in your Mail preferences. When you compose a new message, reply to a message, or forward a message, you can click a button to have Mail add the signature block to your outgoing message.

Signature blocks usually contain personal contact information, such as your phone numbers, business address, and email and website addresses. Mail supports multiple signature blocks, which is useful if you use multiple accounts or for different purposes such as business and personal.

Add a Signature Block

Create a Signature Block

1 Click **Mail**.

2 Click **Preferences**.

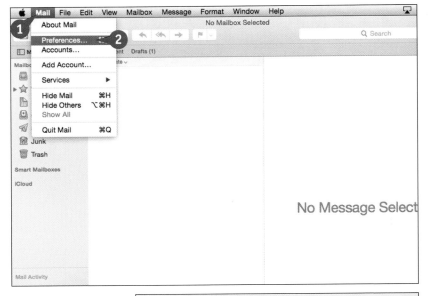

The Mail preferences appear.

3 Click **Signatures**.

4 Click the account for which you want to use the signature.

5 Click **Create a signature** (⊞).

Mail adds a new signature.

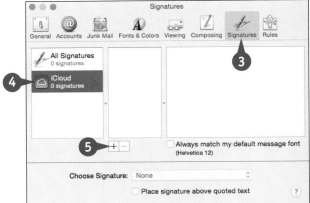

6 Type a name for the signature.

7 Type the signature text.

8 Repeat steps **4** to **7** to add other signatures, if required.

Note: You can add as many signatures as you want. For example, you may want to have one signature for business use and another for personal use.

9 Click **Close** (■).

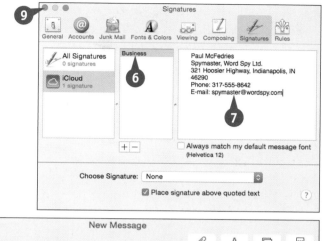

Insert the Signature

1 Click **New Message** (✉) to start a new message.

Note: To start a new message, see the task "Send an Email Message."

2 In the message text area, move the insertion point to the location where you want the signature to appear.

3 Click the **Signature** ◙ and then click the signature you want to insert.

A The signature appears in the message.

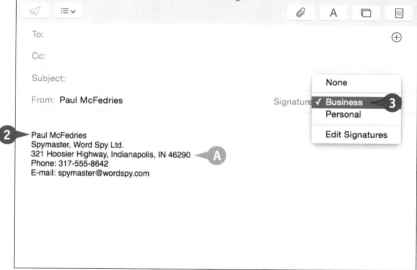

When I have multiple signatures, how can I choose which signature Mail adds automatically?
Follow steps **1** to **4** to display the Signatures preferences and choose an account. Click the **Choose Signature** ◙ and then click the signature you want to insert automatically into each message. If you prefer to add a signature manually, click **None** instead of a signature. Click **Close** (■) to close the Mail preferences.

Receive and Read Email Messages

When another person sends you an email, that message ends up in your account mailbox on the incoming mail server maintained by your ISP or email provider. Therefore, you must connect to the incoming mail server to retrieve and read messages sent to you. You can do this using Mail, which takes care of the details behind the scenes. By default, Mail automatically checks for new messages while you are online, but you can also check for new messages at any time.

Receive and Read Email Messages

Receive Email Messages

1 Click **Get Mail** (⊠).

A The Mail Activity area lets you know if you have any incoming messages.

B If you have new messages, they appear in your Inbox folder with a blue dot in this column.

C The Mail icon (▦) in the Dock shows the number of unread messages in the Inbox folder.

Read a Message

1 Click the message.

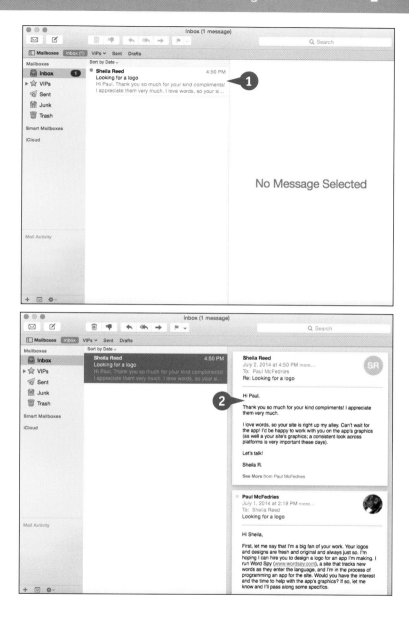

Mail displays the message
text in the preview pane.

2 Read the message text in the
preview pane.

Note: If you want to open the
message in its own window,
double-click the message.

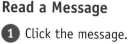

Can I change how often Mail automatically checks for messages?
Yes. Click **Mail** and then click **Preferences**. The Mail preferences appear. Click the **General** tab. Click the
Check for new messages ▣ and then click the time interval that you want Mail to use when checking for
new messages automatically. If you do not want Mail to check for messages automatically, click **Manually**
instead. Click **Close** (▣) to close the Mail preferences.

Reply to a Message

When a message you receive requires a response — whether it is answering a question, supplying information, or providing comments — you can reply to that message. Most replies go only to the person who sent the original message. However, it is also possible to send the reply to all the people who were included in the original message's To and Cc fields. Mail includes the text of the original message in the reply, but you should edit the original message text to include only enough of the original message to put your reply into context.

Reply to a Message

1 Click the message to which you want to reply.

2 Click the reply type you want to use.

Click **Reply** (⬅) to respond only to the person who sent the message.

Click **Reply All** (⬅) to respond to all the addresses in the message's From, To, and Cc fields.

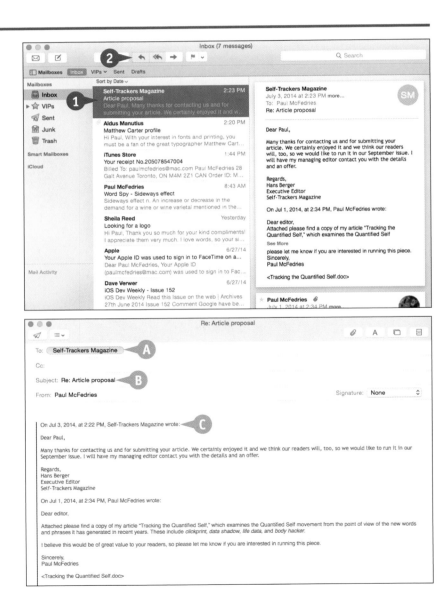

A message window appears.

Ⓐ Mail automatically inserts the recipient addresses.

Ⓑ Mail also inserts the Subject field, preceded by Re:.

Ⓒ Mail includes the original message text at the bottom of the reply.

③ Edit the original message to include only the text relevant to your reply.

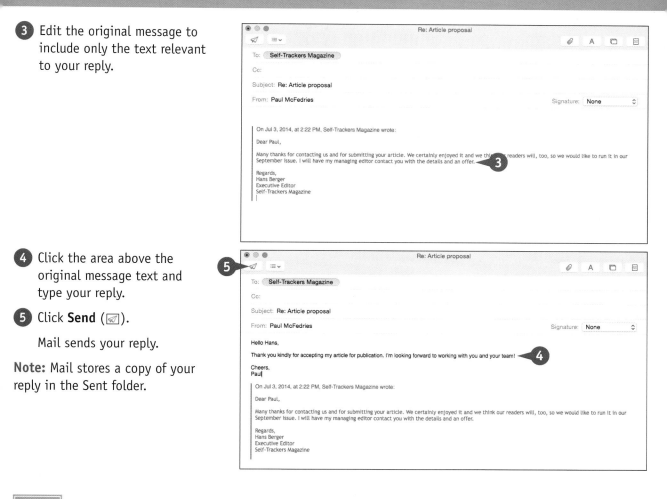

④ Click the area above the original message text and type your reply.

⑤ Click **Send** (⟋).

Mail sends your reply.

Note: Mail stores a copy of your reply in the Sent folder.

TIP

I received a message inadvertently. Is there a way that I can pass it along to the correct recipient?
Yes. Mail comes with a feature that enables you to pass along inadvertent messages to the correct recipient. Click the message that you received inadvertently, click **Message**, and then click **Redirect** (or press **Shift**+**⌘**+**E**). Type the recipient's address and then click **Send**. Replies to this message will be sent to the original sender, not to you.

Forward a Message

If a message has information relevant to or that concerns another person, you can forward a copy of the message to that person. You can also include your own comments in the forward.

In the body of the forward, Mail includes the original message's addresses, date, and subject. Below this information, Mail also includes the text of the original message. In most cases, you will leave the entire message intact so your recipient can see it. However, if only part of the message is relevant to the recipient, you should edit the original message accordingly.

Forward a Message

1 Click the message that you want to forward.

2 Click **Forward** (⇥).

Note: You can also press
Shift + ⌘ + F.

A message window appears.

A Mail inserts the Subject field, preceded by Fwd:.

B The original message's addressees (To and From), date, subject, and text are included at the top of the forward.

3 Type the email address of the person to whom you are forwarding the message.

4 To send a copy of the forward to another person, type that person's email address in the Cc field.

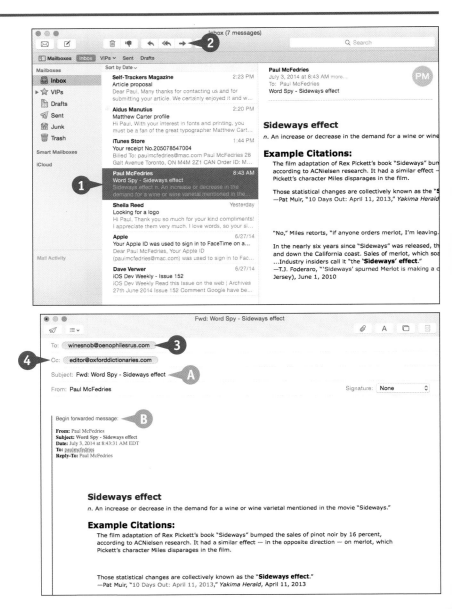

5 Edit the original message to include only the text relevant to your forward.

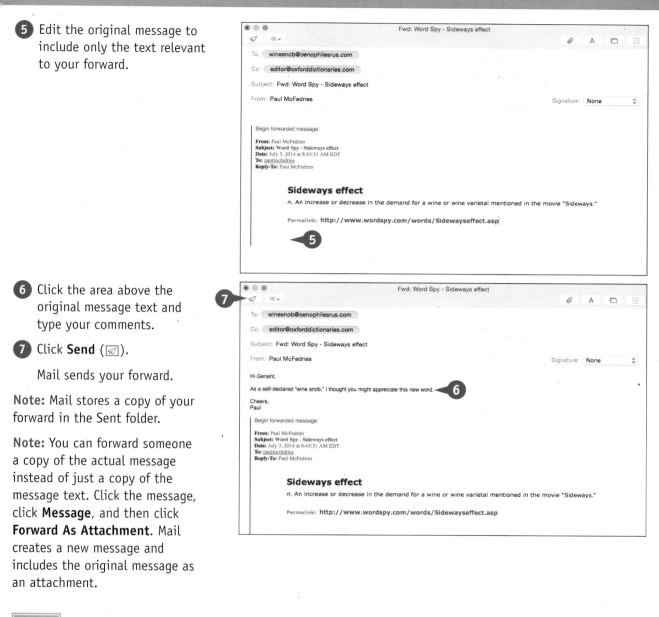

6 Click the area above the original message text and type your comments.

7 Click **Send** (✈).

Mail sends your forward.

Note: Mail stores a copy of your forward in the Sent folder.

Note: You can forward someone a copy of the actual message instead of just a copy of the message text. Click the message, click **Message**, and then click **Forward As Attachment**. Mail creates a new message and includes the original message as an attachment.

TIP

Mail always formats my replies as rich text, even when the original message is plain text. How can I fix this problem?

You can configure Mail to always reply using the same format as the original message. To do this, click **Mail** and then click **Preferences** to open the Mail preferences. Click the **Composing** tab. Click **Use the same message format as the original message** (☐ changes to ☑) and then click **Close** (⬛) to close the Mail preferences.

Open and Save an Attachment

If you receive a message that has a file attached, you can open the attachment to view the contents of the file. However, although some attachments require only a quick viewing, other attachments may contain information that you want to keep. In this case, you should save these files to your Mac's hard drive so that you can open them later without having to launch Mail.

Be careful when dealing with attached files. Computer viruses are often transmitted by email attachments.

Open and Save an Attachment

Open an Attachment

1 Click the message that has the attachment, as indicated by the Attachment symbol (📎).

A An icon appears for each message attachment.

2 Double-click the attachment you want to open.

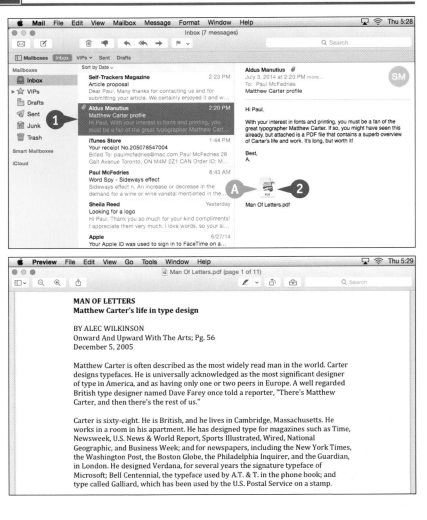

The file opens in the associated application.

Save an Attachment

1 Click the message that has the attachment, as indicated by the Attachment symbol (📎).

2 Right-click the attachment you want to save.

3 Click **Save Attachment**.

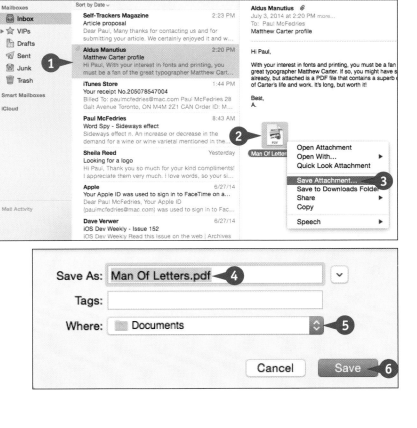

Mail prompts you to save the file.

4 Click in the Save As text box and edit the filename, if desired.

5 Click the **Where** 🔽 and select the folder into which you want the file saved.

6 Click **Save**.

TIPS

Can I open an attachment using a different application?

In most cases, yes. OS X usually has a default application that it uses when you double-click a file attachment. However, it also usually defines one or more other applications capable of opening the file. To check this out, right-click the icon of the attachment you want to open and then click **Open With**. In the menu that appears, click the application that you prefer to use to open the file.

Are viruses a big problem on the Mac?

No, not yet. Most viruses target Windows PCs, and only a few malicious programs target the Mac. However, as the Mac becomes more popular, expect to see more Mac-targeted virus programs. Therefore, you should still exercise caution when opening email attachments.

Create a Mailbox for Saving Messages

After you have used Mail for a while, you may find that you have many messages in your Inbox. To keep the Inbox uncluttered, you can create new mailboxes and then move messages from the Inbox to the new mailboxes.

You should use each mailbox you create to save related messages. For example, you could create separate mailboxes for people you correspond with regularly, projects you are working on, different work departments, and so on.

Create a Mailbox for Saving Messages

Create a Mailbox

1. Click **Mailbox**.

2. Click **New Mailbox**.

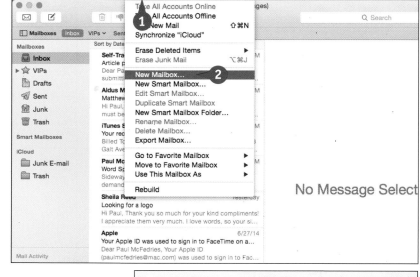

The New Mailbox dialog appears.

3. Click the **Location** ⬦ and then click where you want the mailbox located.

4. Type the name of the new mailbox.

5. Click **OK**.

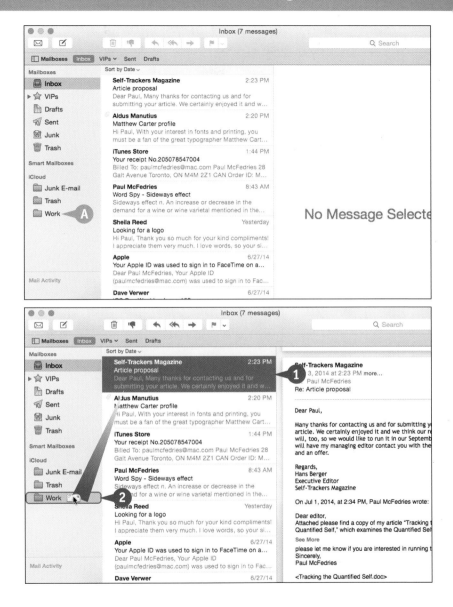

A The new mailbox appears in the Mailboxes list.

Move a Message to Another Mailbox

1 Position the mouse ▮ over the message you want to move.

2 Click and drag the message and drop it on the mailbox to which you want to move it.

Mail moves the message.

How do I rename a mailbox?

Right-click the mailbox and then click **Rename Mailbox**. Type the new name and then press Return. Note that Mail does not allow you to rename any of the built-in mailboxes, including Inbox, Drafts, and Trash.

How do I delete a mailbox?

Right-click the mailbox and then click **Delete**. When Mail asks you to confirm the deletion, click **Delete**. Note that Mail does not allow you to delete any of the built-in mailboxes, including Inbox, Drafts, and Trash. Remember, too, that when you delete a mailbox, you also delete any messages stored in that mailbox.

CHAPTER 5

Talking via Messages and FaceTime

OS X comes with the Messages application, which you use to exchange instant messages with other OS X users, as well as anyone with an iPhone, iPad, or iPod touch. You can also use FaceTime to make video calls to other people.

Configure Messages

OS X includes the Messages application to enable you to use the iMessage technology to exchange instant messages with other people who are online. The first time you open Messages, you must run through a short configuration process to set up your account. This process involves signing in with your Apple ID and deciding whether you want Messages to send out notifications that tell people when you have read the messages they send to you.

Configure Messages

1 Click the **Messages** icon (⬜).

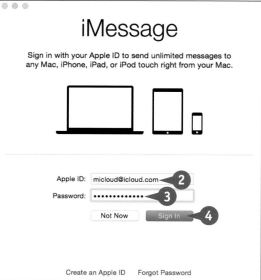

The iMessage dialog appears.

2 Type your Apple ID.

3 Type your Apple ID password.

4 Click **Sign In**.

5 Click to deselect the check box beside each phone number and email address that you do not want to use with Messages (☑ changes to ☐).

6 If you want other people to know when you have read their messages, click **Send read receipts** (☐ changes to ☑).

iMessage

Apple ID: micloud@icloud.com

You can be reached for messages at:

5 ☑ +1 (888) 888-8888

☑ micloud@icloud.com

☑ micloud@me.com

6 ☑ Send read receipts
Allow others to be notified when you have read their messages.

[Go Back] [Done]

7 Click **Done**.

Messages is now ready to use.

iMessage

Apple ID: micloud@icloud.com

You can be reached for messages at:

☑ +1 (888) 888-8888

☑ micloud@icloud.com

☑ micloud@me.com

☑ Send read receipts
Allow others to be notified when you have read their messages.

[Go Back] [Done] **7**

TIP

What if I do not have an Apple ID?

You can create a new Apple ID during the configuration process. Follow steps **1** and **2** to open the iMessage dialog and then click **Create an Apple ID**. In the dialog that appears, type your name, the email address you want to use as your Apple ID, and the password you want to use. You must also choose a secret question and specify your birthday. Click **Create Apple ID** to complete the operation.

Send a Message

In the Messages application, an instant messaging conversation is most often the exchange of text messages between two or more people who are online and available to chat.

An instant messaging conversation begins with one person inviting another person to exchange messages. In Messages, this means sending an initial instant message, and the recipient either accepts or rejects the invitation.

Send a Message

1. Click **Compose new message** (⬚).

Note: You can also click **File** and then click **New Message**, or press ⌘+N.

Messages begins a new conversation.

2. In the To field, type the message recipient using one of the following:

The person's email address.

The person's mobile phone number.

The person's name, if that person is in your Contacts list.

Ⓐ You can also click **Add Contact** (⊕) to select a name from your Contacts list.

③ Type your message.

Ⓑ You can also click 🙂 if you want to insert an emoji symbol into your message.

④ Press **Return**.

Messages sends the text to the recipient.

Ⓒ The recipient's response appears in the transcript window.

Ⓓ You see the ellipsis symbol (⬚) when the other person is typing.

⑤ Repeat steps **3** and **4** to continue the conversation.

TIPS

What is an emoji?
An *emoji* is a pictograph similar to a smiley or emoticon. Many emojis represent an emotional state, such as happy, sad, or angry. There are also many emojis that show symbols such as flowers or animals that you can use to add a bit of visual interest to your messages.

How do I make the Messages text a bit bigger?
To change the size of the text that appears in the Messages window, click **Messages** and then click **Preferences**. In the Messages preferences, click the **General** tab. Drag the **Text size** slider to the right to make the text bigger, or to the left to make the text smaller.

Send a File in a Message

I f, during an instant messaging conversation, you realize you need to send someone a file, you can save time by sending the file directly from the Messages application.

When you need to send a file to another person, your first thought might be to attach that file to an email message. However, if you happen to be in the middle of an instant messaging conversation with that person, it is easier and faster to use Messages to send the file.

Send a File in a Message

1 Start the conversation with the person to whom you want to send the file.

2 Click **Buddies**.

3 Click **Send File**.

Note: You can also press
Option + ⌘ + F .

Messages displays a file selection dialog.

④ Click the file you want to send.

⑤ Click **Send**.

Ⓐ Messages adds an icon for the file to the message box.

⑥ Type your message.

⑦ Press **Return**.

Messages sends the message and adds the file as an attachment.

TIP

How do I save a file that I receive during a conversation?
When you receive a message that has a file attachment, the message shows the name of the file, with the file's type icon to the left. Right-click the file attachment and then click **Save to Downloads** to save the file to your Downloads folder. Messages saves the file and then displays the Downloads folder.

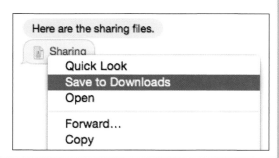

Sign In to FaceTime

FaceTime is a video and audio chat feature that enables you to see and speak to another person over the Internet. To use FaceTime to conduct video chats with your friends, you must each first sign in using your Apple ID. This could be an iCloud account that uses the Apple icloud.com address, or it could be your existing email address.

After you create your Apple ID, you can use it to sign in to FaceTime. Note that you only have to do this once. In subsequent sessions, FaceTime automatically signs you in.

Sign In to FaceTime

1 In the Dock, click the **FaceTime** icon ( ).

The FaceTime window appears.

2 Type your Apple ID email address.

3 Type your Apple ID password.

④ Click **Sign in**.

FaceTime verifies your Apple
ID and then displays the
regular FaceTime window.

TIPS

What equipment do I and the person I am calling need to use FaceTime?
For video calls, your computer must have a web camera, such as the iSight camera that comes with many Macs. For both video and audio calls, your computer must have a microphone, such as the built-in microphone that is part of the iSight camera.

Which devices support FaceTime?
You can use FaceTime on any Mac running OS X 10.6.6 or later. For OS X Snow Leopard (10.6.6), FaceTime is available through the App Store for 99 cents. For all later versions of OS X, FaceTime is installed by default. FaceTime is also available as an app that runs on the iPhone 4 and later, the iPad 2 and later, and the iPod touch fourth generation and later.

Connect Through FaceTime

Once you sign in with your Apple ID, you can use the FaceTime application to connect with another person and conduct a video or audio chat. You connect using whatever email address or phone number the person has associated with her FaceTime account. FaceTime will attempt to connect to that person on any of her devices, which can include a Mac, an iPhone, an iPod touch, or an iPad.

Connect Through FaceTime

1 Begin typing the name of the contact or the phone number you want to call.

A Contacts that support FaceTime calling appear with the FaceTime icon (■■).

2 If you are calling a contact, click the contact's FaceTime icon (■■).

FaceTime sends a message to the contact asking if he or she would like a FaceTime connection.

③ The other person must click or tap **Accept** to complete the connection.

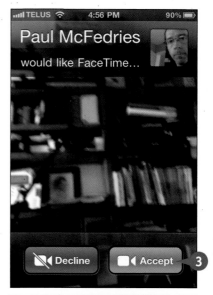

FaceTime connects with the other person.

Ⓑ The other person's video takes up the bulk of the FaceTime screen.

Ⓒ Your video appears in the picture-in-picture (PiP) window.

Note: You can click and drag the PiP to a different location within the FaceTime window.

④ When you finish your FaceTime call, click **End**.

TIP

Can I use FaceTime to call a person without using video?

Yes, FaceTime also supports audio calls, which is useful if the other person does not have a device that supports FaceTime, or if you feel you do not know the other person well enough to place a video call. Use FaceTime to start typing the person's name and then click the **Audio** icon (▨) that appears to the right of the person's name. If you have an iPhone running iOS 8 nearby, then you can click the phone number that appears below the Call Using iPhone text; otherwise, click **FaceTime Audio**.

CHAPTER 6

Tracking Contacts and Events

In OS X, you use the Contacts application to manage your contacts by storing information such as phone numbers, email addresses, street addresses, and much more. You also use the Calendar application to enter and track events and to-do items.

Add a New Contact

OS X includes the Contacts application for managing information about the people you know, whether they are colleagues, friends, or family members. The Contacts app refers to these people as *contacts*, and you store each person's data in an object called a *card*. Each card can store a wide variety of information. For example, you can store a person's name, company name, phone numbers, email address, instant messaging data, street address, notes, and much more. Although you will mostly use Contacts cards to store data about people, you can also use a card to keep information about companies.

Add a New Contact

1 In the Dock, click the **Contacts** icon (▨).

2 Click **File**.

3 Click **New Card**.

A You can also begin a new contact by clicking **Add** (⊞) and then clicking **New Contact**.

Note: You can also invoke the New Card command by pressing ⌘+N.

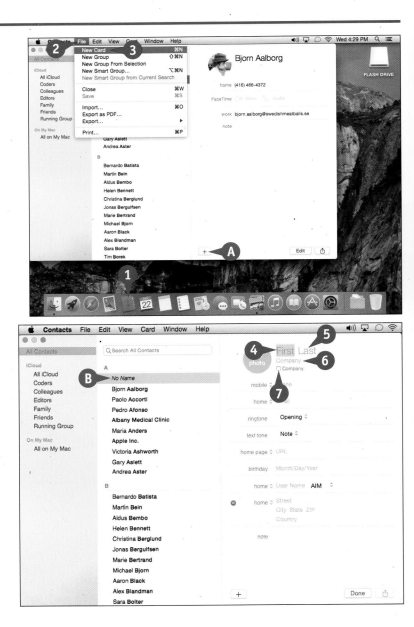

B Contacts adds a new card.

4 In the First field, type the contact's first name.

5 In the Last field, type the contact's last name.

6 In the Company field, type the contact's company name.

7 If the contact is a company, click **Company** (☐ changes to ☑).

8 In the first Phone field, click ⬚ and then click the category you want to use.

9 Type the phone number.

10 Repeat steps 8 and 9 to enter data in some or all of the other fields.

Note: To learn how to add more fields to the card, see the next task, "Edit a Contact."

11 Click **Done**.

Contacts saves the new card.

If I include a contact's email address, is there a way to send that person a message without having to type the address?

Yes. Click the contact's card, click the email address category (such as **work** or **home**), and then click **Send Email**. Mail displays a new email message with the contact already added in the To field. Fill in the rest of the message as required and then click **Send** (✉).

Edit a Contact

If you need to make changes to the information already in a contact's card, or if you need to add new information to a card, you can edit the card from within Contacts. The default fields you see in a card are not the only types of data you can store for a contact. Contacts offers a large number of extra fields. These include useful fields such as Middle Name, Nickname, Job Title, Department, URL (web address), and Birthday. You can also add extra fields for common data items such as phone numbers, email addresses, and dates.

Edit a Contact

1 Click the card you want to edit.

2 Click **Edit**.

A Contacts makes the card's fields available for editing.

3 Edit the existing fields as required.

4 To add a field, click an empty placeholder and then type the field data.

5 To remove a field, click **Delete** (⊖).

6 To add a new field type, click **Card**.

7 Click **Add Field**.

8 Click the type of field you want.

Ⓑ Contacts adds the field to the card.

9 When you complete your edits, click **Done**.

Contacts saves the edited card.

Create a Contact Group

You can organize your contacts into one or more groups, which is useful for viewing just a subset of your contacts. For example, you could create separate groups for friends, family, work colleagues, or business clients. Groups are handy if you have many contacts in your address book. By creating and maintaining groups, you can navigate your contacts more easily. You can also perform groupwide tasks, such as sending a single email message to everyone in the group. You can create a group first and then add members, or you can select members in advance and then create the group.

Create a Contact Group

Create a Contact Group

1 Click **File**.

2 Click **New Group**.

Note: You can also run the New Group command by pressing `Shift`+`⌘`+`N`.

A Contacts adds a new group.

3 Type a name for the group.

4 Press `Return`.

5 Click and drag a contact to the group.

Contacts adds the contact to the group.

6 Repeat step **5** for the other contacts you want to add to the group.

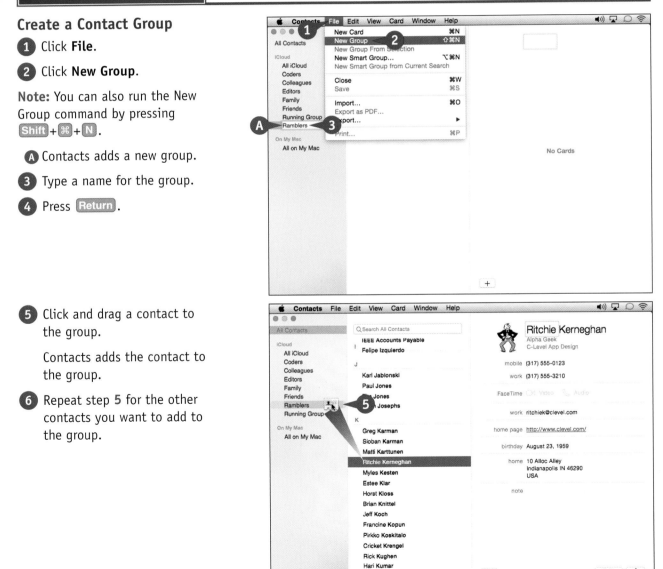

Create a Group of Selected Contacts

1 Select the contacts you want to include in the new group.

Note: To select multiple contacts, press and hold ⌘ and click each card.

2 Click **File**.

3 Click **New Group From Selection**.

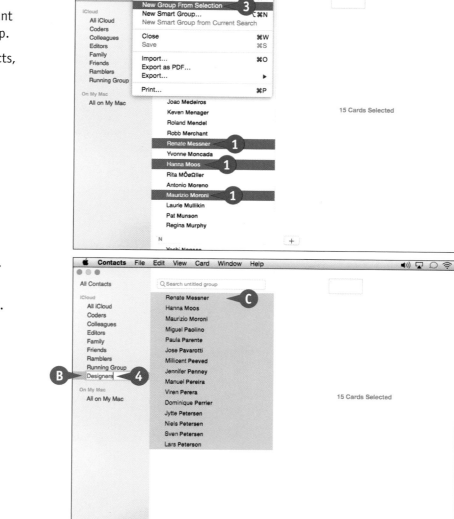

B Contacts adds a new group.

C Contacts adds the selected contacts as group members.

4 Type a name for the group.

5 Press **Return**.

Can I send an email message to the group?

Yes. With a group, you send a single message to the group, and Mail automatically sends a copy to each member. Right-click the group and then click **Send Email to "*Group*"** where *Group* is the name of the group.

What is a Smart Group?

A *Smart Group* is a group where each member has one or more fields in common, such as the company name or city. When you create the Smart Group, you specify one or more criteria, and then Contacts automatically adds members to the group who meet those criteria. To create a Smart Group, click **File**, click **New Smart Group**, and then enter your group criteria.

Navigate the Calendar

Calendar enables you to create and work with events, which are either scheduled appointments or activities such as meetings and lunches, or all-day activities such as birthdays or vacations. Before you create an event, you must first select the date on which the event occurs. You can do this in Calendar by navigating the built-in calendar or by specifying the date that you want.

Calendar also lets you change the calendar view to suit your needs. For example, you can show just a single day's worth of events or a week's worth of events.

Navigate the Calendar

Use the Calendar

1 In the Dock, click the **Calendar** icon (📅).

2 Click **Month**.

3 Click the **Next Month** button (▷) until the month of your event appears.

A If you go too far, click the **Previous Month** button (◁) to move back to the month you want.

B To see a specific date, click the day and then click **Day** (or press ⌘+1).

C To see a specific week, click any day within the week and then click **Week** (or press ⌘+2).

D To return to viewing the entire month, click **Month** (or press ⌘+3).

E If you want to return to today's date, click **Today** (or press ⌘+T).

Go to a Specific Date

1 Click **View**.

2 Click **Go to Date**.

Note: You can also select the Go to Date command by pressing `Shift`+`⌘`+`T`.

The Go to Date dialog appears.

3 In the Date text box, type the date you want using the format mm/dd/yyyy.

F You can also click the month, day, or year and then click ⬍ to increase or decrease the value.

4 Click **Show**.

5 Click **Day**.

G Calendar displays the date.

TIP

In the Week view, the week begins on Sunday. How can I change this to Monday?
Calendar's default Week view has Sunday on the left and Saturday on the right. To display the weekend days together, with Monday on the left signaling the start of the week, follow these steps. Click **Calendar** in the menu bar and then click **Preferences**. The Calendar preferences appear. Click the **General** tab. Click the **Start week on** ⬍, select **Monday** from the pop-up menu, and then click **Close** (■).

Create an Event

You can help organize your life by using Calendar to record your events — such as appointments, meetings, phone calls, and dates — on the date and time they occur.

If the event has a set time and duration — for example, a meeting or a lunch date — you add the event directly to the calendar as a regular appointment. If the event has no set time — for example, a birthday, anniversary, or multiple-day event such as a convention or vacation — you can create an all-day event.

Create an Event

Create a Regular Event

1 Navigate to the date when the event occurs.

2 Click **Calendars**.

3 Click the calendar you want to use.

4 Double-click the time when the event starts.

Note: If the event is less than or more than an hour, you can also click and drag the mouse ▶ over the full event period.

Ⓐ Calendar adds a one-hour event.

5 Type the name of the event.

6 Press Return.

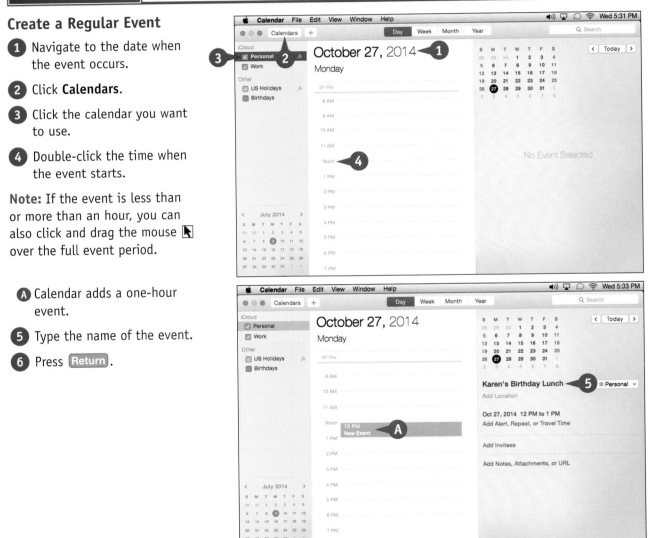

Create an All-Day Event

1 Click **Week**.

2 Navigate to the week that includes the date when the event occurs.

3 Click **Calendars**.

4 Click the calendar you want to use.

5 Double-click anywhere inside the event date's all-day section.

Ⓑ Calendar adds a new all-day event.

6 Type the name of the event.

7 Press **Return**.

TIP

How can I specify event details such as the location and a reminder message?

Follow the steps in this task to create an event and then double-click the event. Type the location of the event in the Add Location text box. Click the event's date or time, click **alert**, and then click the amount of time before the event that you want to receive the reminder. To add notes, attach a file, or add a web address, click **Add Notes, URL, or Attachments**, and then click the type of information you want to add. Click outside the event. Calendar saves the new event configuration.

Create a Repeating Event

If you have an activity or event that recurs at a regular interval, you can create an event and configure it to repeat in Calendar automatically. This saves you from having to add the future events repeatedly yourself because Calendar adds them for you.

You can repeat an event daily, weekly, monthly, or yearly. For even greater flexibility, you can set up a custom interval. For example, you could have an event repeat every five days, every second Friday, on the first Monday of every month, and so on.

Create a Repeating Event

1 Create an event.

Note: To create an event, follow the steps in the task "Create an Event."

2 Double-click the event.

3 Click the event's date and time.

Calendar displays information for the event.

Calendar opens the event for editing.

④ Click the **repeat** 🔽.

⑤ Click the interval you want to use.

Ⓐ If you want to specify a custom interval such as every two weeks or the first Monday of every month, click **Custom** and configure your interval in the dialog that appears.

⑥ Press **Return**.

Ⓑ Calendar adds the repeating events to the calendar.

TIPS

How do I configure an event to stop after a certain number of occurrences?

Follow steps **1** to **5** to select a recurrence interval. Click the **end repeat** 🔽 and then select **After** from the pop-up menu. Type the number of occurrences you want. Click outside the event.

Can I delete a single occurrence from a recurring series of events?

Yes, you can delete one occurrence from the calendar without affecting the rest of the series. Click the occurrence you want to delete, and then press **Delete**. Calendar asks whether you want to delete all the occurrences or just the selected occurrence. Click **Delete Only This Event**.

Send or Respond to an Event Invitation

You can include other people in your event by sending them invitations to attend. If you receive an event invitation yourself, you can respond to it to let the person organizing the event know whether you will attend.

If you have an event that requires other people, Calendar has a feature that enables you to send invitations to other people who use a compatible email program. The advantage of this approach is that when other people respond to the invitation, Calendar automatically updates the event. If you receive an event invitation yourself, the email message contains buttons that enable you to respond quickly.

Send or Respond to an Event Invitation

Send an Event Invitation

1 Create an event.

Note: To create an event, follow the steps in the task "Create an Event."

2 Double-click the event.

3 Click **Add Invitees**.

④ Begin typing the name of a person you want to invite.

⑤ Click the person you want to invite.

⑥ Repeat steps **4** and **5** to add more invitees.

⑦ Click **Send** (not shown).

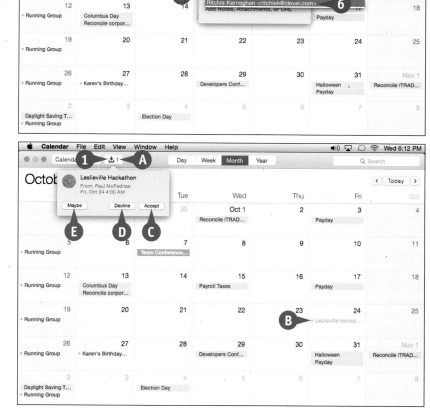

Handle an Event Invitation

Ⓐ The Invitation button shows the number of pending invitations you have received via iCloud.

Ⓑ The event appears tentatively in your calendar.

① Click the **Invitation** button (⬇).

② Click the button that represents your reply to the invitation:

Ⓒ Click **Accept** if you can attend the event.

Ⓓ Click **Decline** if you cannot attend the event.

Ⓔ Click **Maybe** if you are currently not sure whether you can attend.

Is it possible to see emailed invitations in Calendar before I decide whether to accept them?

Yes. Open Mail, click **Mail** in the menu bar, click **Preferences**, click **General**; click the **Add invitations to Calendar** 🔲, and then click **Automatically**.

How do I know when a person has accepted or declined an invitation?

Double-click the event. In the list of invitees, you see a check mark beside each person who has accepted the invitation; you see a question mark beside each person who has not made a choice or who has selected Maybe; and you see a red Not symbol beside each person who has declined the invitation.

CHAPTER 7

Playing and Organizing Music

You can use iTunes to create a library of music and use that library to play songs, albums, and collections of songs called playlists. You can also purchase music from the iTunes Store and more.

Understanding the iTunes Library

OS X includes iTunes to enable you to play back and manage various types of audio files. iTunes also includes features for organizing and playing videos, watching movies and TV shows, and organizing apps, but iTunes is mostly concerned with audio-related media and content.

Most of your iTunes time will be spent in the library, so you need to understand the various categories — such as music and audiobooks — that iTunes uses to organize the library's audio content. You also need to know how to configure the library to show only the categories with which you will be working.

The iTunes Library

The iTunes library is where your Mac stores the files that you can play and work with in the iTunes application. Although iTunes has some video components, its focus is on audio features, so most of the library sections are audio-related. These sections enable you to work with music, podcasts, audiobooks, ringtones, and Internet radio.

Understanding Library Categories

The Sources section in the upper left corner of the iTunes window displays the various categories that are available in the iTunes library. The audio-related categories include Music, Podcasts, Audiobooks, Tones, and Internet Radio.

Each category shows you the contents of that category and the details for each item. For example, in the Music category, you can see details such as the name of each album and the artist who recorded it.

Configuring the Library

You can configure which categories of the iTunes library appear in the Sources section on the left side of the iTunes window. Click **iTunes**, click **Preferences** to open the iTunes preferences, and then click the **General** tab. In the Show section, click the check box for each type of content you want to work with (☐ changes to ☑) and then click **OK**.

Navigate the iTunes Window

Familiarizing yourself with the various elements of the iTunes window is a good idea so that you can easily navigate and activate elements when you are ready to play audio files, music CDs, or podcasts; import and burn audio CDs; create your own playlists; or listen to Internet radio. In particular, you need to learn the iTunes playback controls, because you will use them to control the playback of almost all music you work with in iTunes.

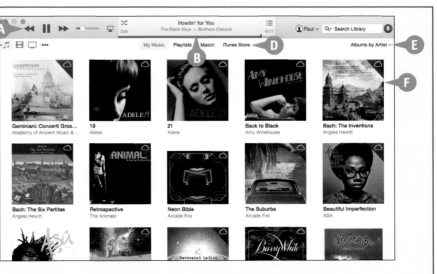

Ⓐ Playback Controls

These buttons control media playback and enable you to adjust the volume.

Ⓑ Status Area

This area displays information about the item currently playing or the action that iTunes is currently performing.

Ⓒ Sources

Click the buttons in this section to select the type of content you want to view.

Ⓓ iTunes Store

Click this command to access the iTunes Store, which enables you to purchase songs and albums, subscribe to podcasts, and more.

Ⓔ Sort List

The commands in this list sort the contents of the current iTunes category.

Ⓕ Contents

The contents of the current iTunes library source appear here.

Play a Song

You use the Music category of the iTunes library to play a song that is stored on your computer. Although iTunes offers several methods to locate the song you want to play, the easiest method is to display the albums you have in your iTunes library, and then open the album that contains the song you want to play. While the song is playing, you can control the volume to suit the music or your current location. If you need to leave the room or take a call, you can pause the song currently playing.

Play a Song

1 Click **Music**.

2 Select **Albums by Artist**.

You can also click a sort option such as Song List, Artists, or Genres.

3 Click the album that contains the song you want to play.

Ⓐ If you want to play the entire album, click **Play** (▶).

4 Double-click the song you want to play.

iTunes begins playing the song.

B Information about the song playback appears here.

C iTunes displays a speaker icon (🔊) beside the currently playing song.

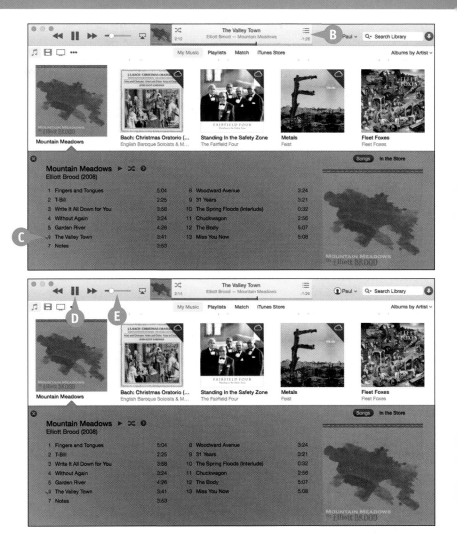

D If you need to stop the song temporarily, click the **Pause** button (⏸).

Note: You can also pause and restart a song by pressing Spacebar.

E You can use the Volume slider to adjust the volume (see the Tip).

TIP

How do I adjust the volume?

To turn the volume up or down, click and drag the **Volume** slider to the left (to reduce the volume) or to the right (to increase the volume). You can also press ⌘+⬇ to reduce the volume, or ⌘+⬆ to increase the volume.

To mute the volume, either drag the **Volume** slider all the way to the left, or press Option+⌘+⬇. To restore the volume, adjust the **Volume** slider or press Option+⌘+⬆.

Create a Playlist

A *playlist* is a collection of songs that are related in some way. Using your iTunes library, you can create customized playlists that include only the songs that you want to hear. For example, you might want to create a playlist of upbeat or festive songs to play during a party or celebration. Similarly, you might want to create a playlist of your current favorite songs to burn to a CD. Whatever the reason, once you create the playlist you can populate it with songs using a simple drag-and-drop technique.

Create a Playlist

Create the Playlist

1 Click **File**.

2 Click **New**.

3 Click **Playlist**.

Note: You can create a new playlist by pressing ⌘+N.

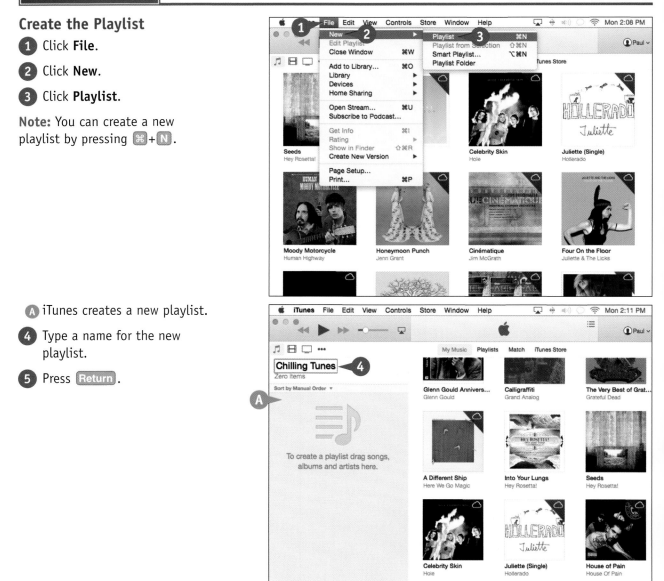

A iTunes creates a new playlist.

4 Type a name for the new playlist.

5 Press Return.

Add Songs to the Playlist

1. Click **Music** (♫).

2. Open an album that has one or more songs you want to add to the playlist.

3. Click a song that you want to add to the playlist.

Note: If you want more than one song from the album's playlist, hold down ⌘ and click each of the songs you want to add.

4. Drag the selected track and drop it on your playlist.

5. Repeat steps **2** to **4** to add more songs to the playlist.

6. Click **Done**.

Ⓑ To access your playlists, click **Playlists**.

Is there a faster way to create and populate a playlist?

Yes. Press and hold ⌘ and then click each song you want to include in your playlist. Click **File**, click **New**, and then click **Playlist from Selection** (you can also press Shift + ⌘ + N). Type the playlist name and then press Return.

Can iTunes add songs to a playlist automatically?

Yes, you can create a *Smart Playlist* where the songs have one or more properties in common, such as the genre or text in the song title. Click **File**, click **New**, and then click **Smart Playlist** (you can also press Option + ⌘ + N). Use the Smart Playlist dialog to create rules that define what songs appear in the playlist.

Purchase Music from the iTunes Store

You can add music to your iTunes library by purchasing songs or albums from the iTunes Store. iTunes downloads the song or album to your computer and then adds it to both the Music category and the Purchased playlist. You can then play and manage the song or album just like any other content in the iTunes library. To purchase music from the iTunes Store, you must have an Apple ID, which you can obtain from https://appleid.apple.com. You can also use an AOL account, if you have one.

Purchase Music from the iTunes Store

1 Click **iTunes Store**.

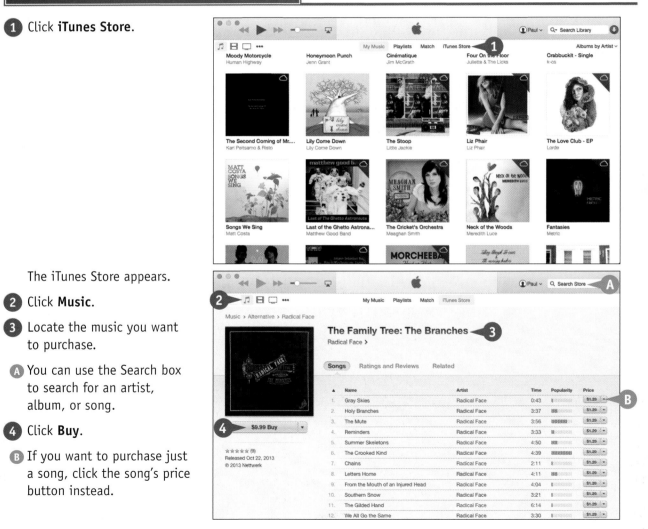

The iTunes Store appears.

2 Click **Music**.

3 Locate the music you want to purchase.

Ⓐ You can use the Search box to search for an artist, album, or song.

4 Click **Buy**.

Ⓑ If you want to purchase just a song, click the song's price button instead.

iTunes asks you to sign in to your iTunes Store account.

5 If you have not signed in to your account, you must type your Apple ID.

6 Type your password.

7 Click **Buy**.

iTunes charges your credit card and begins downloading the music to your Mac.

C The status area displays the progress of the download.

D To return to the iTunes library, click **My Music**.

Sign In to the iTunes Store

If you have an Apple ID and password, enter them here. If you've used the iTunes Store or iCloud, for example, you have an Apple ID.

Apple ID

myappleid@icloud.com

Password

Forgot?

Remember password

Create New Apple ID

Cancel

Buy

Downloading 12 items

Gray Skies / The Family Tree: The Branches / Radical Face (2 seconds remaini...

Paul ⌄   Q Search Store

My Music   Playlists   Match   iTunes Store

Music > Alternative > Radical Face

The Family Tree: The Branches

Radical Face >

Songs   Ratings and Reviews   Related

▲	Name	Artist	Time	Popularity	Price
1.	Gray Skies	Radical Face	0:43		Downloading
2.	Holy Branches	Radical Face	3:37		Downloading
3.	The Mute	Radical Face	3:56		Downloading
4.	Reminders	Radical Face	3:33		Downloading
5.	Summer Skeletons	Radical Face	4:50		Downloading
6.	The Crooked Kind	Radical Face	4:39		Downloading
7.	Chains	Radical Face	2:11		Downloading
8.	Letters Home	Radical Face	4:11		Downloading
9.	From the Mouth of an Injured Head	Radical Face	4:04		Downloading
10.	Southern Snow	Radical Face	3:21		Downloading
11.	The Gilded Hand	Radical Face	6:14		Downloading
12.	We All Go the Same	Radical Face	3:30		Downloading

★★★★★ (9)
Released Oct 22, 2013
℗ 2013 Nettwerk

Purchased

TIPS

Can I use my purchased music on other computers and devices?

Yes. Although many iTunes Store media, particularly movies and TV shows, have digital rights management (DRM) restrictions applied to prevent illegal copying, the songs and albums in the iTunes Store are DRM-free, and so do not have these restrictions. You can play them on multiple devices (such as iPods, iPads, and iPhones), and burn them to multiple CDs.

How do I redeem an iTunes gift card?

On the back of the card, scratch off the sticker that covers the redeem code. Access the iTunes Store, click **Redeem** at the bottom of the screen, and then enter your account password. In the Redeem Code screen, type the redemption code and then click **Redeem**.

Apply Parental Controls

If you are setting up a user account in OS X for a child, you can use iTunes' parental controls to ensure that the child does not have access to music that has been marked as having explicit content. You can also disable certain content types — such as podcasts, the iTunes Store, and Internet radio stations — that could potentially offer content not suitable for the child. Finally, you can also disable access to shared iTunes libraries, which might contain unsuitable music.

Apply Parental Controls

1 Log in to OS X using the child's user account.

2 Click **iTunes**.

3 Click **Preferences**.

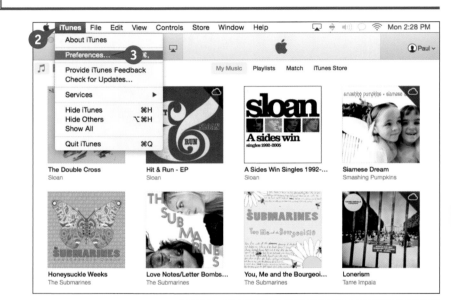

The iTunes preferences appear.

4 Click the **Parental** tab.

5 In the Disable section, click the check box beside each type of content you do not want the user to access (☐ changes to ☑).

6 Click the **Ratings for** ◙ and then click the country ratings you want to use.

7 To ensure that the user cannot access explicit musical content, click **Music with explicit content** (☐ changes to ☑).

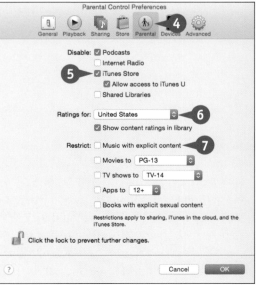

iTunes displays an overview of what it means to restrict explicit content.

8 Click **OK**.

9 Click **OK**.

iTunes puts the parental controls into effect.

TIP

Is it possible that a child could open the iTunes preferences and disable the parent controls?
Yes, although this is not likely to be a concern with young children. However, for older children who know their way around OS X, you should lock the parental controls to avoid having them changed. Follow steps **1** to **4** to open the child's user account and display the Parental tab. Click the lock icon (🔓), type your OS X administrator password, and then click **OK**. 🔓 changes to 🔒, indicating that the controls in the Parental tab are now locked and can be unlocked only with your administrator password. Click **OK**.

Subscribe to a Podcast

You can use iTunes to locate, subscribe, manage, and listen to your favorite podcasts. A *podcast* is an audio feed — or sometimes a feed that combines both audio and video — that a publisher updates regularly with new episodes. The easiest way to get each episode is to subscribe to the podcast. This ensures that iTunes automatically downloads each new episode to your iTunes library. You can subscribe to podcasts either via the publisher's website, or via the iTunes Store.

Subscribe to a Podcast

1 Click **iTunes Store**.

2 Click **More** (•••).

3 Click **Podcasts**.

④ Locate the podcast to which you want to subscribe.

⑤ Click **Subscribe**.

Ⓐ If you want to listen to just one episode before subscribing, click the episode's **Free** button instead.

iTunes asks you to confirm.

⑥ Click **Subscribe**.

iTunes begins downloading the podcast.

To listen to the podcast, click the subscription in the Podcasts category of the library.

TIP

How do I subscribe to a podcast via the web?

Use your web browser to navigate to the podcast's home page, click the **iTunes** link to open a preview of the podcast, click **View in iTunes**, and then follow steps 4 and 5.

If the podcast does not have an iTunes link, copy the address of the podcast feed, switch to iTunes, click **File**, and then click **Subscribe to Podcast**. In the Subscribe to Podcast dialog, use the URL text box to paste the address of the podcast feed and then click **OK**.

CHAPTER 8

Learning Useful OS X Tasks

OS X Yosemite comes with many tools that help you accomplish everyday tasks. In this chapter, you learn how to synchronize an iPod, iPhone, or iPad; work with notes and reminders; post to Facebook or Twitter; share data; and work with notifications, tags, and maps.

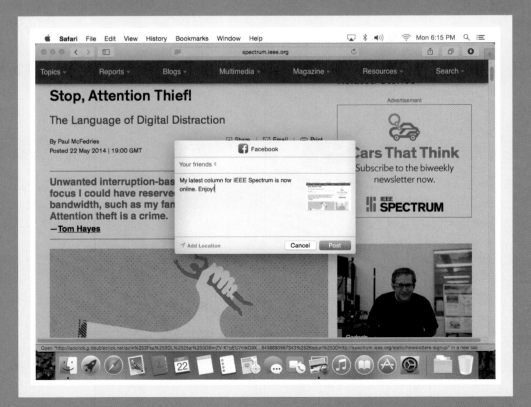

Connect an iPhone, iPad, or iPod touch

To synchronize some or all of your iTunes library — including music, podcasts, audiobooks, TV shows, and movies — as well as your photos and e-books, with your iPhone, iPad, or iPod touch, you can connect the device to your Mac.

Although you can synchronize over Wi-Fi, if your device is not running a recent version of iOS, or if your Mac and your device are not on the same network, you must physically connect your device to your Mac. You need the USB cable that came with the device package. You can also connect using an optional dock.

Connect an iPhone, iPad, or iPod touch

Connect the Device Directly

1 Attach the USB cable's Lightning connector to the device's port.

2 Attach the cable's USB connector to a free USB port on your Mac.

3 If your device asks if you trust this computer, tap **Trust** on the device and click **Continue** on your Mac.

OS X launches iTunes and automatically begins synchronizing the device.

8Learning Useful OS X Tasks

Connect the Device Using the Dock

1 Attach the USB cable's Lightning connector to the dock's port.

2 Insert the device into the dock.

3 Attach the cable's USB connector to a free USB port on your Mac.

4 If your device asks if you trust this computer, tap **Trust** on the device and click **Continue** on your Mac.

OS X launches iTunes and automatically begins synchronizing the device.

TIP

Do I have to eject my device before disconnecting it?

No, you can disconnect the device at any time as long as no sync is in progress. If a sync is in progress and you need to disconnect, first click **Cancel Sync** (⊗) in the iTunes status window and then disconnect your device.

Synchronize an iPod, iPhone, or iPad

You can take your media and other data with you by synchronizing that data from OS X to your iPod touch, iPhone, or iPad. However, you should synchronize movies and TV shows with care. A single half-hour TV episode may be as large as 650MB, and full-length movies can be several gigabytes. To synchronize your device, first connect it to your Mac.

Synchronize an iPod, iPhone, or iPad

Synchronize Music

1. Click your device's icon.

2. Click **Music**.

3. Click **Sync Music** (☐ changes to ☑).

4. Click **Selected playlists, artists, albums, and genres** (☐ changes to ⦿).

5. Click each item you want to synchronize (☐ changes to ☑).

6. Click **Apply**.

7. Click **Music** (♫).

Synchronize Photos

1. Click your device's icon.

2. Click **Photos**.

3. Click **Sync Photos from** (☐ changes to ☑).

4. Click **Selected albums, Events, and Faces, and automatically include** (☐ changes to ⦿).

5. Click each item you want to synchronize (☐ changes to ☑).

6. Click **Apply**.

7. Click **Music** (♫).

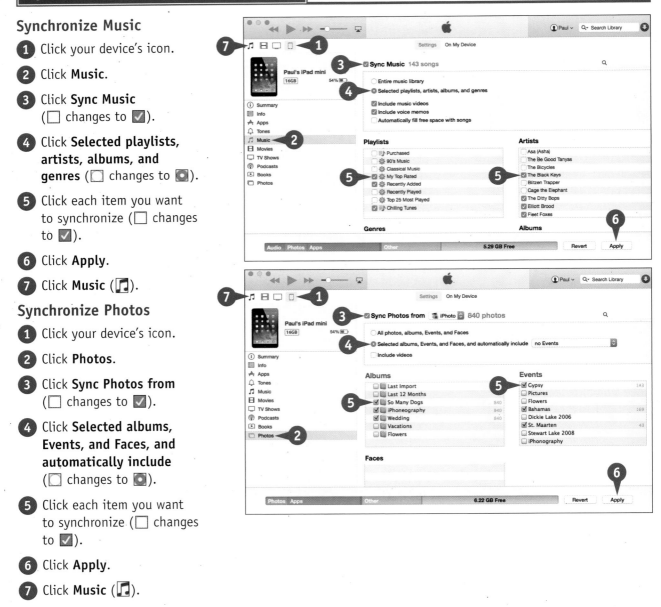

Synchronize Movies

1. Click your device's icon.

2. Click **Movies**.

3. Click **Sync Movies**
   (☐ changes to ✅).

4. Click each movie you
   want to synchronize
   (☐ changes to ✅).

5. Click **Apply**.

6. Click **Music** (🎵).

Synchronize TV Shows

1. Click your device's icon.

2. Click **TV Shows**.

3. Click **Sync TV Shows**
   (☐ changes to ✅).

4. Click each TV show you
   want to synchronize
   (☐ changes to ✅).

5. Click **Apply**.

6. Click **Music** (🎵).

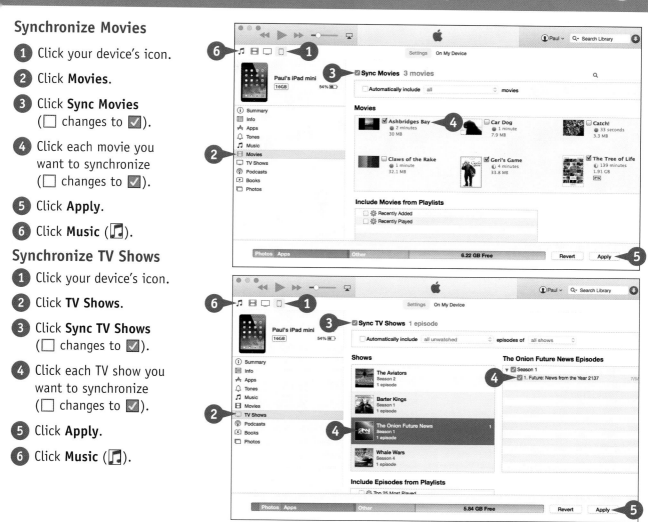

TIPS

Can I sync wirelessly?

Yes. Connect your device and select it in iTunes, click
the **Summary** tab, and then click **Sync with this
device over Wi-Fi**, where *device* is iPhone, iPad, or
iPod (☐ changes to ✅). To sync over Wi-Fi, on your
device tap **Settings**, tap **General**, tap **iTunes Wi-Fi
Sync**, and then tap **Sync Now**.

How do I get my photos from my device to my Mac?

You can view and work with device pictures on your
Mac by importing them into iPhoto. In iPhoto, click
your device and then press and hold ⌘ and click each
photo you want to import. Use the Event Name text
box to type a name for this event and then click
Import Selected.

Integrate OS X and Your iPhone or iPad

Continuity is a set of features that enable you to integrate your Mac and your iPhone or iPad (as well as your iPod touch). Continuity consists of three features: Handoff, for continuing tasks on one device that you started on another; taking phone calls on your Mac or sending Mac calls to your iPhone; and Personal Hotspot for sharing your device's Internet connection with your Mac.

For the Continuity features to work, your Mac must be running OS X Yosemite, and your iPhone or iPad must be running iOS 8. Also, your Mac and your device must be signed in to the same iCloud account.

Handoff

The Handoff feature enables you to begin certain tasks on your iPhone or iPad and then continue those tasks on your Mac. Handoff-compatible tasks include composing an email, writing a text message, browsing a web page, and working with apps such as Maps, Reminders, Calendar, and Contacts. Handoff works both ways, so if you start a task on your Mac, you can continue it on your iPhone or iPad.

Phone Calls

Continuity enables you to initiate iPhone calls from your Mac. For example, if you come across a phone number while using Safari on your Mac, select the number, click the arrow that appears, and then click **Call "*Number*" Using iPhone** (where *Number* is the selected phone number). You can also initiate calls from Contacts or Calendar.

If your iPhone receives an incoming call, your Mac displays a notification that you can click to answer the call on your Mac.

Personal Hotspot

If your Mac cannot connect to a Wi-Fi network for Internet access, you can still get your Mac online by using your iPhone's (or iPad's) cellular connection as a temporary wireless network. When you enable the device's Personal Hotspot (tap **Settings** and then **Personal Hotspot**), your device appears in your Mac's list of nearby Wi-Fi networks. Select the device and type the password to connect.

Enable Handoff in OS X

The Handoff feature enables you to use OS X to continue a task begun on your iPhone or iPad. For Handoff to work, your iPhone or iPad must be running iOS 8 and it must be close to your Mac (usually within about 30 feet or so). Also, your Mac must be running OS X Yosemite and it must be relatively new (no more than two or three years old). Finally, as shown in this task, you must configure OS X to accept Handoff connections between your iPhone or iPad and your Mac.

Enable Handoff in OS X

1 Click the **System Preferences** icon (📷).

2 Click **General**.

The General preferences appear.

3 Click **Allow Handoff between this Mac and your iCloud devices** (☐ changes to ☑).

4 Click **Close** (◉).

OS X now accepts Handoff connections between your Mac and your iPhone or iPad.

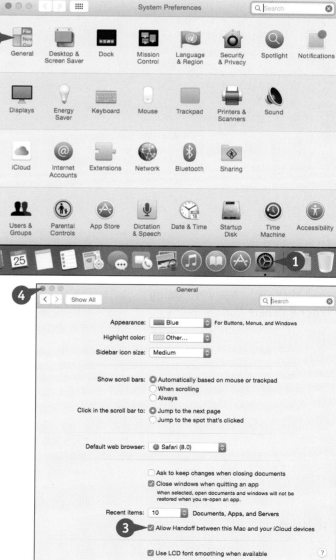

Install a Program Using the App Store

You can enhance and extend OS X by installing new programs from the App Store. OS X comes with an impressive collection of applications — or *apps*. However, OS X does not offer a complete collection of apps. For example, OS X lacks apps in categories such as productivity, personal finance, and business tools. To fill in these gaps, you can use the App Store to locate, purchase, and install new programs, or look for apps that go beyond what the default OS X programs can do.

Install a Program Using the App Store

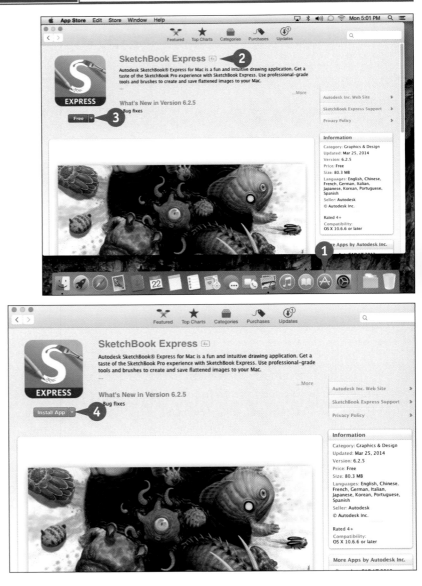

1. In the Dock, click the **App Store** icon (⌾).

   The App Store window appears.

2. Locate the app you want to install.

3. Click the price button, or if the app is free, as shown here, click the **Free** button instead.

The price button changes to a Buy App button, or the Free button changes to an Install App button.

4. Click **Buy App** (or **Install App**).

The App Store prompts you to log in with your Apple ID.

5 Type your Apple ID.

6 Type your password.

7 Click **Sign In**.

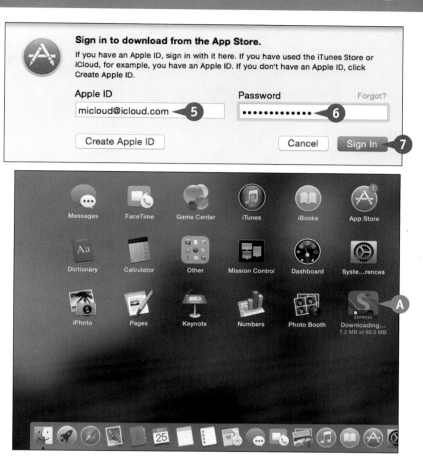

A The App Store begins downloading the app.

When the progress meter disappears, your app is installed. Click the **Launchpad** icon (📍) and then click the app to run it.

TIP

How do I use an App Store gift card to purchase apps?

If you have an App Store or iTunes gift card, you can redeem the card to give yourself store credit in the amount shown on the card. Scratch off the sticker on the back to reveal the code. Click the **App Store** icon (🔲) to open the App Store, click **Featured**, click **Redeem**, type the code, and then click **Redeem**. In the App Store window, the Account item shows your current store credit balance.

Write a Note

You can use the Notes app to create simple text documents for things such as to-do lists and meeting notes. Word processing programs such as Word and Pages are useful for creating complex and lengthy documents. However, these powerful tools feel like overkill when all you want to do is jot down a few notes. For these simpler text tasks, the Notes app that comes with OS X is perfect because it offers a simple interface that keeps all your notes together. As you see in the next task, you can also pin a note to the OS X desktop for easy access.

Write a Note

Create a New Note

1 In the Dock, click the **Notes** icon (☐).

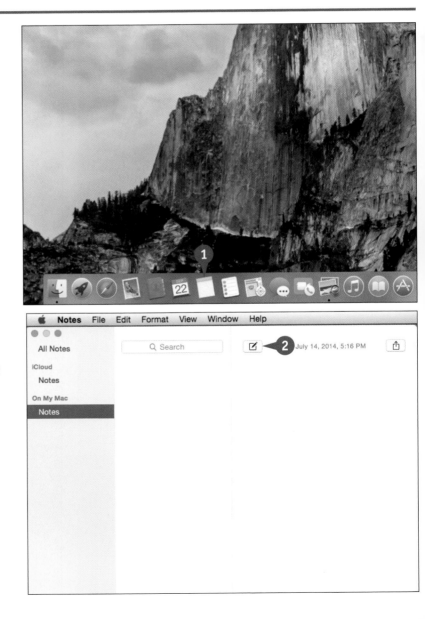

The Notes window appears.

2 Click **New Note** (☑).

Note: You can also click **File** and then click **New Note**, or press ⌘+N.

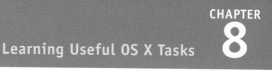

Ⓐ The Notes app creates the new note.

③ Type your note text.

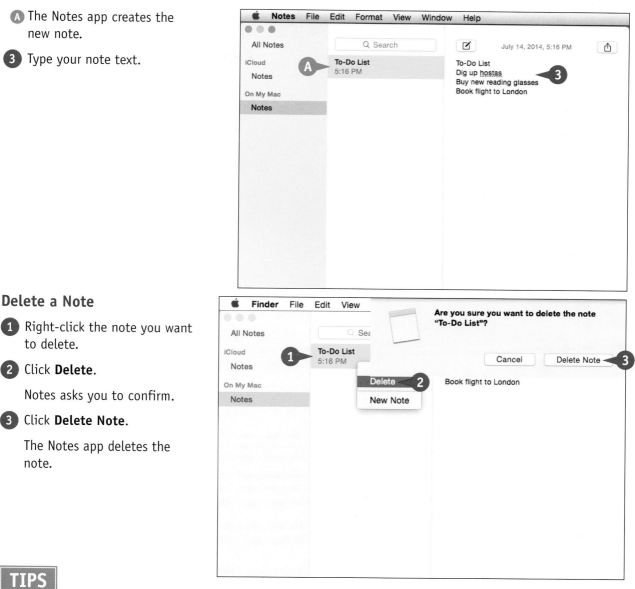

Delete a Note

① Right-click the note you want to delete.

② Click **Delete**.

Notes asks you to confirm.

③ Click **Delete Note**.

The Notes app deletes the note.

TIPS

Can I synchronize my notes with my iPod touch, iPhone, or iPad?

Yes, as long as you have an iCloud account, you have set up that account in OS X, as described in Chapter 14, and you are syncing notes between your Mac and iCloud. To create a new note using iCloud, click **Notes** under the iCloud folder and then follow the steps in this task.

How do I create a bulleted or numbered list?

Position the cursor where you want the list to begin, click **Format**, and then click **Lists**. In the menu that appears, click **Insert Bulleted List**, **Insert Dashed List**, or **Insert Numbered List**.

Pin a Note to the Desktop

You can ensure that you always see the content of a note by pinning that note to the OS X desktop. The Notes app is useful for setting up to-do lists, jotting down things to remember, and creating similar documents that contain text that you need to refer to while you work. Rather than constantly switching back and forth between Notes and your working application, you can pin a note to the desktop, which forces the note to stay visible, even when you switch to another application.

Pin a Note to the Desktop

① Double-click the note you want to pin.

The Notes app opens the note in its own window.

② Click and drag the note title to the position you want.

3 Click **Window**.

4 Click **Float on Top**.

A The Notes app keeps each opened note on top of any other window you open.

Is it possible to pin the Notes app window to the desktop, so that it always remains in view?

No, OS X does not allow you to keep the Notes window on top of other windows on your desktop. The pinning technique in this task applies only to open note windows.

Am I only able to pin one note at a time to the desktop?

No, the Notes app enables you to pin multiple notes to the OS X desktop. This is useful if you have different notes that apply to the same task that you are working on in another application. However, you need to exercise some caution because the pinned notes take up space on the desktop.

Create a Reminder

Y ou can use Reminders to have OS X display a notification when you need to perform a task. You can use Calendar to schedule important events, but you likely have many tasks during the day that cannot be considered full-fledged events: returning a call, taking clothes out of the dryer, turning off the sprinkler. If you need to be reminded to perform such tasks, Calendar is overkill, but OS X offers a better solution: Reminders. You use this app to create reminders, which are notifications that tell you to do something or to be somewhere.

Create a Reminder

1 In the Dock, click the **Reminders** icon (▣).

The Reminders app appears.

2 Click **New Reminder** (▦).

Ⓐ You can also click the next available line in the Reminders list.

Note: You can also click **File** and then click **New Reminder**, or press ⌘+N.

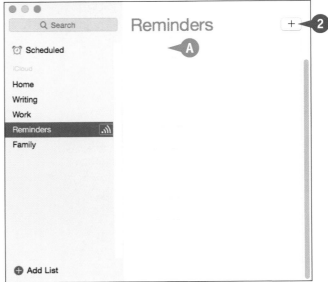

3 Type the reminder title.

4 Click the **Show Info** icon (ⓘ).

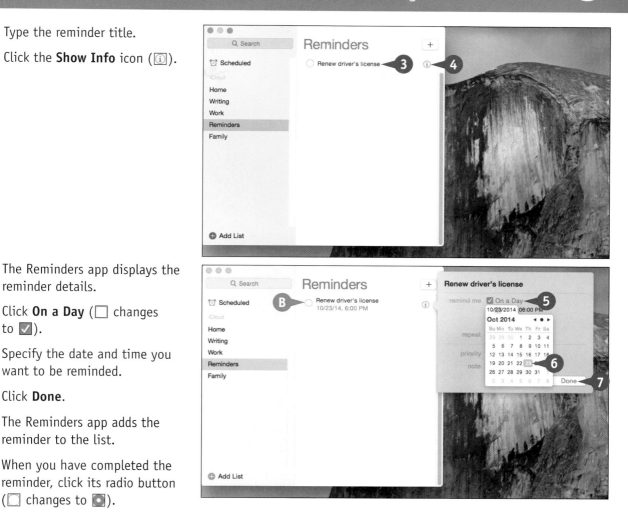

The Reminders app displays the reminder details.

5 Click **On a Day** (☐ changes to ☑).

6 Specify the date and time you want to be reminded.

7 Click **Done**.

The Reminders app adds the reminder to the list.

B When you have completed the reminder, click its radio button (☐ changes to ⊙).

TIP

What does the At a Location option do?
The At a Location option allows the Reminders app to display a notification for a task when you arrive at or leave a location and you have your Mac notebook with you. To set this up, follow steps **1** to **4**, click **At a Location** (☐ changes to ☑), and then type the address or choose a contact that has a defined address. Click either **Leaving** or **Arriving** (☐ changes to ⊙) and then click **Done**.

Create a New Reminder List

You can organize your reminders and make them easier to locate by creating new reminder lists. By default, Reminders comes with a single list called Reminders. However, if you use reminders frequently, the Reminders list can become cluttered, making it difficult to locate reminders. To solve this problem, you can organize your reminders by creating new lists. For example, you could have one list for personal tasks and another for business tasks. After you create one or more new lists, you can move some or all of your existing reminders to the appropriate lists.

Create a New Reminder List

Create a Reminder List

1 Click **Add List**.

Note: You can also click **File** and then click **New List**, or press ⌘+L.

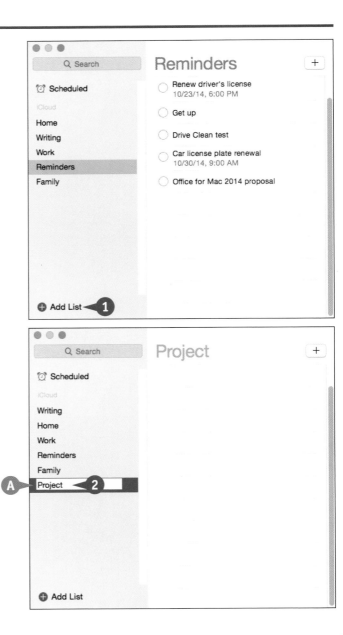

A The Reminders app adds the new list to the sidebar.

2 Type the list name.

3 Press Return.

Move a Reminder to a Different List

1 Click the list that contains the reminder you want to move.

2 Click and drag the reminder and drop it on the destination list.

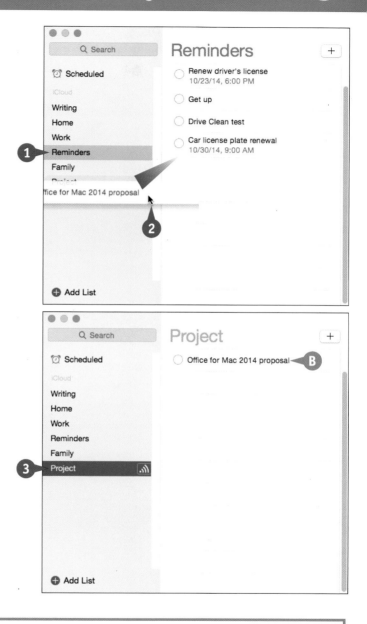

3 Click the destination list.

Ⓑ The reminder now appears in the destination list.

Note: You can also right-click the reminder, click **Move to List**, and then click the destination list.

Why does my Reminders app not have a Completed list?

The Reminders app does not show the Completed list when you first start using the program. When you mark a reminder as complete (☐ changes to ◉), Reminders creates the Completed list and moves the task to that list.

Can I change the order of the lists in the sidebar?

Yes. By default, the Reminders app displays the new lists in the order you create them. To move a list to a new position, click and drag the list up or down in the sidebar. When the horizontal blue bar shows the list to be in the position you want, release the mouse button.

Sign In to Your Facebook Account

If you have a Facebook account, you can use it to share information with your friends directly from your Mac because OS X has built-in support for Facebook accounts. This enables you to post status updates and other data directly from many OS X apps. For example, you can send a link to a web page from Safari or post a photo from Photo Booth. OS X also displays notifications when your Facebook friends post to your News Feed. Before you can post or see Facebook notifications, you must sign in to your Facebook account.

Sign In to Your Facebook Account

1 Click the **System Preferences** icon (⬚).

Note: You can also click the **Apple** menu (⬚) and then click **System Preferences**.

The System Preferences window appears.

2 Click **Internet Accounts**.

The Internet Accounts preferences appear.

3 Click **Facebook**.

System Preferences prompts you for your Facebook username and password.

4 Type your Facebook username.

5 Type your Facebook password.

6 Click **Next**.

System Preferences displays information detailing what signing in to Facebook entails.

7 Click **Sign In**.

OS X signs in to your Facebook account.

TIPS

Is there an easy way to add my Facebook friends' profile pictures to the Contacts app?
Yes. Follow steps **1** and **2** to open the Internet Accounts window, click your Facebook account, and then click **Get Profile Photos**. When System Preferences asks you to confirm, click **Update Contacts**.

Can I prevent Facebook friends and events from appearing in the Contacts and Calendar apps?
Yes. Follow steps **1** and **2** to open the Internet Accounts window and then click your Facebook account. If you do not want to clutter Contacts with all your Facebook friends, click **Contacts** (☑ changes to ☐). If you do not want your Facebook events or friends' birthdays to appear in Calendar, click **Calendars** (☑ changes to ☐).

Post to Facebook

Once you sign in to your Facebook account, you begin seeing notifications whenever your friends post to your News Feed. However, OS X Yosemite's Facebook support also enables you to use various OS X apps to post information to your Facebook News Feed. For example, if you surf to a web page that you want to share, you can post a link to that page. You can also post a photo to your News Feed.

Post to Facebook

Post a Web Page

1. Use Safari to navigate to the web page you want to share.

2. Click **Share** (⬆).

3. Click **Facebook**.

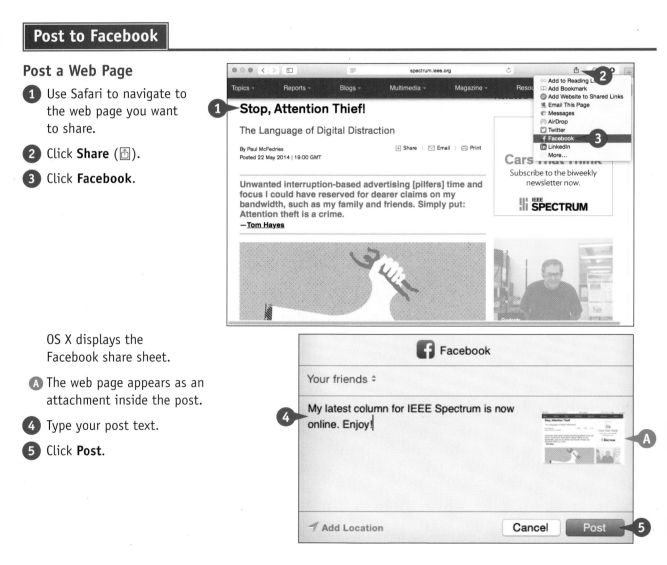

OS X displays the Facebook share sheet.

Ⓐ The web page appears as an attachment inside the post.

4. Type your post text.

5. Click **Post**.

Post a Photo

1 In Finder, click the photo you want to post.

2 Click **Share** (⬆).

3 Click **Facebook**.

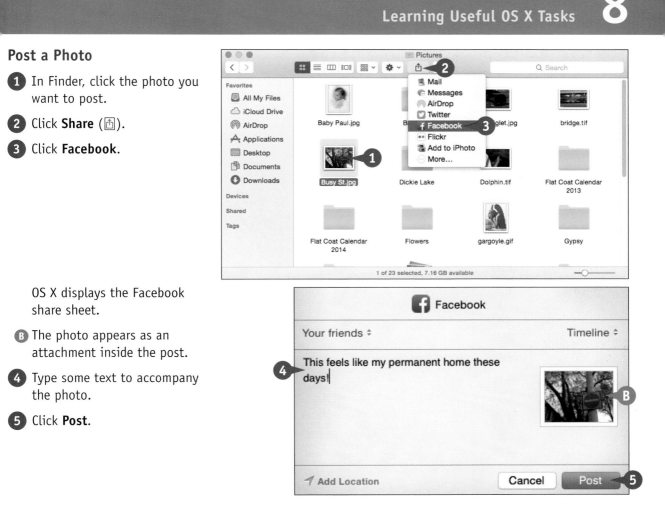

OS X displays the Facebook share sheet.

Ⓑ The photo appears as an attachment inside the post.

4 Type some text to accompany the photo.

5 Click **Post**.

TIP

Can I use OS X Yosemite to post information to my LinkedIn connections?

Yes. OS X Yosemite also comes with support for the LinkedIn social network. To sign in to your LinkedIn account, click the **System Preferences** icon (⬚), click **Internet Accounts**, and then click **LinkedIn**. Type your LinkedIn username and password, click **Next**, and then click **Sign In**.

To share information with your LinkedIn connections, open the app that contains the data, click **Share** (⬆), click **LinkedIn**, type some text to accompany the post, and then click **Send**.

Sign In to Your Twitter Account

If you have a Twitter account, you can use it to share information with your followers directly from OS X Yosemite, which comes with built-in support for Twitter. This enables you to send tweets directly from many OS X apps. For example, you can send a link to a web page from Safari or tweet a photo from Photo Booth. OS X also displays notifications if you are mentioned on Twitter or if a Twitter user sends you a direct message. Before you can tweet or see Twitter notifications, you must sign in to your Twitter account.

Sign In to Your Twitter Account

1 Click the **System Preferences** icon (🎛).

Note: You can also click the **Apple** icon (🍎) and then click **System Preferences**.

The System Preferences window appears.

2 Click **Internet Accounts**.

The Internet Accounts preferences appear.

3 Click **Twitter**.

System Preferences prompts you for your Twitter username and password.

4 Type your Twitter username.

5 Type your Twitter password.

6 Click **Next**.

Twitter 🐦

To get started, fill out the following information:

User Name: | paulmcf | ◀ **4**

Password: | •••••••••••• | ◀ **5**

By clicking "Next", you represent that you are legally permitted to upload the content and that the content does not violate Twitter's Terms of Use.

Cancel | Next ◀ **6**

System Preferences displays information detailing what signing in to Twitter entails.

7 Click **Sign In**.

OS X signs in to your Twitter account.

Twitter 🐦

Signing into Twitter will:

Allow you to tweet and post photos and links to Twitter.

Show links from your Twitter timeline in Safari.

Enable apps to work with your Twitter account, with your permission.

You can disable Contacts syncing and disallow any app on this Mac from accessing your Twitter account in System Preferences.

Cancel | Sign In ◀ **7**

TIP

Some of the people in my contacts list are on Twitter. Is there an easy way to add their Twitter usernames to the Contacts app?

Yes, OS X has a feature that enables you to give permission for Twitter to update your contacts. Twitter examines the email addresses in the Contacts app, and if it finds any that match Twitter users, it updates Contacts with each person's username and account photo.

Follow steps **1** and **2** to open the Internet Accounts window, click your Twitter account, and then click **Update Contacts**. When OS X asks you to confirm, click **Update Contacts**.

Send a Tweet

After you sign in to your Twitter account in OS X Yosemite, you can send tweets from various OS X apps. Although signing in to your Twitter account is useful for seeing notifications that tell you about mentions and direct messages, you will mostly use it for sending tweets to your followers. For example, if you come across a web page that you want to share, you can tweet a link to that page. You can also write a note using the Notes app and tweet that note to your followers.

Send a Tweet

Tweet a Web Page

1 Use Safari to navigate to the web page you want to share.

2 Click **Share** (⬆).

3 Click **Twitter**.

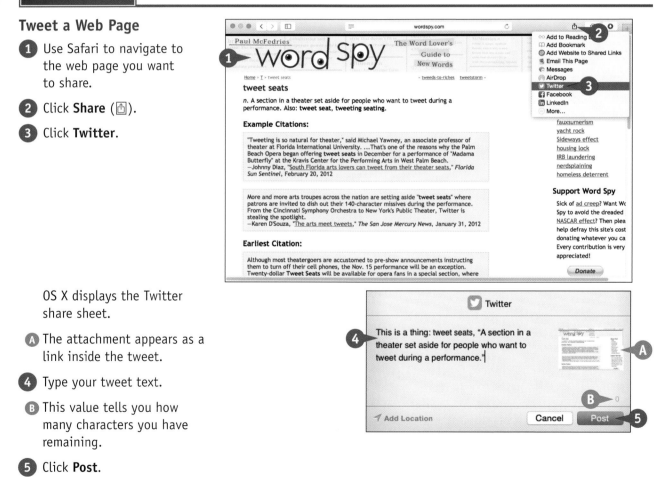

OS X displays the Twitter share sheet.

Ⓐ The attachment appears as a link inside the tweet.

4 Type your tweet text.

Ⓑ This value tells you how many characters you have remaining.

5 Click **Post**.

Tweet a Note

1 In Notes, click the note you want to share.

2 Click **Share** (🔗).

3 Click **Twitter**.

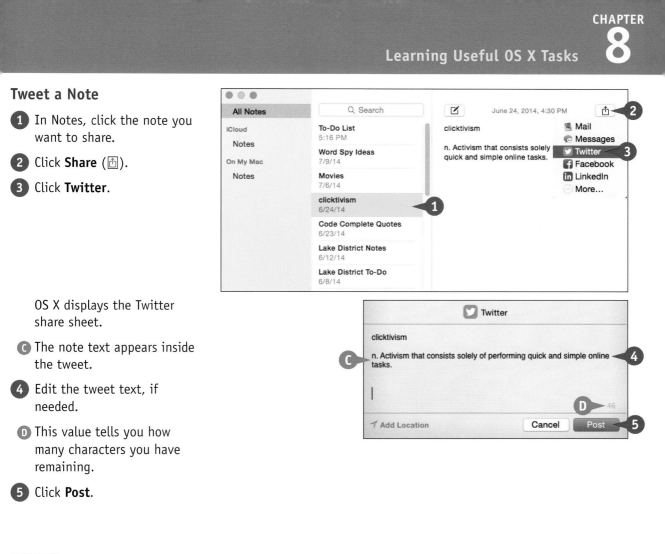

OS X displays the Twitter share sheet.

ⓒ The note text appears inside the tweet.

4 Edit the tweet text, if needed.

ⓓ This value tells you how many characters you have remaining.

5 Click **Post**.

TIP

Are there other apps I can use to send tweets?

Yes. If you open a photo using Quick Look (click the photo in Finder and then press `Spacebar`), you can click **Share** (🔗) and then click **Twitter**. Similarly, you can open a photo in Preview, click **Share** (🔗), and then click **Twitter**. Also, with your permission, many third-party apps are able to use your sign-in information to send tweets from the apps without requiring separate Twitter logins for each program.

Share Information with Other People

You can use OS X Yosemite to share information with other people, including web pages, maps, notes, pictures, videos, and photos. OS X Yosemite was built with sharing in mind, and so it implements a feature called the *share sheet*, which makes it easy to share data using multiple methods, such as email and instant messaging, as well as Facebook and Twitter. Please note that you can share via Facebook and Twitter if you have configured those accounts in OS X, as described earlier in this chapter.

Share Information with Other People

Share a Web Page

1. Use Safari to navigate to the web page you want to share.

2. Click **Share** (□).

3. Click the method you want to use to share the web page.

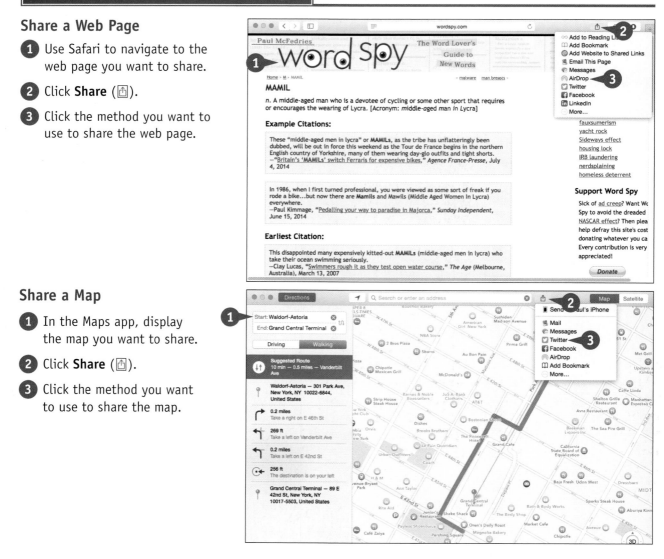

Share a Map

1. In the Maps app, display the map you want to share.

2. Click **Share** (□).

3. Click the method you want to use to share the map.

Share an Image

1. In Finder, click the image you want to share.

2. Click **Share** (⬆).

3. Click the method you want to use to share the image.

Share a Video

1. In QuickTime Player, open the video you want to share.

2. Click **Share** (⬆).

3. Click the method you want to use to share the video.

TIP

Do I need to configure OS X to use some of the sharing methods?
Yes. You cannot use the Mail method unless you configure Mail with an email account, and you cannot use the Message method until you configure Messages with an account. Flickr and Vimeo must be configured in System Preferences. Click the **System Preferences** icon (⬛) in the Dock, click **Internet Accounts**, and then click the type of account you want to add.

Work with the Notification Center

You can keep on top of what is happening while you are using your Mac by taking advantage of the Notification Center. Several apps take advantage of a feature called *notifications*, which enables them to send messages to OS X about events that are happening on your Mac. For example, the App Store uses the Notification Center to let you know when OS X updates are available. There are two types of notifications: a banner that appears temporarily and an alert that stays on-screen until you dismiss it. You can also open the Notification Center to view recent notifications.

Work with the Notification Center

Handle Alert Notifications

A An alert notification displays one or more buttons.

1 Click a button to dismiss the notification.

Note: In a notification about new OS X updates, click **Update** to open the App Store and see the updates. For details about the updates, click **Details**.

Handle Banner Notifications

B A banner notification does not display any buttons.

Note: The banner notification stays on-screen for about 5 seconds and then disappears.

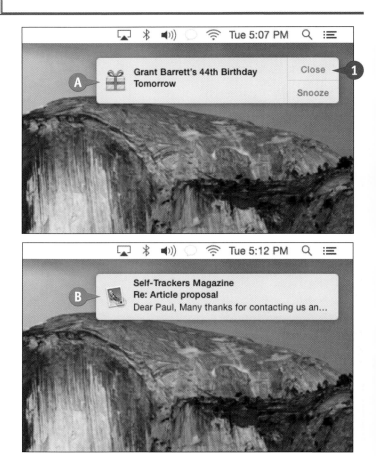

View Recent Notifications

1 Click **Notification Center** (▭).

Note: If your Mac has a trackpad, you can also open the Notification Center by using two fingers to swipe left from the right edge of the trackpad.

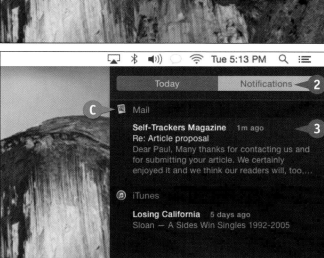

2 Click **Notifications**.

C OS X displays your recent notifications.

3 Click a notification to view the item in the original application.

TIP

Can I control which apps use the Notification Center and how they use it?
Yes. Click the **System Preferences** icon (▦) in the Dock and then click **Notifications**. Click an app on the left side of the window and then click a notification style: None, Banners, or Alerts. To control the number of items the app can display in the Notification Center, click the **Show in Notification Center** option menu and select a number. To remove an app from the Notification Center, click **Show in Notification Center** (☑ changes to ☐).

Organize Files with Tags

You can describe many of your files to OS X by adding one or more tags that indicate the content or subject matter of the file. A *tag* is a word or short phrase that describes some aspect of a file. You can add as many tags as you need. Adding tags to files makes it easier to search and organize your documents.

For an existing file, you can add one or more tags within Finder. If you are working with a new file, you can add tags when you save the file to your Mac's hard drive.

Organize Files with Tags

Add Tags with Finder

1 Click the **Finder** icon ([image]) in the Dock.

2 Open the folder that contains the file you want to tag.

3 Click the file.

4 Click **Edit Tags** ([image]).

OS X displays the Tags sheet.

5 Type the tag.

Note: To assign multiple tags, separate each one with a comma.

6 Press Return.

OS X assigns the tag or tags.

7 Press Return.

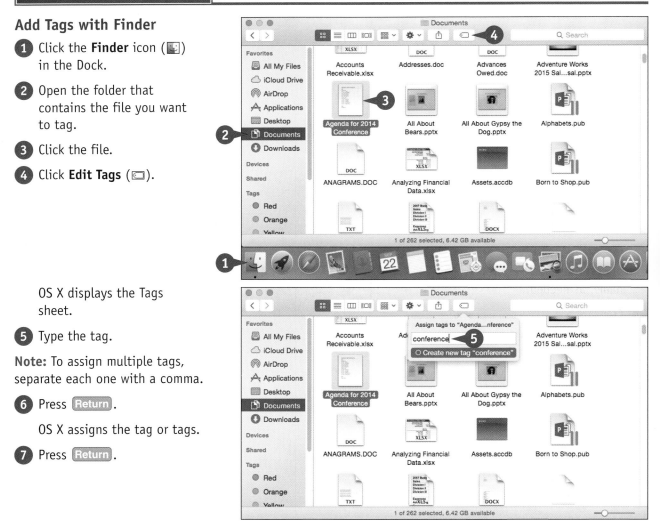

Add Tags When Saving

1 In the application, select the command that saves the new file.

The application displays the Save sheet.

2 Use the Tags text box to type the tag.

Note: To assign multiple tags, separate each one with a comma.

3 Choose the other save options, such as the file name, as needed.

4 Click **Save**.

The application saves the file and assigns that tag or tags.

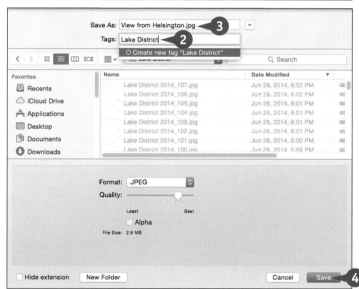

Is there an easier method I can use to assign an existing tag to another file?

Yes. OS X keeps a list of your tags, and it displays that list each time you display the Tags sheet. You can assign the same tag to another file by displaying the Tags sheet and clicking the tag in the list that appears.

Can I assign the same tag or tags to multiple files?

Yes. First, use Finder to select all the files in advance. Click **Edit Tags** (☐), type the tag, and OS X automatically assigns the tag to all the selected files.

Search Files with Tags

After you assign tags to your files, you can take advantage of those tags to make it easier to find and group related files.

Although keeping related files together in the same folder is good practice, that is not always possible. It can make locating and working with related files difficult. However, if you assign the same tag or tags to those files, you can use those tags to quickly and easily search for the files. No matter where the files are located, Finder shows them all together in a single window for easy access.

Search Files with Tags

Search for a Tag

1. Use Finder's Search box to type the first few letters of the tag.

2. When the tag appears, click it.

A Finder displays the files assigned that tag.

Select a Tag

1 In the Finder sidebar, click the tag.

B If you do not see the tag you want, click **All Tags** to display the complete list.

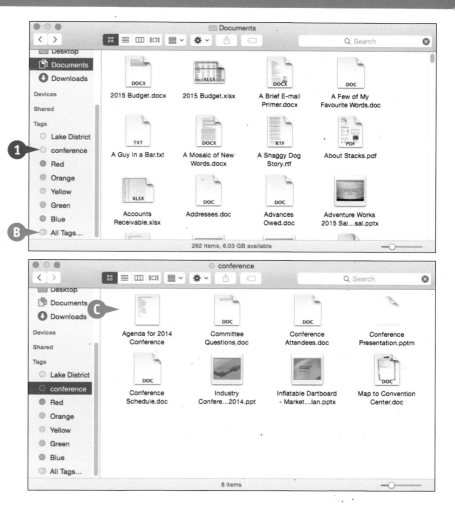

C Finder displays the files assigned that tag.

Note: With the tag folder displayed, you can automatically assign that tag to other files by dragging the files from another Finder window and dropping them within the tag folder.

TIP

Can I control what tags appear in Finder's sidebar?
Yes, by following these steps:

1 Open Finder.

2 Click **Finder**.

3 Click **Preferences**.

4 Click the **Tags** tab.

5 For each tag you do not want to appear in the sidebar, click the check box to the right of the tag (☑ changes to ☐).

6 Click **Close** (▣).

Search for a Location

You can use the Maps app to display a location on a map. Maps is an OS X app that displays digital maps that you can use to view just about any location by searching for an address or place name.

Maps comes with a Search box that enables you to search for locations by address or by name. If Maps finds the place, it zooms in and drops a pin on the digital map to show you the exact location. For many public locations, Maps also offers an info screen that shows you the location's address, phone number, and more.

Search for a Location

1 Click the **Maps** icon (▣).

OS X starts the Maps app.

2 Use the Search box to type the address or name of the location.

A If Maps displays the name of the location as you type, click the location.

B Maps drops a pin on the location.

C Click **Zoom In** (⊞) or press ⌘+➕ to get a closer look.

D Click **Zoom Out** (⊟) or press ⌘+➖ to see more of the map.

3 If Maps offers more data about the location, click **Show Info** (ⓘ).

E Maps displays the Info screen for the location.

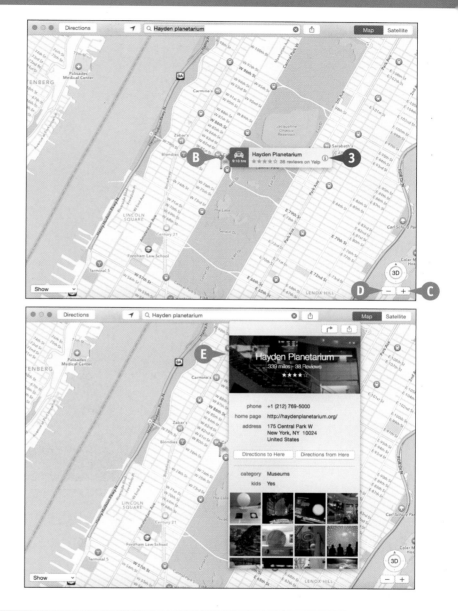

Get Directions to a Location

Besides displaying locations, Maps also understands the roads and highways found in most cities, states, and countries. This means that you can use the Maps app to get specific directions for traveling from one location to another. You specify a starting point and destination for a trip, and Maps then provides you with directions for getting from one point to the other. Maps highlights the trip route on a digital map and also gives you specific details for negotiating each leg of the trip.

Get Directions to a Location

① Add a pin to the map for your destination.

Note: See the previous task, "Search for a Location," to learn how to add a pin.

② Click **Directions**.

The Directions pane appears.

Ⓐ Your pinned location appears in the End text box.

Ⓑ Maps assumes you want to start the route from your current location.

③ To start the route from another location, type the name or address in the Start text box.

④ Select how you intend to travel to the destination:

Click **Driving** if you plan to drive.

Click **Walking** if plan to walk.

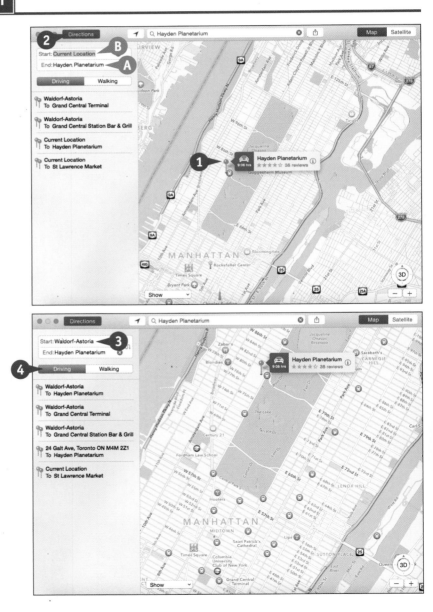

C Maps displays the suggested route for your journey.

D This area tells the distance and approximate traveling time.

E This area displays the various legs of the journey.

F If Maps displays alternate routes, you can click these banners to view the routes.

5 Click the first leg of the trip.

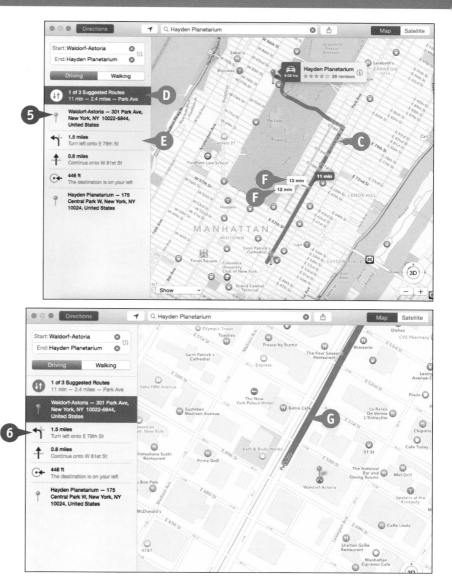

G Maps zooms in to show you just that leg of the trip.

6 As you complete each leg of the trip, click the next leg for further instructions.

TIPS

Can I get traffic information?
Yes, Maps can display current traffic conditions for most major cities. Click **View** and then click **Show Traffic**. On the map, you see a sequence of red dots where traffic is slow, and a sequence of red dashes where traffic is heavy.

Can I get directions even though I do not have an exact address?
Yes. You can give Maps the approximate location and it generates the appropriate directions. To specify a location without knowing its address, click **Edit** and then click **Drop Pin** (or press **Shift** + **⌘** + **D**). Maps drops a purple pin randomly on the map. Click and drag the pin to the location you want.

Search Your Mac

You can save time and make your Mac easier to use by learning how to search for the apps, settings, or files that you need.

After you have used your Mac for a while and have created many documents, you might have trouble locating a specific file. You can save a great deal of time by using OS X's Spotlight search feature to search for your document. You can also use Spotlight to search for apps as well as information from the Internet, the iTunes Store, the App Store, and more. Alternatively, you can use Finder's Search box to search just your Mac.

Search Your Mac

Search with Spotlight

1 Click **Spotlight** (🔍).

You can also press
⌘ + Spacebar.

Ⓐ The Spotlight window appears.

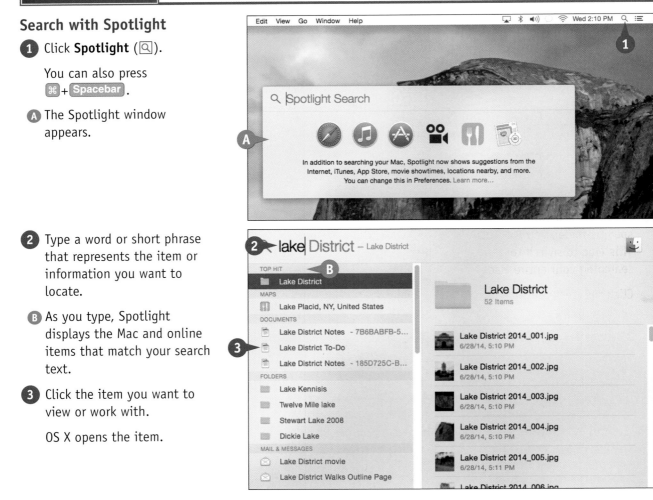

2 Type a word or short phrase that represents the item or information you want to locate.

Ⓑ As you type, Spotlight displays the Mac and online items that match your search text.

3 Click the item you want to view or work with.

OS X opens the item.

Search Your Mac

1 Click the **Finder** icon (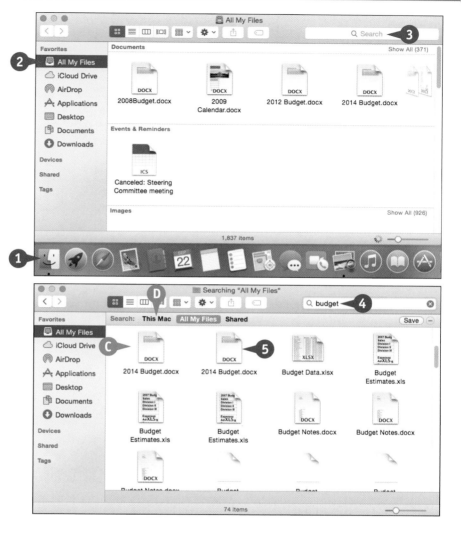).

2 If you want to search within a specific folder, open that folder.

3 Click inside the Search box.

4 Type a word or short phrase that represents the item you want to locate.

C As you type, Spotlight displays the items that match your search text.

D If you are searching a specific folder, you can click **This Mac** to switch to searching your entire Mac.

5 Click the item you want to work with.

OS X opens the item.

TIP

Can I remove item types from the Spotlight search results?

Yes. Spotlight supports a number of different *categories*, such as Applications, Documents, and Contacts. If there are categories that you never search for, such as system preferences or movies, you should remove them to make it easier to navigate the Spotlight search results.

To remove one or more categories from the Spotlight results, click the **System Preferences** icon (▣) in the Dock and then click **Spotlight**. In the Search Results pane, click the check box beside each category you want to remove (☑ changes to ☐).

Install a Font

OS X ships with a large collection of fonts, but if you require a different font for a project, you can download the font files and then install them on your Mac.

Macs have always placed special emphasis on typography, so it is no surprise that OS X ships with nearly 300 fonts. However, typography is a personal, exacting art form, so your Mac might not have a particular font that would be just right for a newsletter, greeting card, or similar project. In that case, you can download the font you need and then install it.

Install a Font

1 Click **Spotlight** (🔍).

You can also press ⌘ + **Spacebar**.

Note: For more about the Spotlight search feature, see the previous task, "Search Your Mac."

The Spotlight window appears.

2 Type **font**.

3 Click **Font Book**.

You can also open Finder, click **Applications**, and then click **Font Book** (📖).

The Font Book application appears.

4 Click **File**.

5 Click **Add Fonts**.

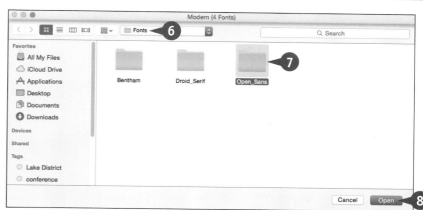

⑥ Open the location that contains the font you want to install.

⑦ Click the folder that contains the font files.

⑧ Click **Open**.

OS X installs the font.

Ⓐ The typeface name appears in the Fonts list.

⑨ Click ▶ to open the typeface and see its individual fonts.

⑩ Click a font.

Ⓑ A preview of the font appears here.

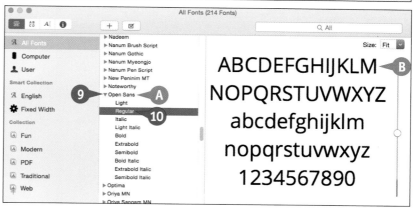

TIPS

What is the difference between a font and a typeface?

A *typeface* is a unique design applied to each letter, number, and symbol. A *font* is a particular style of a typeface, such as regular, bold, or italic. However, in everyday parlance, most people use the terms typeface and font interchangeably.

What is a font collection?

A *collection* is a group of related fonts. For example, the Fun collection contains fonts normally used with informal designs, whereas the Web collection contains fonts that render well on web pages. To add your new font to an existing collection, drag it from the **Fonts** list and drop it on the collection. To create your own collection, click **File** and then click **New Collection** (or press ⌘+Ⓝ).

CHAPTER 9

Viewing and Editing Photos

Whether you just want to look at your photos, or you want to edit them to crop out unneeded portions or fix problems, OS X comes with a number of useful tools for viewing and editing photos.

View a Preview of a Photo

OS X offers several tools you can use to see a preview of any photo on your Mac. The Finder application has a number of methods you can use to view your photos, but here you learn about the two easiest methods. First, you can preview any saved image file using the OS X Quick Look feature; second, you can see photo previews by switching to the Cover Flow view. You can also preview photos using the Preview application.

View a Preview of a Photo

View a Preview with Quick Look

1 In Finder, open the folder that contains the photo you want to preview.

2 Click the photo.

3 Press Spacebar.

A Finder displays a preview of the photo.

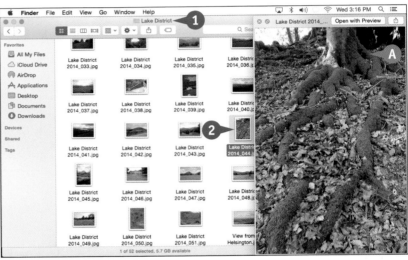

View a Preview with Cover Flow

1 In Finder, open the folder that contains the photo you want to preview.

2 Click the photo.

3 Click **Cover Flow** ( ).

B Finder displays a preview of the photo.

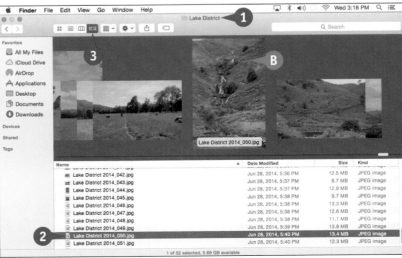

View a Preview in the Preview Application

1. In Finder, open the folder that contains the photo you want to preview.

2. Click the photo.

3. Click **File**.

4. Click **Open With**.

5. Click **Preview**.

Note: In many cases, you can also simply double-click the photo to open it in the Preview application.

The Preview application opens and displays the photo.

6. Use the toolbar buttons to change how the photo appears in the Preview window.

C. More commands are available on the View menu.

7. When you finish viewing the photo, click **Close** (■).

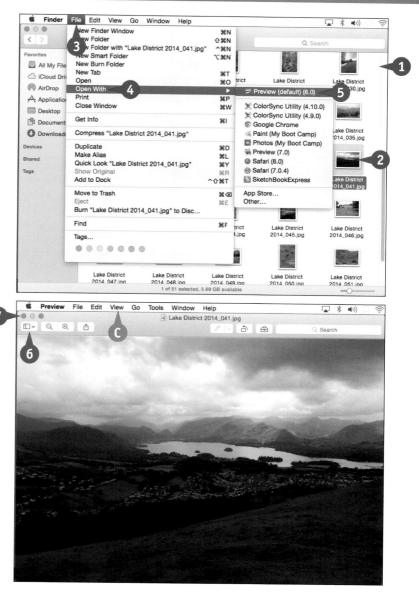

TIPS

Is there an easier way to preview multiple photos using the Preview application?
Yes. In Finder, navigate to the folder that contains the photos and then select each file that you want to preview. Either click and drag the mouse ▶ over the photos, or press and hold ⌘ and click each one. In Preview, click **Next** and **Previous** to navigate the photos.

Is there a way that I can zoom in on just a portion of a photo?
Yes. In Preview, click and drag your mouse ▶ to select the portion of the photo that you want to magnify. Click **View** and then click **Zoom to Selection** (or press ⌘+*).

View a Slideshow of Your Photos

Instead of viewing your photos one at a time, you can easily view multiple photos by running them in a slideshow. You can run the slideshow using the Preview application or Quick Look. The slideshow displays each photo for a few seconds and then Preview automatically displays the next photo. Quick Look also offers several on-screen controls that you can use to control the slideshow playback. You can also configure Quick Look to display the images full screen.

View a Slideshow of Your Photos

1 In Finder, open the folder that contains the photos you want to view in the slideshow.

2 Select the photos you want to view.

3 Click **File**.

4 Click **Open With**.

5 Click **Preview**.

The Preview window appears.

6 Click **View**.

7 Click **Slideshow**.

You can also select Slideshow by pressing Shift + ⌘ + F.

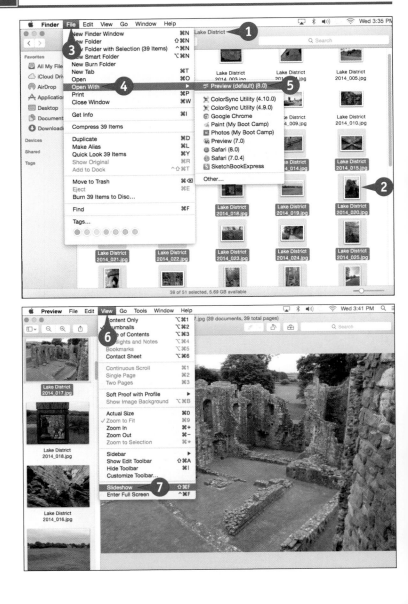

Preview opens the slideshow window.

8 Move the mouse.

Ⓐ Preview displays the slideshow controls.

9 Click **Play**.

Preview begins the slideshow.

Ⓑ Click **Next** to move to the next photo.

Ⓒ Click **Back** to move to the previous photo.

Ⓓ Click **Pause** to suspend the slideshow.

10 When the slideshow is over or when you want to return to Finder, click **Close** or press Esc.

TIPS

Can I jump to a specific photo during the slideshow?
Yes. With the slideshow running, press Spacebar to stop the show. Use the arrow keys to select the photo that you want to view in the slideshow. Click **Play** to resume the slideshow.

What keyboard shortcuts can I use when viewing a slideshow?
Press → or ↑ to display the next photo, and press ← or ↓ to display the previous photo. Press Esc to end the slideshow.

Import Photos from a Digital Camera

You can import photos from a digital camera and save them on your Mac. If you have the iLife suite installed on your Mac, you can use the iPhoto application to handle importing photos. iPhoto is also available separately through the App Store. iPhoto enables you to add a name and a description to each import, which helps you to find your photos after the import is complete. To perform the import, you need a cable to connect your digital camera to your Mac. Most digital cameras come with a USB cable.

Import Photos from a Digital Camera

Import Photos from a Digital Camera

1 Connect one end of the cable to the digital camera.

2 Connect the other end of the cable to a free USB port on your Mac.

3 Turn the camera on and put it in either playback or computer mode.

Your Mac launches the iPhoto application.

Note: You can also launch the application by clicking the **iPhoto** icon (🖼) in the Dock.

Ⓐ Your digital camera appears in the Devices section.

Ⓑ iPhoto displays previews of the camera's photos.

4 Use the Event Name text box to type a name for the group of photos you are going to import.

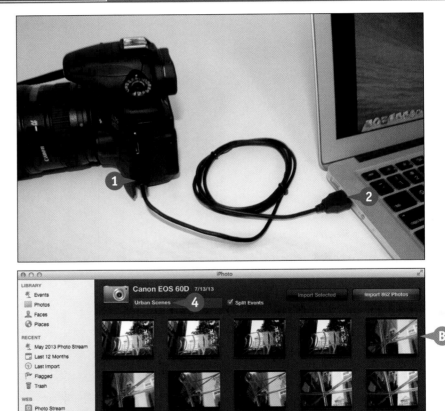

⑤ Click and drag the mouse 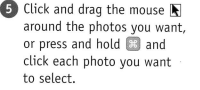 around the photos you want, or press and hold ⌘ and click each photo you want to select.

⑥ Click **Import Selected**.

Ⓒ To import all the photos from the digital camera, click **Import X Photos**, where X is the number of photos stored in the camera.

iPhoto imports the photos from the digital camera.

iPhoto asks if you want to delete the original photos from the digital camera.

⑦ If you no longer need the photos on the camera, click **Delete Photos**.

Ⓓ To keep the photos on the camera, click **Keep Photos**.

View the Imported Photos

① Click **Events**.

② Double-click the event name that you specified in step 4.

Ⓔ You can also click **Last Import**.

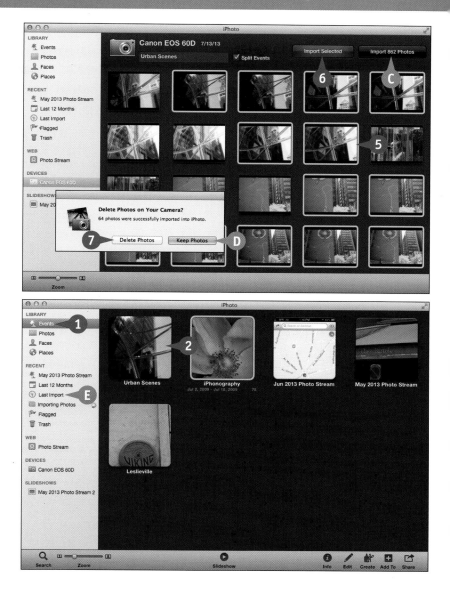

TIP

When I connect my digital camera, why do I see Image Capture instead of iPhoto?
Your Image Capture is not configured to open iPhoto when you connect your camera. To fix this, connect your digital camera to your Mac; the Image Capture application opens. (If you do not see the Image Capture application, click **Finder** in the Dock, click **Applications**, and then double-click **Image Capture**.) Click the **Connecting** 🔲 and then click **iPhoto**. Click **Image Capture** in the menu bar and then click **Quit Image Capture**.

View Your Photos

If you want to look at several photos, you can use the iPhoto application, which is available with the Apple iLife suite or separately via the App Store. iPhoto offers a feature called full-screen mode, which hides everything else and displays your photos using the entire screen. Once you activate full-screen mode, iPhoto offers several on-screen controls that you can use to navigate backward and forward through the photos. Full-screen mode also shows thumbnail images of each photo, so you can quickly jump to any photo you want to view.

View Your Photos

1 In iPhoto, click **Events**.

2 Double-click the event that contains the photos you want to view.

3 Double-click the first photo you want to view.

iPhoto displays the photo.

④ Click **Next** (▶) to view the next photo in the event.

Ⓐ You can also click **Previous** (◀) to see the previous photo in the event.

Note: You can also navigate photos by pressing ▶ and ◀.

⑤ When you are done, click the name of the event.

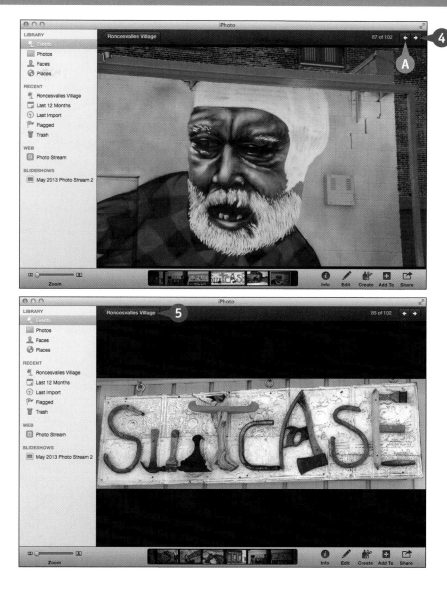

TIP

Is there a way that I can jump quickly to a particular photo in full-screen mode?
Yes. Move the mouse ▸ to the thumbnails at the bottom of the iPhoto window and use the horizontal scroll bar to bring the thumbnail of the photo you want into view. Click the photo's thumbnail. iPhoto displays the photo in full-screen mode.

Create an Album

You can use iPhoto to organize your photos into albums. You can get iPhoto either via the iLife suite, which is installed on all new Macs, or via the App Store. In iPhoto, an *album* is a collection of photos that are usually related in some way. For example, you might create an album for a series of vacation photos, for photos taken at a party or other special event, or for photos that include a particular person, pet, or place. Using your iPhoto library, you can create customized albums that include only the photos that you want to view.

Create an Album

Create the Album

1 Click **File**.

2 Click **New Album**.

Note: You can also start a new album by pressing ⌘+N.

3 Type a name for the new album.

4 Click **Continue**.

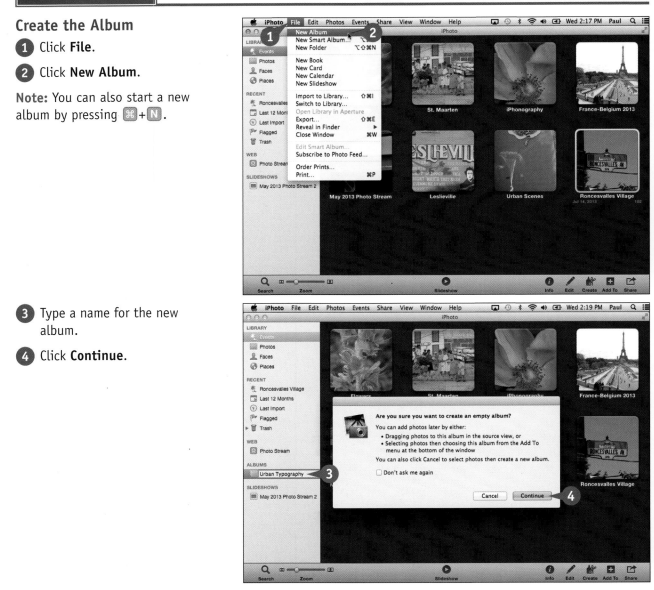

Add Photos to the Album

1 Click **Photos**.

2 Click ▶ beside an event that contains photos you want to work with (▶ changes to ▼).

3 Click and drag a photo and drop it on the new album.

4 Repeat steps **2** and **3** to add other photos to the album.

5 Click the album.

Ⓐ iPhoto displays the photos you added to the album.

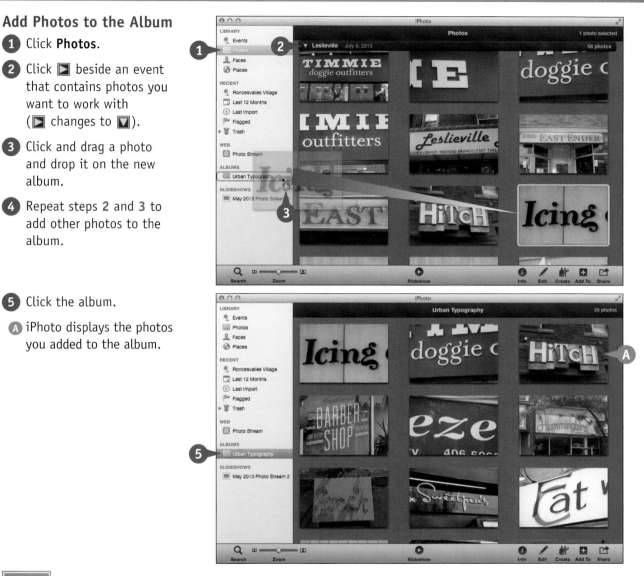

TIP

Is there any way to make iPhoto add photos to an album automatically?

Yes, you can create a *Smart Album* where the photos that appear in the album have one or more properties in common, such as the description, rating, date, or text in the photo title. Click **File** and then click **New Smart Album** (you can also press Option+⌘+N). Use the Smart Album dialog to create one or more rules that define what photos you want to appear in the album.

Crop a Photo

If you have a photo containing elements that you do not want to see, you can often cut out those elements. This is called *cropping*, and you can do this with iPhoto, which comes with iLife or via the App Store. When you crop a photo, you specify a rectangular area of the photo that you want to keep. iPhoto discards everything outside of the rectangle. Cropping is a useful skill because it can help give focus to the true subject of a photo. Cropping is also useful for removing extraneous elements that appear near the edges of a photo.

Crop a Photo

1 Click the photo you want to crop.

2 Click **Edit**.

iPhoto displays its editing tools.

3 Click **Crop**.

iPhoto displays a cropping rectangle on the photo.

④ Click and drag a corner or side to define the area you want to keep.

Note: Remember that iPhoto keeps the area inside the rectangle.

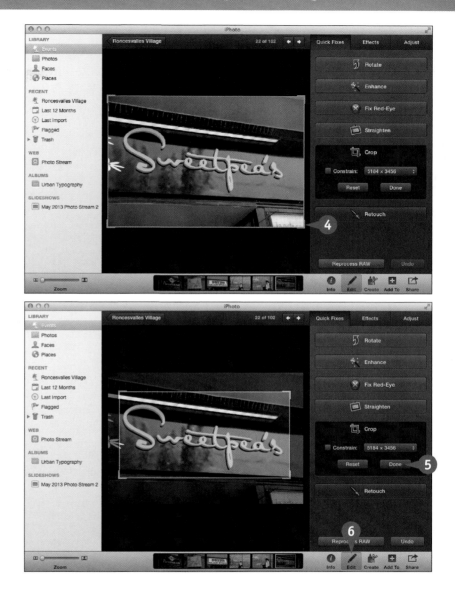

⑤ Click **Done**.

iPhoto saves the cropped photo.

⑥ Click **Edit**.

iPhoto exits edit mode.

TIP

Is there a quick way to crop a photo to a certain size?
Yes, iPhoto enables you to specify either a specific size, such as 640 × 480, or a specific ratio, such as 4 × 3 or 16 × 9. Follow steps **1** to **3** to display the Crop tool. Click **Constrain** (☐ changes to ☑) (Ⓐ). Click the **Constrain** 🔽 and then click the size or ratio you want to use (Ⓑ). Click **Done** and then click **Edit** to exit edit mode.

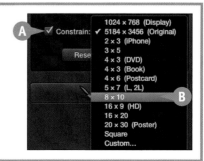

Rotate a Photo

You can rotate a photo using the iPhoto application, which comes with all new Macs as part of iLife, and is also available separately via the App Store. Depending on how you held your camera when you took a shot, the resulting photo might show the subject sideways or upside down. This may be the effect you want, but more likely this is a problem. To fix this problem, you can use iPhoto to rotate the photo so that the subject appears right-side up. You can rotate a photo either clockwise or counterclockwise.

Rotate a Photo

1 Click the photo you want to rotate.

Note: A quick way to rotate a photo is to right-click the photo and then click **Rotate** (⟳).

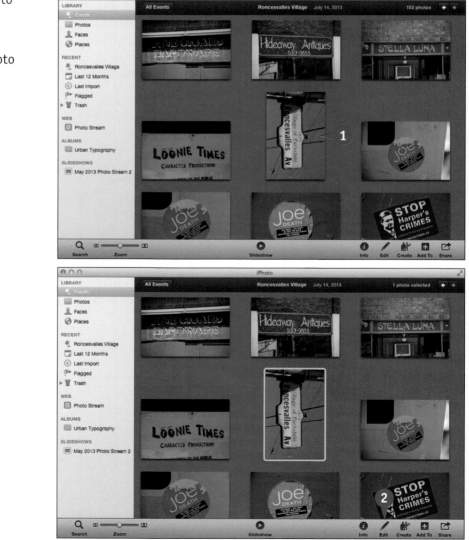

2 Click **Edit**.

iPhoto displays its editing tools.

③ Click **Rotate** (⟲).

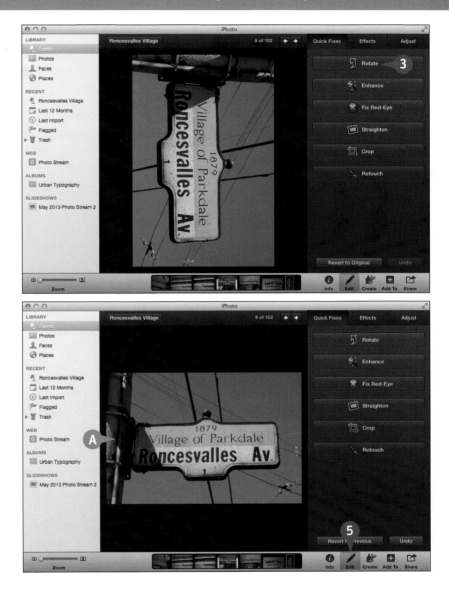

Ⓐ iPhoto rotates the photo 90 degrees counterclockwise.

④ Repeat step **3** until the subject of the photo is right-side up.

⑤ Click **Edit**.

iPhoto exits edit mode.

Straighten a Photo

You can straighten a crooked photo using the iPhoto application, which comes with all new Macs as part of iLife, and is also available separately via the App Store. If you do not use a tripod when taking pictures, getting your camera perfectly level when you take a shot is very difficult and requires a lot of practice and a steady hand. Despite your best efforts, you might end up with a photo that is not quite level. To fix this problem, you can use iPhoto to nudge the photo clockwise or counterclockwise so that the subject appears straight.

Straighten a Photo

1 Click the photo you want to straighten.

2 Click **Edit**.

iPhoto displays its editing tools.

3 Click **Straighten**.

iPhoto displays a grid over the photo.

④ Click and drag the **Angle** slider.

Drag the slider to the left to angle the photo counterclockwise.

Drag the slider to the right to angle the photo clockwise.

⑤ Click **Done**.

⑥ Click **Edit**.

iPhoto exits edit mode.

TIP

How do I know when my photo is level?
Use the gridlines that iPhoto places over the photo. Locate a horizontal line in your photo and then rotate the photo so that this line is parallel to the nearest horizontal line in the grid. You can also match a vertical line in the photo with a vertical line in the grid.

Remove Red Eye from a Photo

You can remove red eye from a photo using the iPhoto application, which comes with all new Macs as part of iLife, and is also available separately via the App Store. When you use a flash to take a picture of one or more people, in some cases the flash may reflect off the subjects' retinas. The result is the common phenomenon of *red eye*, where each person's pupils appear red instead of black. If you have a photo where one or more people have red eyes due to the camera flash, you can use iPhoto to remove the red eye and give your subjects a more natural look.

Remove Red Eye from a Photo

1 Click the photo that contains the red eye.

2 Click **Edit**.

iPhoto displays its editing tools.

A If needed, you can click and drag this slider to the right to zoom in on the picture.

B You can click and drag this rectangle to bring the red eye into view.

3 Click **Fix Red-Eye**.

iPhoto displays its Red-Eye controls.

Ⓒ You may be able to fix the red eye automatically by clicking **Auto-fix red-eye** (☐ changes to ☑). If that does not work, continue with the rest of these steps.

④ Move the red eye pointer over a red eye in the photo.

⑤ Click the red eye.

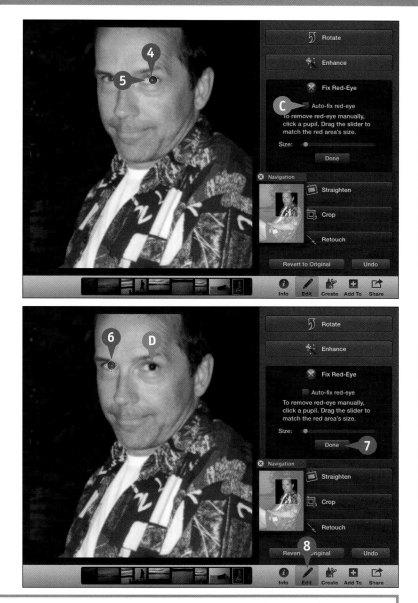

Ⓓ iPhoto removes the red eye.

⑥ Repeat steps **4** and **5** to fix any other instances of red eye in the photo.

⑦ Click **Done**.

⑧ Click **Edit**.

iPhoto exits edit mode.

TIP

Why does iPhoto remove only part of the red eye in my photo?
The Red-Eye tool may not be set to a large enough size. The tool should be approximately the same size as the subject's eye. If it is not, as shown here (Ⓐ), follow steps **1** to **3** to display the Red-Eye controls. Click and drag the **Size** slider until the Red-Eye tool is the size of the red-eye area. Use your mouse to move the circle over the red eye and then click.

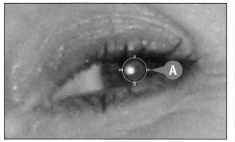

Add Names to Faces in Your Photos

You can make your photos easier to manage and navigate by adding names to the faces that appear in each photo. This is sometimes called *tagging*, and it enables you to navigate your photos by name.

Specifically, iPhoto includes a special Faces section in its library, which organizes your faces according to the names you assign when you tag your photos. This makes it easy to view all your photos in which a certain person appears.

Add Names to Faces in Your Photos

1 Click the photo that you want to tag.

2 Click **Info**.

3 Click **X unnamed** (where X is the number of faces iPhoto identifies in the photo).

iPhoto displays its naming tools.

4 Click **unnamed**.

5 Type the person's name.

6 Press **Return**.

7 Repeat steps **3** to **5** to name each person in the photo.

A If iPhoto did not mark a face in the photo, click **Add a face**, size and position the box over the face, and then type the name in the **click to name** box.

8 Click **Info**.

iPhoto exits naming mode.

How do I view all the photos that contain a particular person?
You can open a photo, click **Info**, and then click the **Show All** arrow (▶) beside the person's name. You can also click **Faces** in the iPhoto sidebar. iPhoto displays the names and sample photos of each person you have named. Double-click the person you want to view. iPhoto displays all the photos that contain the person.

Map Your Photos

You can view your photos by location if you edit each photo to include the location where you took the image. Most modern cameras, particularly smartphone cameras such as those found on the iPhone and iPad, include location information for each photo. If your camera does not add location data automatically, you can tell iPhoto the locations where your photos were taken and then display a map that shows those locations. This enables you to view all your photos taken in a particular place.

Map Your Photos

1. Click the event that you want to map.

   If you want to map a single photo, open the event and then open the photo.

2. Click **Info**.

3. Click **Assign a Place**.

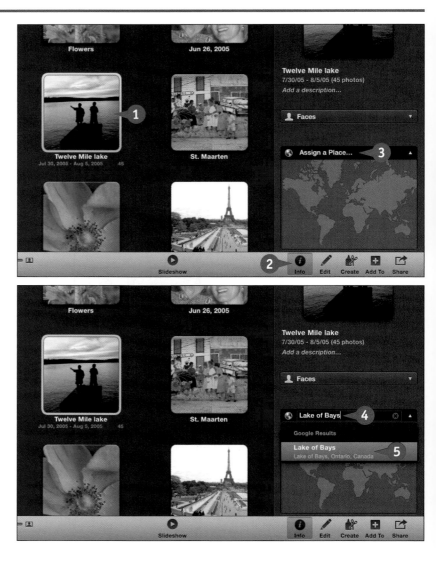

4. Type the location.

   iPhoto displays a list of locations that match what you typed.

5. When you see the place you want to use, click it.

iPhoto displays the location on a Google map.

⑥ Click and drag the pin to the correct location, if necessary.

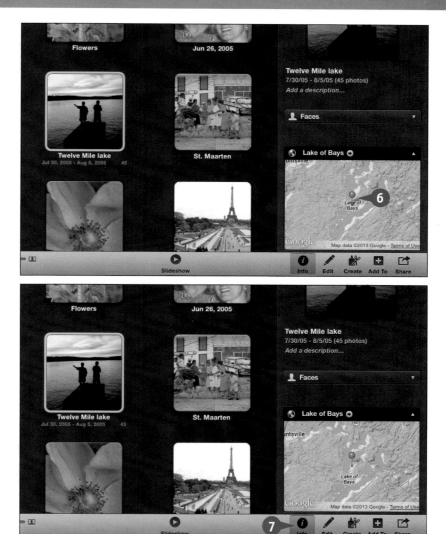

⑦ Click **Info**.

iPhoto closes the info window.

Is there a way to have the location data added automatically?

Yes. To activate this feature, click **iPhoto** in the menu bar, click **Preferences**, and then click the **Advanced** tab. Click the **Look up Places** ⊙ and then click **Automatically**. Note that you may still have to add or edit location names for your photos.

How do I view all the photos that were taken in a particular place?

Click **Places** in the iPhoto sidebar to see a map of the world with pins for each of your photo locations. Position the mouse ▶ over the location's pin and then click the **Show All** arrow (⊙). iPhoto displays all the photos that were taken in that location.

Email a Photo

If you have a photo that you want to share with someone, and you know that person's email address, you can send the photo in an email message. Using iPhoto, you can specify what photo you want to send, and iPhoto creates a new message. Even if a photo is very large, you can still send it via email because you can use iPhoto to shrink the copy of the photo that appears in the message.

Email a Photo

1. Click the photo you want to send.

2. Click **Share**.

3. Click **Email**.

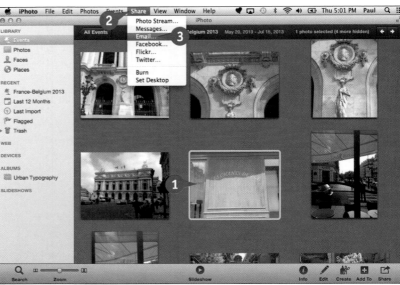

A. iPhoto creates a new message and adds the photo to the message body.

4. Type the address of the message recipient.

5. Type the message subject.

6 Click here and then type your message text.

B You can use these controls to format the text.

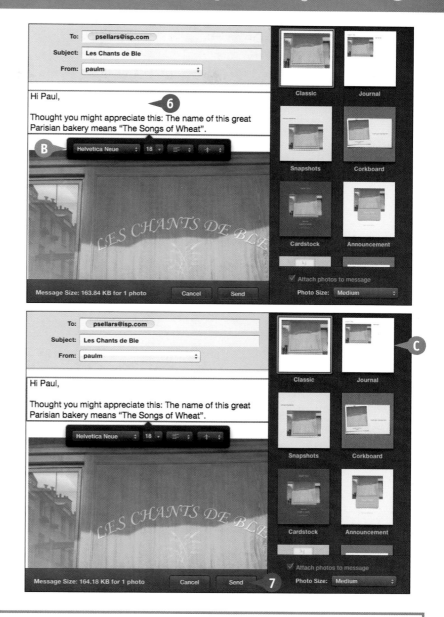

C You can click these thumbnails to apply a special effect to the message.

7 Click **Send**.

iPhoto sends the message with the photo as an attachment.

How do I change the size of the photo?

You need to be careful when sending photos because a single image can be several megabytes in size. If your recipient's email system places restrictions on the size of messages it can receive, your message might not go through.

To change the size of the photo, click the **Photo Size** 🔘 and then click the size you want to use for the sent photo, such as Small or Medium. Note that this does not affect the size of the original photo, just the copy that is sent with the message.

Take Your Picture

You can use your Mac to take a picture of yourself. If your Mac comes with a built-in iSight or FaceTime HD camera, or if you have an external camera attached to your Mac, you can use the camera to take a picture of yourself using the Photo Booth application. After you take your picture, you can email that picture, add it to iPhoto, or set it as your user account or Messages buddy picture.

Take Your Picture

Take Your Picture with Photo Booth

1 Click the **Photo Booth** icon ( ).

The Photo Booth window appears.

A The live feed from the camera appears here.

2 Click **Take a still picture** ( ).

B Click **Take four quick pictures** ( ) if you want Photo Booth to snap four successive photos, each about 1 second apart.

C Click **Take a movie clip** ( ) if you want Photo Booth to capture the live camera feed as a movie.

3 Click **Take Photo** ( ).

Note: You can also press ⌘+T or click **File** and then click **Take Photo**.

Photo Booth counts down 3 seconds and then takes the photo.

Note: When the Mac is taking your picture, be sure to look into the camera, not into the screen.

Work with Your Photo Booth Picture

D Photo Booth displays the picture.

1 Click the picture.

2 Click **Share** (⬆).

E Click **Add to iPhoto** to add the photo to iPhoto.

F Click **Change profile picture** to set the photo as your user account picture.

TIP

Can I make my photos more interesting?
Definitely. Photo Booth comes with around two dozen special effects. Follow these steps:

1 Click **Effects**.

2 Click an icon to select a different page of effects.

A You can also use the arrow buttons to change pages.

3 Click the effect you want to use.

Playing and Creating Videos

Your Mac comes with the tools you need to play movies and digital video as well as to create your own digital videos.

Play a DVD Using DVD Player

If your Mac has a DVD drive, you can insert a movie DVD into the drive and then use the DVD Player application to play the movie on your Mac. You can either watch the movie in full-screen mode, where the movie takes up the entire Mac screen, or play the DVD in a window while you work on other things. DVD Player has features that enable you to control the movie playback and volume.

Play a DVD Using DVD Player

Play a DVD Full Screen

1 Insert the DVD into your Mac's DVD drive.

DVD Player runs automatically and starts playing the DVD full screen.

2 If you get to the DVD menu, click **Play** to start the movie.

3 Move the mouse 🔍 to the bottom of the screen.

The playback controls appear.

Ⓐ Click to pause the movie.

Ⓑ Click to fast-forward the movie.

Ⓒ Click to rewind the movie.

Ⓓ Drag the slider to adjust the volume.

Ⓔ Click to display the DVD menu.

Ⓕ Click to exit full-screen mode.

Play a DVD in a Window

1 Insert the DVD into your Mac's DVD drive.

DVD Player runs automatically and starts playing the DVD full screen.

2 Press ⌘+F.

Note: You can also press Esc or move the mouse ▶ to the bottom of the screen and then click **Exit full screen**.

DVD Player displays the movie in a window.

G DVD Player displays the Controller.

3 When you get to the DVD menu, click **Play** to start the movie.

H Click to pause the movie.

I Click and hold to fast-forward the movie.

J Click and hold to rewind the movie.

K Drag the slider to adjust the volume.

L Click to display the DVD menu.

M Click to stop the movie.

N Click to eject the DVD.

Play Digital Video with QuickTime Player

Your Mac comes with an application called QuickTime Player that can play digital video files in various formats. You will mostly use QuickTime Player to play digital video files stored on your Mac, but you can also use the application to play digital video from the web.

QuickTime Player enables you to open video files, navigate the digital video playback, and control the digital video volume. Although you learn only how to play digital video files in this task, the version of QuickTime that comes with OS X comes with many extra features, including the ability to record movies and audio and to cut and paste scenes.

Play Digital Video with QuickTime Player

① Click the **Finder** icon (⬜).

② Click **Applications**.

③ Double-click **QuickTime Player** (◯).

Note: If you see the QuickTime Player icon in the Dock, you can also click that icon to launch the program.

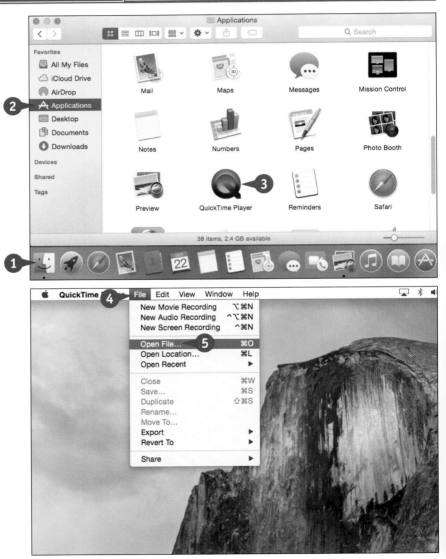

The QuickTime Player application appears. If you see the Open dialog, skip to step **6**.

④ Click **File**.

⑤ Click **Open File**.

Note: You can also press ⌘+O.

The Open dialog appears.

6 Locate and click the video file you want to play.

7 Click **Open**.

QuickTime opens a new player window.

8 Click **Play** (▶).

A Click here to fast-forward the video.

B Click here to rewind the video.

C Click and drag this slider to adjust the volume.

If you want to view the video in full-screen mode, press ⌘+F.

TIP

Can I use QuickTime Player to play a video from the web?
Yes. As long as you know the Internet address of the video, QuickTime Player can play most video formats available on the web. In QuickTime Player, click **File** and then click **Open Location** (or press ⌘+U). In the Open URL dialog, type or paste the video address in the Movie Location text box and then click **Open**.

Create a New Movie Project

The iLife suite installed on your Mac includes iMovie, which enables you to import video from a digital camcorder or video file and use that footage to create your own movies. You do this by first creating a project that holds your video clips, transitions, titles, and other elements of your movie.

When you first start iMovie, the program creates a new project for you automatically. Follow the steps in this task to create subsequent projects. Note, too, that iMovie is also available via the App Store.

Create a New Movie Project

1 Click the **iMovie** icon (⊡) in the Dock.

Note: If you do not see the iMovie icon in the Dock, click **Spotlight** (🔍), type **iMovie**, and then click **iMovie** in the search results.

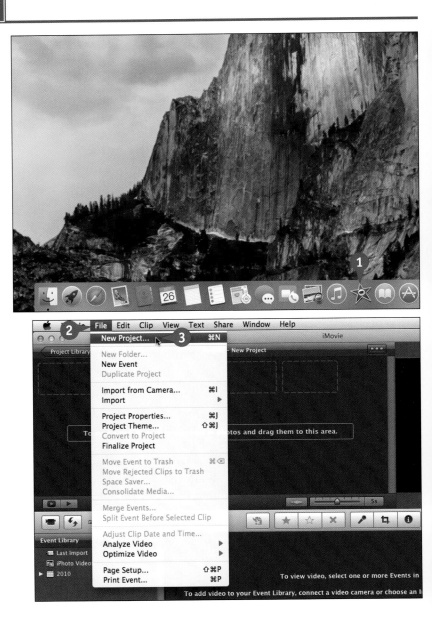

The iMovie window appears.

2 Click **File**.

3 Click **New Project**.

Note: You can also press ⌘+N.

The New Project dialog appears.

④ In the Name text box, type a name for your project.

⑤ Click the **Aspect Ratio** 🖸 and then click the ratio you prefer: **Widescreen** (16:9) or **Standard** (4:3).

⑥ To apply a theme to your project, click the one you want in the Project Themes list.

Note: See the first Tip to learn more about themes.

⑦ To automatically insert transitions between all your clips, click **Automatically add** (☐ changes to ☑) and then click 🖸 to choose the type of transition.

If you chose a theme in step **6**, the check box changes to Automatically Add Transition and Titles by default.

⑧ Click **Create**.

iMovie creates your new project.

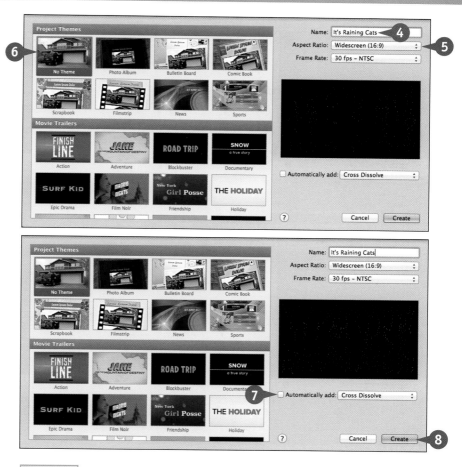

TIPS

What are the iMovie themes?
iMovie offers seven themes that you can apply to a project to save on your production time. Each theme comes with its own set of titles and transitions that are added automatically. Among the themes are Photo Album, Bulletin Board, Comic Book, and Scrapbook.

How do I switch from one project to another?
You use the Project Library, which is a list of your movie projects. To display it, click **Window** and then click **Show Project Library**. You can also click the **Project Library** button in the top left corner of the iMovie window. In the Project Library, double-click the project you want to work with.

Import a Video File

With the iMovie application, you can import digital video from a camera for use in your movie project. If you have video content on a USB digital camcorder or smartphone (such as an iPhone 3GS or later), you can connect the device to your Mac and then import some or all of the video to your iMovie project.

If your Mac or monitor has a built-in iSight or FaceTime HD camera, you can also use iMovie to import live images from that camera to use as digital video footage in your movie project.

Import a Video File

Import All Clips

① Connect the video device to your Mac.

iMovie displays its Import From dialog.

② Click **Import All**.

iMovie prompts you to create a new event.

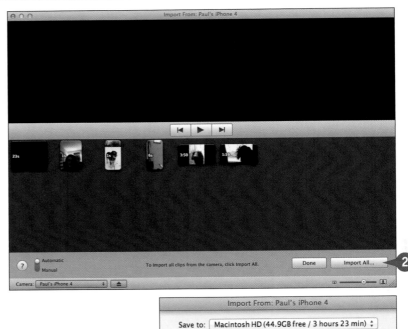

③ Click **Create new Event** (☐ changes to ⦿).

④ Use the Create New Event text box to type a name for the import event.

Ⓐ If you want to add the video to an existing event, click **Add to existing Event** (☐ changes to ⦿) and then choose the event from the pop-up menu.

⑤ Click **Import**.

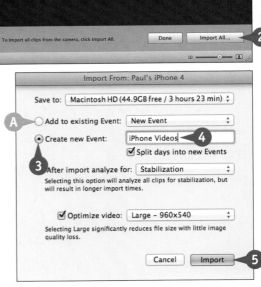

Import Selected Clips

1 Connect the video device to your Mac and place it in playback mode, if necessary.

iMovie displays its Import From dialog.

2 Click **Manual**.

3 Click the check box under each clip you do not want to import (☑ changes to ☐).

4 Click **Import Checked**.

iMovie prompts you to create a new event.

5 Click **Create new Event** (☐ changes to ◉).

6 Use the Create New Event text box to type a name for the import event.

7 Click **Import**.

iMovie begins importing the clips.

8 Click **OK**.

9 Click **Done** to close the Import From dialog (not shown).

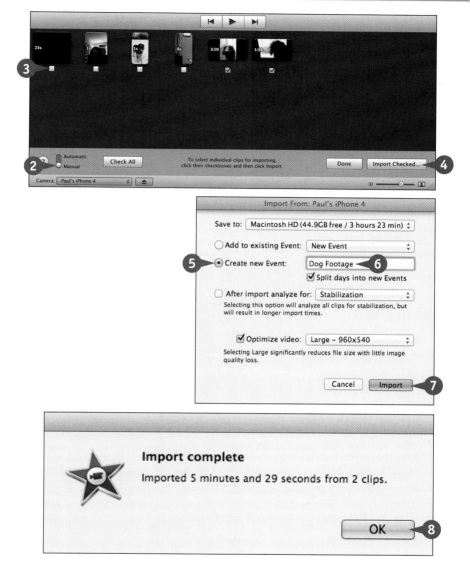

How do I import digital video from my iSight or FaceTime HD camera?
In iMovie, click **File** and then click **Import from Camera** to open the Import dialog. Click **Capture** and then follow steps **5** and **6** in the subtask "Import Selected Clips." Click **Capture** to begin the video capture. When you are done, click **Stop** and then click **Done** to close the Import dialog.

Add Video Clips to Your Project

To create and work with a movie project in iMovie, you must first add some video clips to that project. A *video clip* is a segment of digital video. You begin building your movie by adding one or more video clips to your project.

When you import digital video as described in the previous task, "Import a Video File," iMovie automatically breaks up the video into separate clips, with each clip being the footage shot during a single recording session. You can then decide which of those clips you want to add to your project, or you can add only part of a clip.

Add Video Clips to Your Project

Add an Entire Clip

1 Click the Event Library item that contains the video clip you want to add.

2 Press and hold `Option` and click the clip.

Ⓐ iMovie selects the entire clip.

3 Click and drag the selected clip and drop it in your project at the spot where you want the clip to appear.

Ⓑ iMovie adds the entire video clip to the project.

Ⓒ iMovie adds an orange bar to the bottom of the original clip to indicate that it has been added to the project.

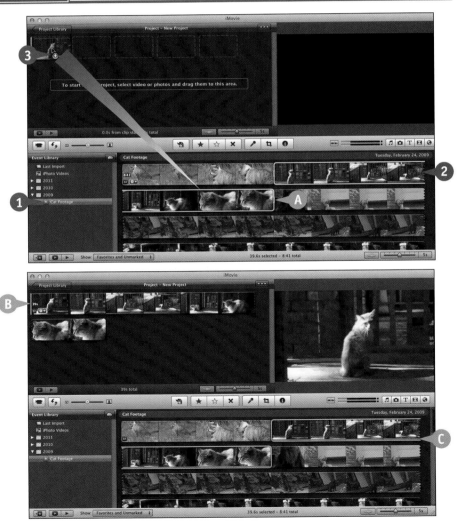

Add a Partial Clip

1 Click the Event Library item that contains the video clip you want to add.

2 Click the clip at the point where you want the selection to begin.

3 Click and drag the right edge of the selection box to the point where you want the selection to end.

4 Click and drag the selected clip and drop it in your project at the spot where you want the clip to appear.

D iMovie adds the selected portion of the video clip to the project.

E iMovie adds an orange bar to the bottom of the original clip to indicate that it has been added to a project.

TIPS

Is it possible to play a clip before I add it?
Yes. The easiest way to do this is to click the clip at the point where you want the playback to start and then press Spacebar. iMovie plays the clip in the Viewer in the top right corner of the window. Press Spacebar again to stop the playback.

I added a clip in the wrong place. Can I move it?
Yes. Click the added clip to select it. Use your mouse to click and drag the clip to the correct location within the project. If you want to delete the clip, click it, click **Edit**, and then click **Delete Entire Clip** (or press Option+Delete).

Trim a Clip

If you have a video clip that is too long or contains footage you do not need, you can shorten the clip or remove the extra footage. Removing parts of a video clip is called *trimming* the clip.

Trimming a clip is particularly useful if you recorded extra, unneeded footage before and after the action you were trying to capture. By trimming this unneeded footage, your movie will include only the material you really require.

Trim a Clip

1 In your project, click the clip you want to trim.

Ⓐ iMovie selects the entire clip.

2 Use your mouse 🔺 to click and drag the left edge of the selection box to the starting position of the part of the clip you want to keep.

3 Use your mouse 🔺 to click and drag the right edge of the selection box to the ending position of the part of the clip you want to keep.

4 Click **Clip**.

5 Click **Trim to Selection**.

Note: You can also press ⌘+B.

B iMovie trims the clip.

How can I trim one frame at a time from either the beginning or the end of the clip?
In your project, click the clip you want to trim. Click the **Clip** menu and then click **Trim Clip End**. Select the trim direction by clicking **Move Left** or **Move Right** and repeat until you reach the number of frames that you want to trim.

Add a Transition Between Clips

You can use the iMovie application to enhance the visual appeal of your digital movie by inserting transitions between some or all of the project's video clips. By default, iMovie jumps immediately from the end of one clip to the beginning of the next clip, a transition called a *jump cut*. You can add more visual interest to your movie by adding a transition between the two clips.

iMovie offers 24 different transitions, including various fades, wipes, and dissolves. More transitions are available if you applied a theme to your iMovie project.

Add a Transition Between Clips

1 Click the **Transitions Browser** button (⬛), or press ⌘+4.

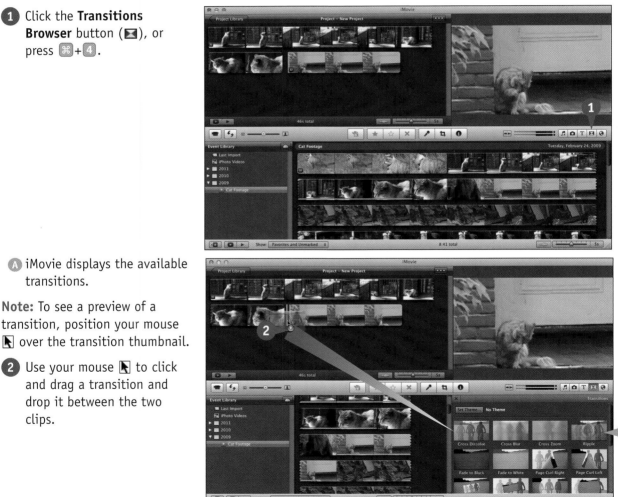

Ⓐ iMovie displays the available transitions.

Note: To see a preview of a transition, position your mouse 🖰 over the transition thumbnail.

2 Use your mouse 🖰 to click and drag a transition and drop it between the two clips.

B iMovie adds an icon for the transition between the two clips.

3 Position your mouse ▶ over the beginning of the transition and move the mouse ▶ to the right.

C iMovie displays a preview of the transition.

How can I change the duration of the transition?

Double-click the transition icon in your project. The Inspector appears. Use the Duration text box to set the number of seconds you want the transition to take (**A**). If you want to change only the current transition, click **Applies to all transitions** (☑ changes to ☐) (**B**). Click **Done** to close the Inspector.

Add a Photo

You can use the iMovie application to enhance your movie projects with still photos. Although most movie projects consist of several video clips, you can also add a photo to your project. By default, iMovie displays the photo for 4 seconds.

You can also specify how the photo fits in the movie frame: You can adjust the size of the photo to fit the frame, you can crop the photo, or you can apply a Ken Burns effect to animate the static photo, which automatically pans and zooms the photo.

Add a Photo

1 Click the **Photos Browser** button (📷), or press ⌘+2.

A iMovie displays the available photos.

2 Click the event or album that contains the photo you want to add.

3 Click and drag the photo and drop it inside your project.

B iMovie adds the photo to the movie.

4 Click the photo.

5 Click the **Crop** button (🔳).

iMovie displays the cropping options for the photo.

6 Click **Ken Burns**.

C You can also click **Fit** to have iMovie adjust the size of the photo to fit the movie frame.

D You can also click **Crop** and then click and drag the cropping rectangle to specify how much of the photo you want to appear in the movie frame.

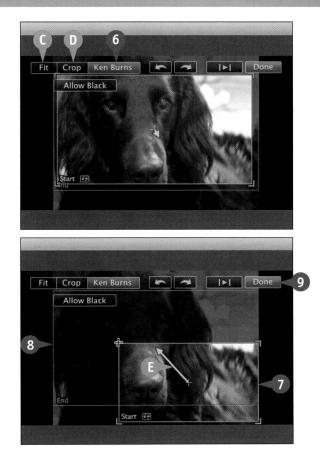

7 Click and drag the green rectangle to set the start point of the Ken Burns animation.

8 Click and drag the red rectangle to set the end point of the Ken Burns animation.

Note: Click and drag the corners and edges of the rectangle to change the size; click and drag the interior of the rectangles to change the position.

E The arrow shows the direction of motion.

9 Click **Done**.

TIP

How can I change the length of time that the photo appears in the movie?
Double-click the photo in your project. The Inspector appears. Click the **Clip** tab (**A**). Use the Duration text box to set the number of seconds you want the photo to appear (**B**). To change the duration for all the photos in your project, click **Applies to all stills** (☐ changes to ☑) (**C**). Click **Done** to close the Inspector.

209

Add a Music Track

Using the iMovie application, you can enhance the audio component of your movie by adding one or more songs that play in the background. With iMovie you can also add sound effects and other audio files that you feel would enhance your project's audio track.

To get the best audio experience, you can adjust various sound properties. For example, you can adjust the volume of the music clip or the volume of the video clip. You can also use iMovie to adjust the time it takes for the song clip to fade in and fade out.

Add a Music Track

1 Click the **Music and Sound Effect Browser** button (⌂), or press ⌘+1.

Ⓐ iMovie displays the available audio files.

2 Click the folder, category, or playlist that contains the track you want to add.

3 Use your mouse ▶ to click and drag the song and drop it on a video clip.

Ⓑ iMovie adds the song to the movie.

Note: iMovie treats the song like a clip, which means you can trim the song as needed, as described earlier in the task "Trim a Clip."

4 Double-click the music clip.

iMovie displays the Inspector.

5 Click the **Audio** tab.

6 Use the **Volume** slider to adjust the volume of the music clip.

7 If you want to reduce the video clip volume, click **Ducking** (☐ changes to ☑) and then click and drag the slider.

8 To adjust the fade-in time, click **Fade In: Manual** (☐ changes to ☑) and then click and drag the slider.

9 To adjust the fade-out time, click **Fade Out: Manual** (☐ changes to ☑) and then click and drag the slider.

10 Click **Done**.

TIP

When I add a video clip before the music clip, the music does not play with the new video clip. How can I work around this?

You need to add your song as a background track instead of as a clip. Follow these steps:

1 Click the **Music and Sound Effect Browser** button (♫).

2 Click and drag a song onto the project background, not on a clip or between two clips.

Ⓐ The background turns green when the song is positioned correctly.

Record a Voiceover

You can use the iMovie application to augment the audio portion of your movie with a voiceover. A *voiceover* is a voice recording that you make using audio equipment attached to your Mac.

A voiceover is useful for explaining a video clip, introducing the movie, or giving the viewer background information about the movie. To record a voiceover, your Mac must have either a built-in microphone, such as the one that comes with the iSight or FaceTime HD camera, or an external microphone connected via an audio jack, USB port, or Bluetooth.

Record a Voiceover

1 If your Mac does not have a built-in microphone, attach a microphone.

Note: You may need to configure the microphone as the sound input device. Click the **System Preferences** icon (🖼️), click **Sound**, click **Input**, and then click your microphone.

2 Click the **Voiceover** button (🎤).

The Voiceover dialog appears.

3 Click the spot in the movie at which you want the voiceover to begin.

iMovie counts down and then begins the recording.

4 Speak your voiceover text into the microphone.

Ⓐ The progress of the recording appears here.

5 When you finish, click **Recording**.

Ⓑ iMovie adds the voiceover to the clip.

6 Click **Close** (⊠).

You can double-click the voiceover to adjust the audio, as described in the previous task, "Add a Music Track."

TIP

Is there a way to tell if my voice is too loud or too soft?
Yes. Use the controls in the Voiceover dialog to check your voice level by talking into the microphone and then watching the Left and Right volume meters. No green bars or just a few green bars indicate the voice level is too low (Ⓐ). Yellow or red bars indicate the voice level is too high (Ⓑ). Use the Input Volume slider to adjust the voice level up or down.

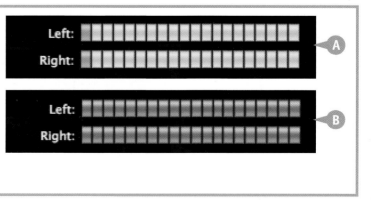

Add Titles and Credits

You can use the iMovie application to enhance your movie project with titles and scrolling credits. You can get your movie off to a proper start by adding a title and a subtitle at or near the beginning of the movie. iMovie offers a number of title styles you can choose from, and you can also change the title font.

You can also enhance your movie with *scrolling credits*. This is a special type of title that you place at the end of the movie and that scrolls the names of the people responsible for the project.

Add Titles and Credits

1. Click the **Titles browser** button (▮).

Ⓐ iMovie displays the available title types.

2. Use your mouse ▶ to click and drag a title and drop it where you want the titles to appear.

Note: To see just the titles, drop the title thumbnail at the beginning of the movie or between two clips. To superimpose the titles on a video clip, drop the title thumbnail on the clip.

Ⓑ If you want to add credits, click and drag the **Scrolling Credits** thumbnail and drop it at the end of the movie.

C iMovie adds a clip for the title.

3 Replace this text with the movie title.

4 Replace this text with the movie subtitle.

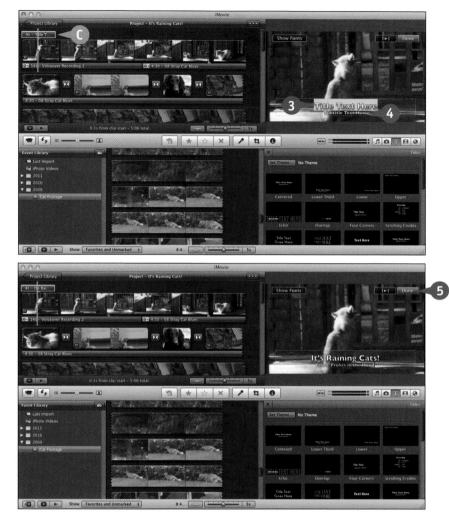

5 Click **Done**.

Note: iMovie treats the title like a clip, which means you can lengthen or shorten the title duration by clicking and dragging the beginning or end, as described earlier in the task "Trim a Clip."

TIP

How do I change the font of the titles?

The Text menu offers several font-related commands, including Bold, Italic, Bigger, and Smaller. You can also click the **Show Fonts** command to display the Choose Font dialog. If you do not see the Choose Font dialog shown here, you can switch to iMovie's predefined fonts by clicking **iMovie Font Panel**. You can then click a typeface, font color, and type size; click **Done** to close the dialog.

Play the Movie

The iMovie application offers the Viewer pane, which you can use to play your movie. While you are building your iMovie project, it is a good idea to occasionally play some or all of the movie to check your progress. For example, you can play the entire movie to make sure the video and audio are working properly and are synchronized correctly. You can also play parts of the movie to ensure that your transitions appear when you want them to.

Play the Movie

Play from the Beginning

1. Click **View**.

2. Click **Play from Beginning**.

Note: You can also press [\] or click the **Play Project from beginning** button ().

Play from a Specific Location

1. Position the mouse over the spot where you want to start playing the movie.

2. Press [Spacebar].

Play a Selection

1 Select the video clips you want to play.

Note: See the first Tip to learn how to select multiple video clips.

2 Click **View**.

3 Click **Play Selection**.

Note: You can also press /.

How do I select multiple video clips?

To select multiple video clips, press and hold ⌘ and then click anywhere inside each clip you want to select. If you select a clip by accident, ⌘+click it again to deselect it. If you want to skip just a few clips, first press ⌘+A to select all the clips, and then press and hold ⌘ and click the clips you do not want in the selection.

Can I enlarge the size of the playback pane?

Yes, you can play your movie in full-screen mode. To do this, click **View** and then click **Play full-screen**. You can also press ⌘+G or click the **Play Project full screen** button (▶).

Publish Your Movie to YouTube

W hen your movie project is complete, you can send it to YouTube for viewing on the web. To publish your movie to YouTube, you must have a YouTube account, available from www.youtube. com. You must also know your YouTube username, which you can see by clicking your account icon on YouTube and then clicking **Settings**. Your movie must be no more than 15 minutes long. Before you can publish your movie, you must select a YouTube category, such as Entertainment or Pets and Animals, provide a title and description, and enter at least one tag, which is a word or short phrase that describes some aspect of the movie's content.

Publish Your Movie to YouTube

① Click **Share**.

② Click **YouTube**.

③ Click **Add**.

iMovie prompts you for your YouTube username.

4 Type your username.

5 Click **Done**.

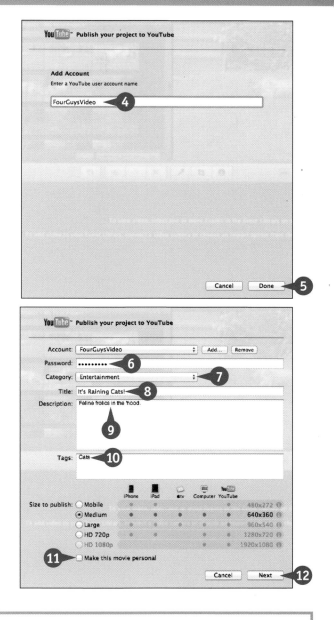

6 Type your YouTube password.

7 Select a category.

8 Type a title.

9 Type a description.

10 Type one or more tags for the video.

11 If you do not want to allow anyone to view the movie, click **Make this movie personal** (☑ changes to ☐).

12 Click **Next**.

iMovie displays the YouTube terms of service.

13 Click **Publish** (not shown).

iMovie prepares the movie and then publishes it to YouTube.

14 Click **OK** (not shown).

TIPS

How do I publish my movie to Facebook?
Click **Share** and then click **Facebook**. Click **Add**, type your Facebook email address, and then click **Done**. Type your Facebook password. Use the **Viewable by** 🔘 to choose who can see the video. Type a title and description, select a size, click **Next**, and then click **Publish**.

How do I view my movie outside of iMovie?
Beyond viewing it on YouTube or Facebook, you need to export the movie to a digital video file. Click **Share** and then click **Export Movie** (or press ⌘+E). Type a title for the movie and then click a Size to Export option, such as **Large** or **HD 720p** (☐ changes to 🔘). Click **Export**.

CHAPTER 11

Securing OS X

Threats to your computing-related security and privacy often come from the Internet and from someone simply using your Mac while you are not around. To protect yourself and your family, you need to understand these threats and know what you can do to thwart them.

Change Your Password

You can make OS X more secure by changing your password. For example, if you turn on file sharing, as described in Chapter 15, you can configure each shared folder so that only someone who knows your password can get full access to that folder. Similarly, you should change your password if other network users know your current password and you no longer want them to have access to your shared folders. Finally, you should also change your password if you feel that your current password is not secure enough. See the Tip to learn how to create a secure password.

Change Your Password

1 Click the **System Preferences** icon (■).

The System Preferences window appears.

2 Click **Users & Groups**.

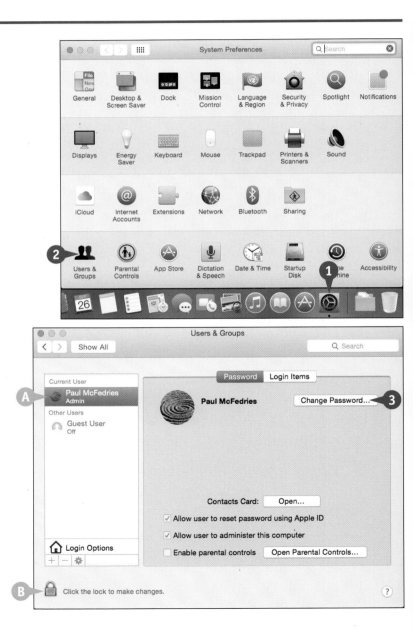

The Users & Groups preferences appear.

Ⓐ Your user account is selected automatically.

Ⓑ If you want to work with a different user account, you must click the lock icon (🔒), type your administrator password (🔒 changes to 🔓), and then click the account.

3 Click **Change Password**.

System Preferences asks whether you want to use your iCloud password.

④ Click **Change Password**.

Ⓒ If you prefer to log in to OS X with your iCloud password, click **Use iCloud Password**, instead.

The Change Password dialog appears.

⑤ Type your current password.

⑥ Type your new password.

⑦ Retype the new password.

⑧ Type a hint that OS X will display if you forget the password.

Note: Construct the hint in such a way that it makes the password easy for you to recall, but hard for a potential snoop to guess.

⑨ Click **Change Password**.

OS X changes your password.

Would you like to change the password for "Paul McFedries", or begin using your iCloud password to log in and unlock this Mac?

You will only need to remember one password if you use your iCloud password to log in to this Mac.

Ⓒ Use iCloud Password... — Cancel — Change Password... ④

Old password: •••••••• ⑤

New password: •••••••••• ⑥ ♀

Verify: •••••••••• ⑦

Password hint: Mom's maiden name, year of birth, and
(Recommended) month of birth ⑧

Cancel — Change Password ⑨

TIP

How do I create a secure password?
Follow these steps:

① Follow steps 1 to 4 in this task.

② Click the **Password Assistant** icon (♀).

The Password Assistant dialog appears.

③ Click the **Type** 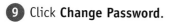 and then click a password type.

④ Click and drag the **Length** slider to set the password length you want to use.

⑤ Click the **Suggestion** and then click the password you want to use.

⑥ Click **Close** (▨).

⑥ ○ ○ ○ Password Assistant

Type: Memorable ③

Suggestion: aims17[mimed ⑤

Length: ——————⬤—————————— 12

Quality: [▨▨▨▨▨ ④   ]

Require a Password on Waking

You can enhance your Mac's security by configuring OS X to ask for your user account password when the system wakes up from either the screen saver or sleep mode. Protecting your account with a password prevents someone from logging on to your account, but what happens when you leave your Mac unattended? If you remain logged on to the system, any person who sits down at your computer can use it to view and change files. To prevent this, activate the screen saver or sleep mode before you leave your Mac unattended, and configure OS X to require a password on waking.

Require a Password on Waking

1 Click the **Apple** icon (🍎).

2 Click **System Preferences**.

You can also click the **System Preferences** icon (⚙️) in the Dock.

The System Preferences window appears.

3 Click **Security & Privacy**.

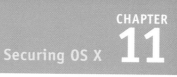

The Security & Privacy preferences appear.

④ Click the **General** tab.

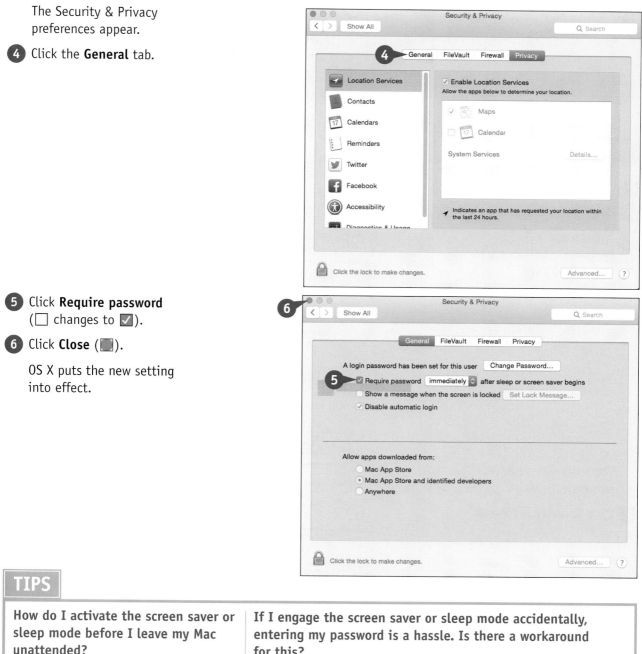

⑤ Click **Require password** (☐ changes to ☑).

⑥ Click **Close** (⬤).

OS X puts the new setting into effect.

How do I activate the screen saver or sleep mode before I leave my Mac unattended?

To put your Mac display to sleep, press `Control` + `Shift` and then press ⏏. To engage full sleep mode, click the **Apple** icon (🍎) and then click **Sleep**.

If I engage the screen saver or sleep mode accidentally, entering my password is a hassle. Is there a workaround for this?

Yes, you can tell OS X to not require the password as soon as the screen saver or sleep mode is activated. Follow steps **1** to **5**, click the **Require password** 🔽, and then click the amount of time you want OS X to wait.

Disable Automatic Logins

Y ou can enhance your Mac's security by preventing OS X from logging in to your user account automatically. If you are the only person who uses your Mac, you can configure OS X to automatically log in to your account. This saves time at startup by avoiding the login screen, but it opens a security hole. If a snoop or other malicious user has access to your Mac, that person can start the computer and gain access to your documents, settings, web browsing history, and network. To prevent this, configure OS X to disable the automatic login.

Disable Automatic Logins

1 Click the **Apple** icon (🍎).

2 Click **System Preferences**.

You can also click the **System Preferences** icon (⚙) in the Dock.

The System Preferences window appears.

3 Click **Security & Privacy**.

The Security & Privacy preferences appear.

④ Click the lock icon (🔒).

OS X prompts you for your administrator password.

⑤ Type the administrator password.

⑥ Click **Unlock**.

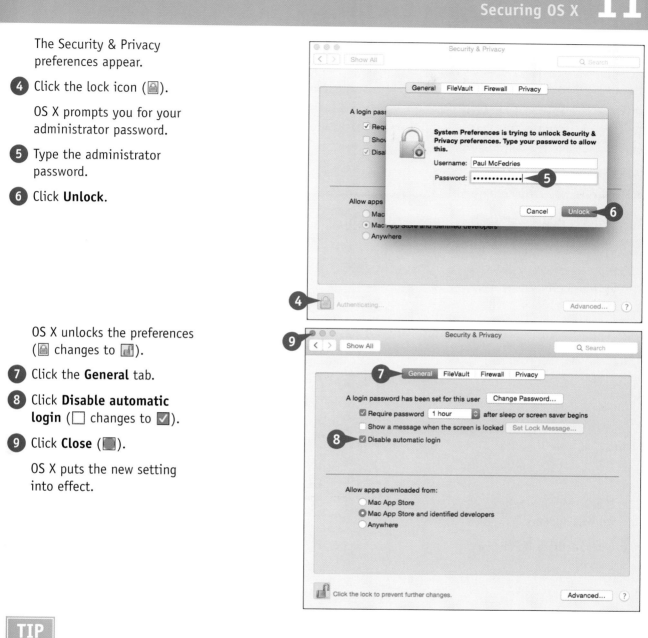

OS X unlocks the preferences (🔒 changes to 🔓).

⑦ Click the **General** tab.

⑧ Click **Disable automatic login** (☐ changes to ☑).

⑨ Click **Close** (⬤).

OS X puts the new setting into effect.

TIP

Is there a way to get OS X to log out of my account automatically?

Yes, you can configure the system to log you out of your account when OS X has been idle for a specified amount of time. Follow steps **1** to **7** to unlock and display the General tab and then click **Advanced**. In the dialog that appears, click **Log out after X minutes of inactivity** (☐ changes to ☑) and then use the spin box to set the amount of idle time after which OS X logs you out automatically. You can select a time as short as 5 minutes and as long as 960 minutes.

Configure App Downloads

You can ensure that malware cannot be installed on your Mac by configuring the system to allow only app downloads from the Mac App Store. By default, OS X allows downloads from the App Store and from so-called *identified developers*. The reason for this heightened security is that malware developers are starting to target Macs now that they have become so popular. The extra security is a response to that and is designed to prevent users from accidentally installing malware. However, you can configure this feature to be even more secure, which is useful if you are setting up a user account for a child.

Configure App Downloads

1 Click the **Apple** icon ().

2 Click **System Preferences**.

You can also click the **System Preferences** icon () in the Dock.

The System Preferences window appears.

3 Click **Security & Privacy**.

The Security & Privacy preferences appear.

④ Click the lock icon (🔒).

OS X prompts you for your administrator password.

⑤ Type the administrator password.

⑥ Click **Unlock**.

OS X unlocks the preferences (🔒 changes to 🔓).

⑦ Click the **General** tab.

⑧ Click **Mac App Store** (☐ changes to ◉).

⑨ Click **Close** (🔴).

OS X puts the new setting into effect.

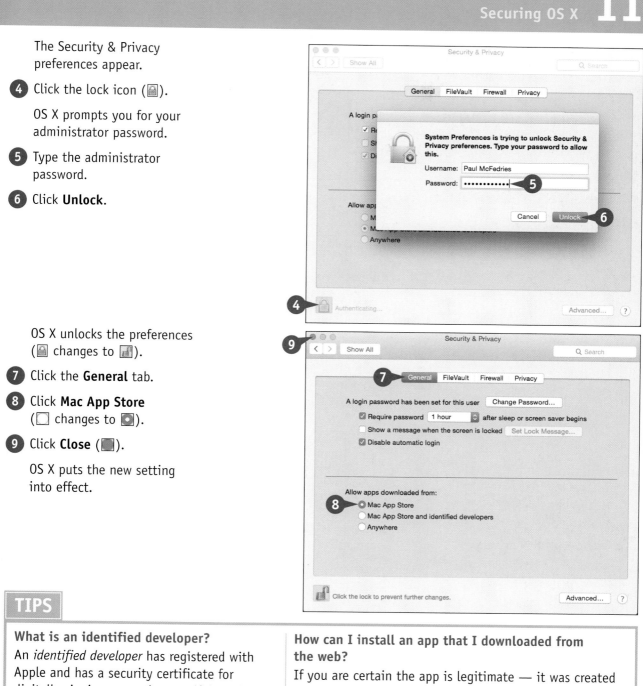

TIPS

What is an identified developer?
An *identified developer* has registered with Apple and has a security certificate for digitally signing apps, thus certifying where the apps came from. There is a possibility that a malicious developer could spoof a digitally signed app, so allowing only App Store apps is the safest option.

How can I install an app that I downloaded from the web?
If you are certain the app is legitimate — it was created by a reputable developer and you purchased it from a reputable dealer — you can temporarily allow it to be installed. Follow steps **1** to **7**, click **Anywhere** (☐ changes to ◉), and then install your app. Follow steps **1** to **9** to restore the secure setting.

Turn On the Firewall

You can make your Mac's Internet connection much more secure by turning on the OS X firewall. A *firewall* is a tool designed to prevent malicious users from accessing a computer connected to the Internet. Chances are your network router already implements a hardware firewall, but you can add an extra layer of protection by also activating the OS X software firewall. This will not affect your normal Internet activities, such as web browsing, emailing, and instant messaging.

Turn On the Firewall

1 Click the **Apple** icon (🍎).

2 Click **System Preferences**.

You can also click the **System Preferences** icon (📷) in the Dock.

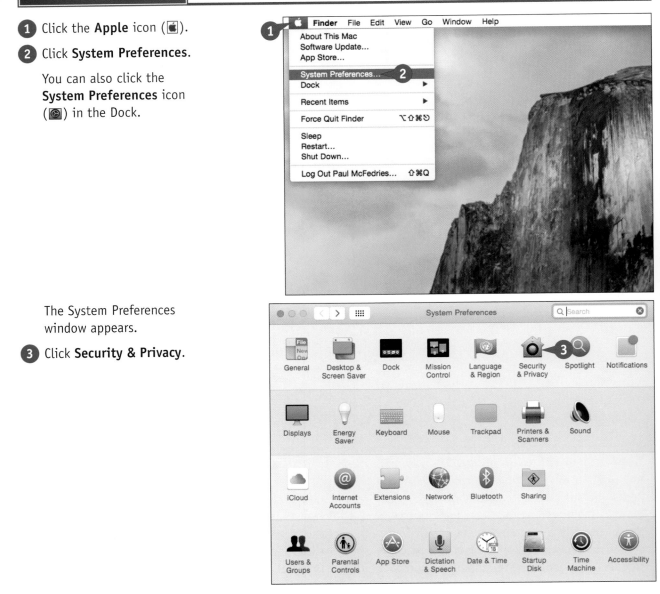

The System Preferences window appears.

3 Click **Security & Privacy**.

The Security & Privacy preferences appear.

4 Click the lock icon (🔒).

OS X prompts you for your administrator password.

5 Type the administrator password.

6 Click **Unlock**.

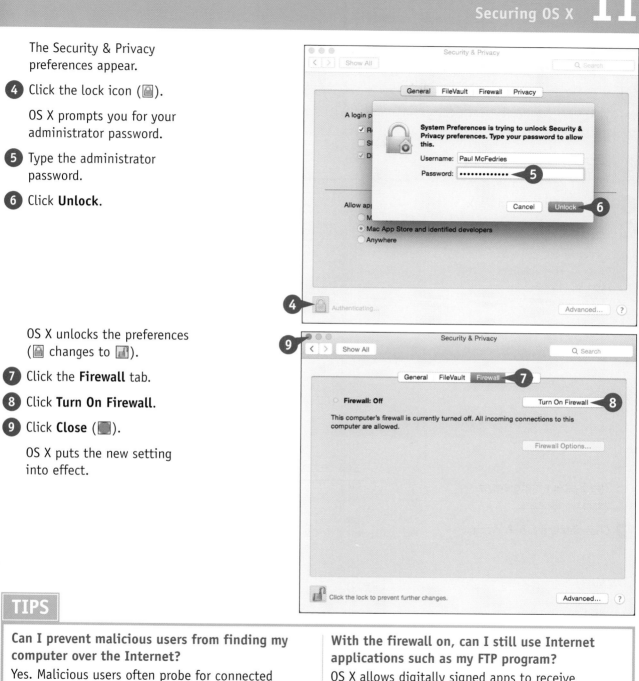

OS X unlocks the preferences (🔒 changes to 🔓).

7 Click the **Firewall** tab.

8 Click **Turn On Firewall**.

9 Click **Close** (⬤).

OS X puts the new setting into effect.

Configure Location Services

Location services refers to the features and technologies that provide apps and system tools with access to location data, particularly the current location of your Mac. This is a handy and useful thing, but it is also something that you need to keep under your control because your location data, especially your current location, is fundamentally private and should not be given to applications thoughtlessly. Fortunately, OS X comes with a few tools for controlling and configuring location services.

Configure Location Services

1 Click the **Apple** icon (■).

2 Click **System Preferences**.

You can also click the **System Preferences** icon (■) in the Dock.

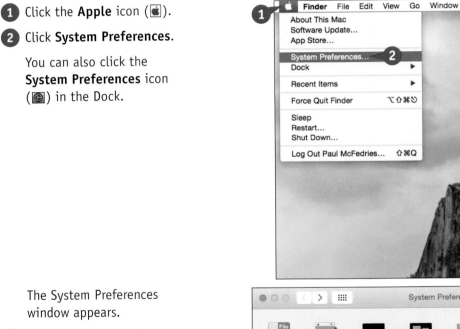

The System Preferences window appears.

3 Click **Security & Privacy**.

The Security & Privacy preferences appear.

4 Click the lock icon (🔒).

OS X prompts you for your administrator password.

5 Type the administrator password.

6 Click **Unlock**.

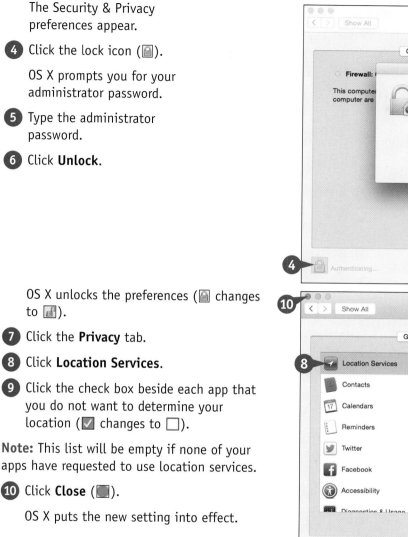

OS X unlocks the preferences (🔒 changes to 🔓).

7 Click the **Privacy** tab.

8 Click **Location Services**.

9 Click the check box beside each app that you do not want to determine your location (☑ changes to ☐).

Note: This list will be empty if none of your apps have requested to use location services.

10 Click **Close** (⬤).

OS X puts the new setting into effect.

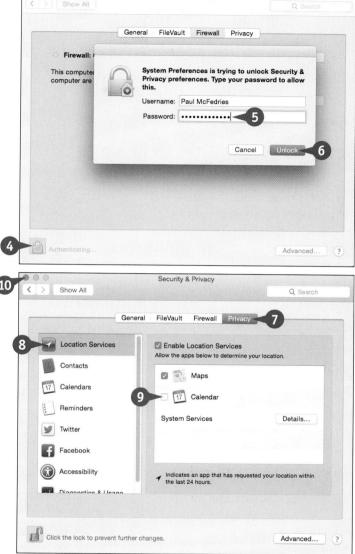

TIPS

How does the location services feature know my location?

Location services uses several bits of data to determine your location. First, it looks for known Wi-Fi networks that are near your location. Second, if you are connected to the Internet, it uses the location information embedded in your unique Internet Protocol (IP) address.

Can I turn off location services?

Yes. Follow steps **1** to **7** to unlock and display the Privacy tab. Click **Location Services** and then click **Enable Location Services** (☑ changes to ☐). Note, however, that by turning off location services, you disable many features in apps such as Reminders and Maps.

Encrypt Your Data

By encrypting data, you can ensure that a malicious user who has physical access to your Mac cannot read the files in your user account. This means that your data appears as gibberish until it is decrypted by entering your user account password. Your password protects your user account from unauthorized access, but a sophisticated user can still access your data by using special tools. If you have sensitive, secret, or private files in your user account, you can protect that data from such access by encrypting it.

Encrypt Your Data

1 Follow steps **1** to **6** in the previous task, "Configure Location Services," to display and unlock the Security & Privacy preferences.

2 Click the **FileVault** tab.

3 Click **Turn On FileVault**.

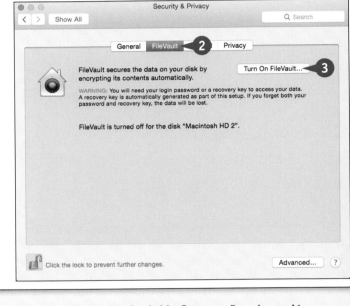

System Preferences asks whether you want to use your iCloud to unlock your disk if you forget your encryption password.

4 Click **Allow my iCloud account to unlock my disk** (☐ changes to ◉).

5 Click **Continue**.

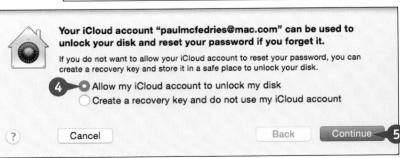

If you have multiple users, OS X prompts you to enable FileVault for the other accounts.

Ⓐ If you want to enable FileVault for a user, click **Enable User**, type the account password, and then click **OK**.

6 Click **Continue**.

OS X prompts you to restart the computer.

7 Click **Restart**.

OS X restarts and begins encrypting your user account data.

Each user must type in their password before they will be able to unlock the disk.

Karen — Enable User... Ⓐ

Paul McFedries
Admin

? | Cancel | Back | Continue **6**

Click "Restart" to restart the Mac and begin the encryption process.

After restarting, you can use your Mac while the encryption process takes place. Return to Security & Privacy preferences to check on the progress.

? | Cancel | Back | Restart **7**

TIP

How do I encrypt my disk if I do not have an iCloud account?
In this case, OS X generates a *recovery key*, which is a code that you must enter to unlock your disk if you forget your password. Follow steps **1** to **3** and, if System Preferences asks whether you want to use an iCloud account, click **Create a recovery key and do not use my iCloud account** (☐ changes to ⦿), and then click **Continue**. When you see the recovery key, write it down and then continue with steps **5** to **7**. Be sure to store the recovery key in a secure, off-site location, such as a safety deposit box. If you lose the recovery key, you will lose access to your data.

CHAPTER 12

Customizing OS X

OS X comes with a number of features that enable you to customize your Mac. For example, you might not like the default desktop background or the layout of the Dock. Not only can you change the appearance of OS X to suit your taste, but you can also change the way OS X works to make it easier and more efficient for you to use.

Display System Preferences

You can find many of the OS X customization features in System Preferences, a collection of settings and options that control the overall look and operation of OS X. You can use System Preferences to change the desktop background, specify a screen saver, set your Mac's sleep options, add user accounts, and customize the Dock, to name some of the tasks that you learn about in this chapter. To use these settings, you must know how to display the System Preferences window.

Display System Preferences

Open System Preferences

1 In the Dock, click the **System Preferences** icon ().

The System Preferences window appears.

Close System Preferences

1 Click **System Preferences**.

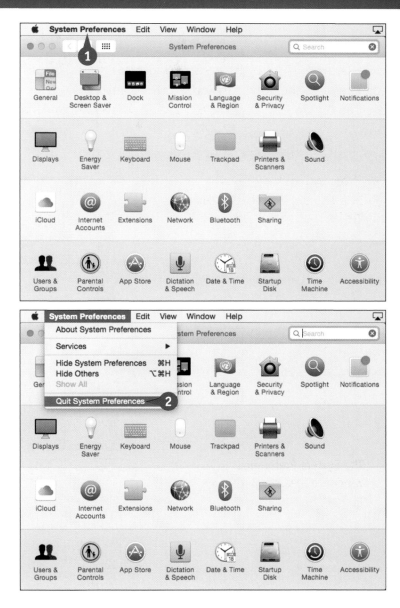

2 Click **Quit System Preferences**.

TIPS

Are there other methods I can use to open System Preferences?
If you have hidden the Dock (see the task "Hide the Dock") or removed the System Preferences icon from the Dock, you can click the **Apple** icon (🍎) and then click **System Preferences**.

Sometimes when I open System Preferences, I do not see all the icons. How can I restore the original icons?
When you click an icon in System Preferences, the window changes to show just the options and settings associated with that icon. To return to the main System Preferences window, click **View** and then click **Show All Preferences** (or press ⌘+L). You can also click ◁ until the main window appears, or click **Show All**.

Change the Desktop Background

To give OS X a different look, you can change the default desktop background. OS X offers a wide variety of desktop background options. For example, OS X comes with several dozen images you can use, from abstract patterns to photos of plants and other natural images. You can also choose a solid color as the desktop background, or you can use one of your own photos. You can change the desktop background to show either a fixed image or a series of images that change periodically.

Change the Desktop Background

Set a Fixed Background Image

1 In the Dock, click the **System Preferences** icon ( ).

2 In the System Preferences window, click **Desktop & Screen Saver**.

Note: You can also right-click the desktop and then click **Change Desktop Background**.

The Desktop & Screen Saver preferences appear.

3 Click **Desktop**.

4 Click the image category you want to use.

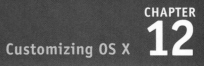
5 Click the image you want to use as the desktop background.

Your Mac changes the desktop background.

6 If you chose a photo in step **5**, click 🔢 and then click an option to determine how your Mac displays the photo.

Note: Another way to set a fixed background image is to select a photo in iPhoto, click **Share**, and then click **Set Desktop**.

Set a Changing Background Image

1 Click **Change picture** (☐ changes to ☑).

2 Click 🔢 and then click how often you want the background image to change.

3 If you want your Mac to choose the periodic image randomly, click **Random order** (☐ changes to ☑).

Your Mac changes the desktop background periodically based on your chosen interval.

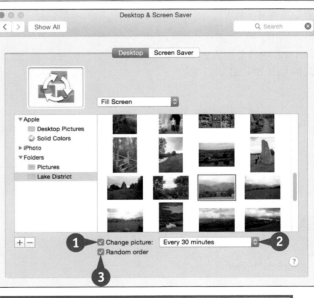

TIP

When I choose a photo, how do the various options differ for displaying the photo?
Your Mac gives you five options for displaying the photo:

- **Fill Screen**. Expands the photo until the desktop is covered.
- **Fit to Screen**. Expands the photo in all four directions until the photo is either the same height as the desktop or the same width as the desktop.
- **Stretch to Fill Screen**. Stretches the photo as needed to make the entire photo fill the desktop.
- **Center**. Displays the photo at its actual size and places the photo in the center of the desktop.
- **Tile**. Repeats your photo multiple times to fill the entire desktop.

Activate the Screen Saver

You can set up OS X to display a *screen saver*, a moving pattern or series of pictures. The screen saver appears after your computer has been idle for a while. If you leave your monitor on for long stretches while your computer is idle, a faint version of the unmoving image can endure for a while on the screen, a phenomenon known as *persistence*. A screen saver prevents this by displaying a moving image. However, persistence is not a major problem for modern screens, so for the most part, you use a screen saver for visual interest.

Activate the Screen Saver

1 In the Dock, click the **System Preferences** icon (⊚).

2 In the System Preferences window, click **Desktop & Screen Saver**.

The Desktop & Screen Saver dialog appears.

3 Click **Screen Saver**.

4 Click the screen saver you want to use.

Ⓐ A preview of the screen saver appears here.

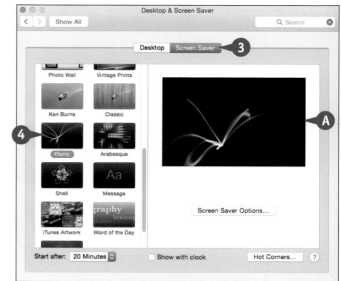

5 Click the **Start after** and then click a time delay until the screen saver begins.

Note: The interval you choose is the number of minutes or hours that your Mac must be idle before the screen saver starts.

B If the screen saver is customizable, click **Screen Saver Options** to configure it.

C If you chose a slideshow instead of a screen saver, click the **Source** to select an image collection.

D If you also want to see the current time when the screen saver is active, click **Show with clock** (☐ changes to ☑).

TIP

What are hot corners and how do I configure them?
A *hot corner* is a corner of your Mac's screen that you have set up to perform an action when you move the mouse ▶ to that specific corner. To configure hot corners, follow steps **1** to **3** and click **Hot Corners**. In the Active Screen Corners dialog, click the upper left and select the action you want to perform when you move the mouse ▶ to the top left corner of the screen. Click the for the remaining corners and select the action you want to perform when you move the mouse ▶ to the specific corner of the screen.

Set Your Mac's Sleep Options

You can make OS X more energy efficient by configuring parts of your Mac to go into sleep mode automatically when you are not using them. *Sleep mode* means that your display or your Mac is in a temporary low-power mode. This saves energy on all Macs, and saves battery power on a notebook Mac. For example, you can set up OS X to put the display to sleep automatically after a period of inactivity. Similarly, you can configure OS X to put your entire Mac to sleep after you have not used it for a specified amount of time.

Set Your Mac's Sleep Options

Open the Energy Saver Preferences

1 In the Dock, click the **System Preferences** icon (⚙).

2 In the System Preferences window, click **Energy Saver**.

The Energy Saver preferences appear.

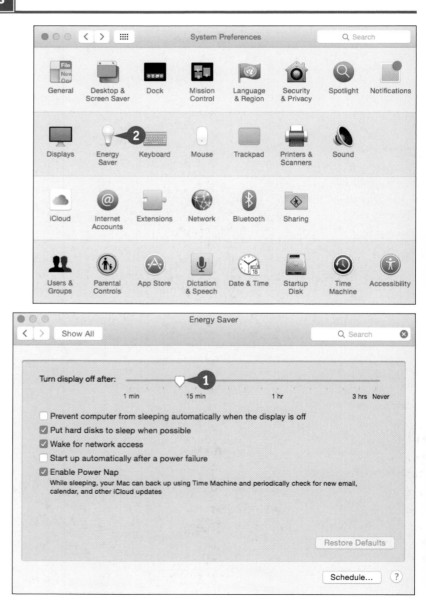

Set Sleep Options for a Desktop Mac

1 Click and drag the slider to set the display sleep timer.

This specifies the period of inactivity after which your display goes to sleep.

Set Sleep Options for a Notebook Mac

1 Click **Battery**.

2 Click and drag the slider to set the computer sleep timer for when your Mac is on battery power.

3 Click and drag the slider to set the display sleep timer for when your Mac is on battery power.

4 Click **Power Adapter**.

5 Click and drag the slider to set the computer sleep timer for when your Mac is plugged in.

6 Click and drag the slider to set the display sleep timer for when your Mac is plugged in.

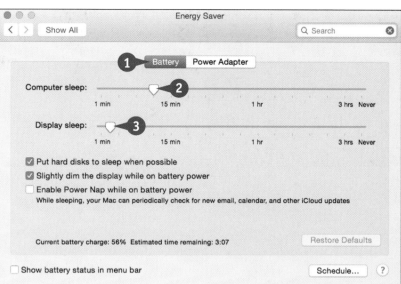

TIPS

How do I wake a sleeping display or computer?

If your Mac's display is in sleep mode, you can wake it by moving your mouse ▶ or sliding your finger on the trackpad. You can also wake up the display or your entire Mac by pressing any key.

I changed the display sleep timer, and now I never see my screen saver. Why?

You set the display sleep timer to a time that is less than your screen saver timer. Suppose you configured OS X to switch on the screen saver after 15 minutes. If you set the display sleep timer to a shorter interval, such as 10 minutes, OS X always puts the display to sleep before the screen saver appears.

Change the Display Resolution and Brightness

You can change the resolution and the brightness of the OS X display. This enables you to adjust the display for best viewing or for maximum compatibility with whatever application you are using.

Increasing the display resolution is an easy way to create more space on the screen for applications and windows, because the objects on the screen appear smaller. Conversely, if you have trouble reading text on the screen, decreasing the display resolution can help, because the screen objects appear larger. If you find that your display is too dark or too bright, you can adjust the brightness for best viewing.

Change the Display Resolution and Brightness

1 In the Dock, click the **System Preferences** icon (⚙).

2 In the System Preferences window, click **Displays**.

The Displays preferences appear.

3 Click **Display**.

4 Select the resolution:

A To have OS X set the resolution based on your display, click **Best for display** (☐ changes to ◉).

B To set the resolution yourself, click **Scaled** (☐ changes to ◉) and then click the resolution you want to use.

OS X adjusts the screen to the new resolution.

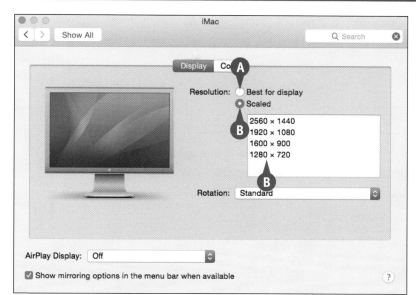

5 For some screens, you can click and drag the **Brightness** slider to set the display brightness.

OS X adjusts the screen to the new brightness.

C If you do not want OS X to adjust the notebook screen brightness based on the ambient light, click **Automatically adjust brightness** (☑ changes to ☐).

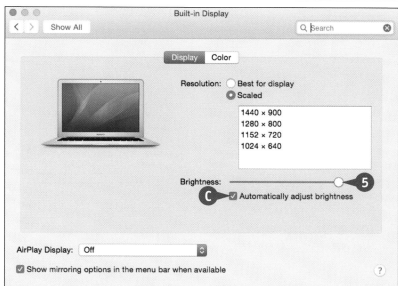

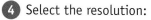
TIPS

What do the resolution numbers mean?
The resolution numbers are expressed in *pixels*, which are the individual dots that make up what you see on your Mac's screen, arranged in rows and columns. So a resolution of 1440 × 900 means that the display is using 1,440-pixel rows and 900-pixel columns.

Why do some resolutions also include the word stretched?
Most older displays use an aspect ratio (width to the height) of 4:3. However, most new Mac displays use an aspect ratio of either 16:9 or 16:10, which is called *widescreen*. Resolutions designed for 4:3 displays take up only part of a widescreen display. To make them take up the entire display, choose the *stretched* version of the resolution.

Create an App Folder in Launchpad

You can make Launchpad easier to use by combining multiple icons into a single storage area called an *app folder*. Normally, Launchpad displays icons in up to five rows per screen, with at least seven icons in each row, so you can have at least 35 icons in each screen. Also, if you have configured your Mac with a relatively low display resolution, you might see only partial app names in Launchpad.

All this can make it difficult to locate your apps. However, app folders can help you organize similar apps and reduce the clutter on the Launchpad screens.

Create an App Folder in Launchpad

1 Click the **Launchpad** icon (▦).

Ⓐ Launchpad displays icons for each installed application.

2 Click the dot for the Launchpad screen you want to work with.

3 Use the mouse ▨ to click and drag an icon that you want to include in the folder, and drop it on another icon that you want to include in the same folder.

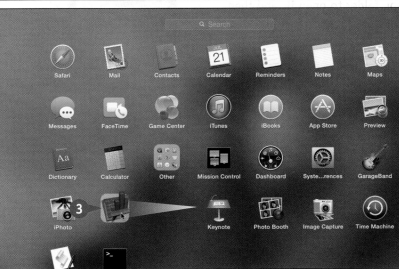

Launchpad creates the app folder.

B Launchpad applies a name to the folder based on the type of applications in the folder.

C Launchpad adds the icons to the app folder.

D To specify a different name, you can click the name and then type the one you prefer.

4 Click the Launchpad screen, outside of the app folder.

E Launchpad displays the app folder.

5 To add more icons to the new app folder, use the mouse **▶** to click and drag each icon and drop it on the folder.

Note: To launch a program from an app folder, click the **Launchpad** icon (🚀), click the app folder to open it, and then click the program's icon.

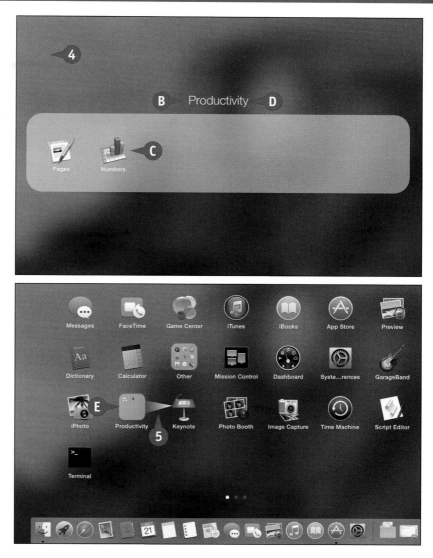

TIPS

How do I make changes to an app folder?
Click the **Launchpad** icon (🚀) and then click the app folder. To rename the app folder, click the current name, type the new name, and then press `Return`. To rearrange the icons, use the mouse **▶** to drag and drop the apps within the folder. When you are done, click outside the app folder to close it.

How do I remove an icon from an app folder?
Click the **Launchpad** icon (🚀) and then click the app folder. To remove an app from a folder, use the mouse **▶** to click and drag the app out of the folder. Launchpad closes the folder, and you can then drop the icon within the Launchpad screen.

Add a User Account

You can share your Mac with another person by creating a user account for that person. This enables the person to log in to OS X and use the system. The new user account is completely separate from your own account. This means that the other person can change settings, create documents, and perform other OS X tasks without interfering with your own settings or data. For maximum privacy for all users, you should set up each user account with a password.

Add a User Account

1 In the Dock, click the **System Preferences** icon (■).

2 In the System Preferences window, click **Users & Groups**.

A In most OS X systems, to modify accounts you must click the lock icon (■) and then type your administrator password (■ changes to ■).

3 Click **Add** (⊞).

The New Account dialog appears.

④ Click the **New Account** ▣ and then click an account type.

⑤ Type the user's name.

⑥ Edit the short username that OS X creates.

⑦ If the user has an iCloud account, click **Use iCloud password**; otherwise, click **Use separate password** (☐ changes to ▣).

⑧ Type and retype the user's password.

⑨ Type a hint that OS X will display if the user forgets the password.

⑩ Click **Create User**.

Ⓑ OS X adds the user account to the Users & Groups preferences.

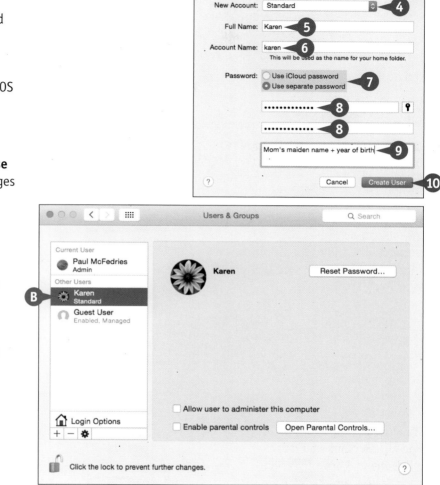

TIPS

Which account type should I use for the new account?

The Standard account type is a good choice because it can make changes only to its own account settings. Avoid the Administrator option because it enables the user to make major changes to the system. Consider the Managed with Parental Controls account type for children.

How do I change the user's picture?

In the Users & Groups preferences, click the user and then click the picture. OS X displays a list of the available images. If you see one you like, click it. If your Mac has a camera attached and the user is nearby, you can click **Camera** and then click the **Camera** icon to take the user's picture.

Customize the Dock

You can customize various aspects of the Dock by using System Preferences to modify a few Dock options. For example, you can make the Dock take up less room on the screen by adjusting the size of the Dock. You can also make the Dock a bit easier to use by turning on the Magnification feature, which enlarges Dock icons when you position the mouse pointer over them. You can also make the Dock easier to access and use by moving it to either side of the screen.

Customize the Dock

1 In the Dock, click the **System Preferences** icon (⚙).

2 In the System Preferences window, click **Dock**.

Note: You can also open the Dock preferences by clicking the **Apple** icon (), clicking **Dock**, and then clicking **Dock Preferences**.

The Dock preferences appear.

3 Click and drag the **Size** slider to make the Dock smaller or larger.

Ⓐ You can also click and drag the Dock divider: Drag up to increase the Dock size, and drag down to decrease the Dock size.

Ⓑ System Preferences adjusts the size of the Dock.

Note: If your Dock is already as wide as the screen, dragging the Size slider to the right (toward the Large value) has no effect.

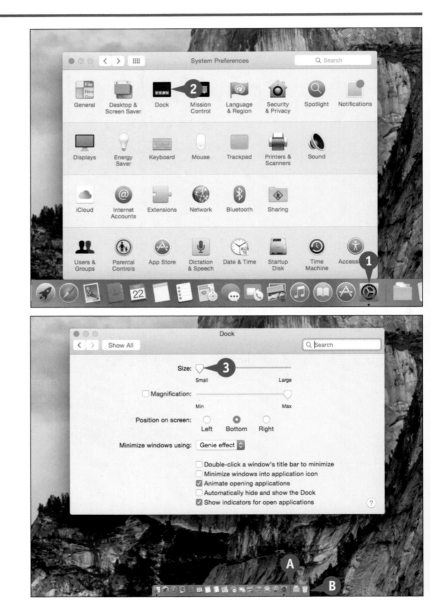

4 Click **Magnification** (☐ changes to ☑).

5 Click and drag the **Magnification** slider to set the magnification level.

C When you position the mouse 🖱 over a Dock icon, your Mac magnifies the icon.

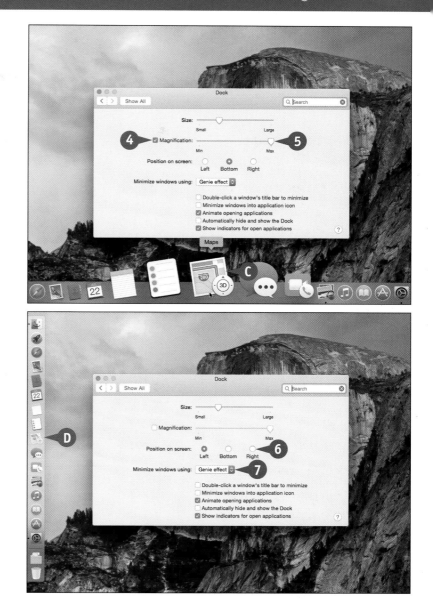

6 Use the **Position on screen** options to click where you want the Dock to appear, such as the **Left** side of the screen (☐ changes to ◉).

D Your Mac moves the Dock to the new position.

7 Click the **Minimize windows using** 🔽 and then click the effect you want your Mac to use when you minimize a window: **Genie effect** or **Scale effect**.

TIP

Is there an easier method I can use to control some of these preferences?

Yes, you can control these preferences directly from the Dock. To set the Dock size, click and drag the Dock divider left or right. For the other preferences, right-click the Dock divider. Click **Turn Magnification On** to enable the magnification feature; click **Turn Magnification Off** to disable this feature. To change the Dock position, click **Position on Screen** and then click **Left**, **Bottom**, or **Right**. To set the minimize effect, click **Minimize Using** and then click either **Genie Effect** or **Scale Effect**. Finally, you can also click **Dock Preferences** to open the Dock pane in System Preferences.

Add an Icon to the Dock

The icons on the Dock are convenient because you can open them with just a single click. You can enhance the convenience of the Dock by adding an icon for an application you use frequently.

The icon remains in the Dock even when the application is closed, so you can always open the application with a single click. You can add an icon to the Dock even if the program is not currently running.

Add an Icon to the Dock

Add an Icon for a Nonrunning Application

1 Click the **Finder** icon (▨).

2 Click **Applications**.

3 Click and drag the application icon, and then drop it inside the Dock.

Ⓐ Be sure to drop the icon anywhere to the left of the Dock divider.

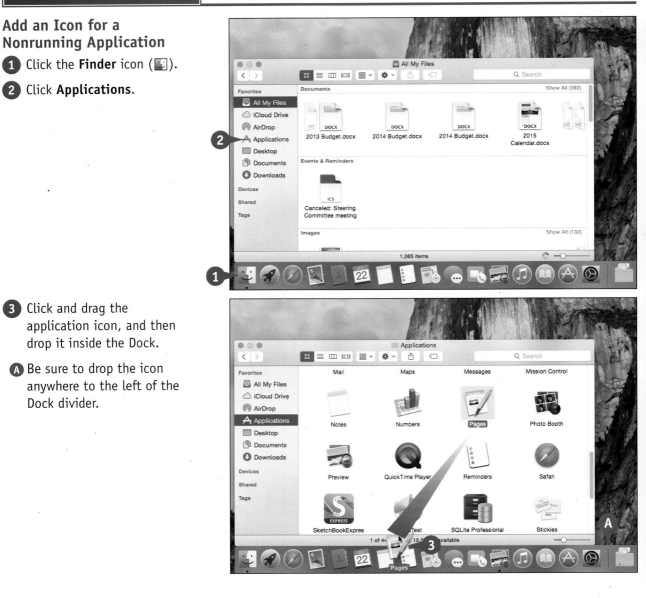

Ⓑ OS X adds the application's icon to the Dock.

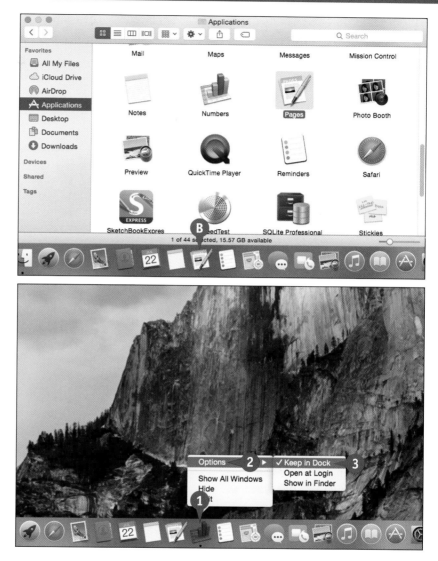

Add an Icon for a Running Application

1 Right-click the application icon in the Dock.

2 Click **Options**.

3 Click **Keep in Dock**.

The application's icon remains in the Dock even after you close the program.

Can my Mac start the application automatically each time I log in?

Yes. Your Mac maintains a list of *login items*, which are applications that run automatically after you log in. You can configure your application as a login item, and your Mac opens it automatically each time you log in. Right-click the application's Dock icon, click **Options**, and then click **Open at Login**.

How do I remove an icon from the Dock?

Right-click the application's Dock icon, click **Options**, and then click **Remove from Dock**. If the application is currently running, OS X removes the icon from the Dock when you quit the program. Note that you can remove any application icon except Finder (🙂).

Hide the Dock

When you are working in an application, you might find that you need to maximize the amount of vertical space the application window takes up on-screen. This might come up, for example, when you are reading or editing a long document or viewing a large photo. In such cases, you can size the window to maximum height, but OS X will not let you go past the Dock. You can work around this by hiding the Dock. When the Dock is hidden, it is still easily accessible whenever you need to use it.

Hide the Dock

Turn On Dock Hiding

1 Click the **Apple** icon (🍎).

2 Click **Dock**.

3 Click **Turn Hiding On**.

Ⓐ You can also right-click the Dock divider and then click **Turn Hiding On**.

Ⓑ OS X removes the Dock from the desktop.

Display the Dock Temporarily

1 Move the mouse 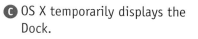 to the bottom of the screen.

C OS X temporarily displays the Dock.

Note: To hide the Dock again, move the mouse ▶ away from the bottom of the screen.

TIPS

Is there a faster way to hide the Dock?
Yes. You can quickly hide the Dock by pressing
`Option`+`⌘`+`D`. This keyboard shortcut is a toggle,
which means that you can also turn off Dock hiding
by pressing `Option`+`⌘`+`D`. When the Dock is
hidden, you can display it temporarily by pressing
`Control`+`F3` (on some keyboards you must press
`Fn`+`Control`+`F3`).

How do I bring the Dock back into view?
When you no longer need the extra screen space
for your applications, you can turn off Dock
hiding to bring the Dock back into view. Click the
Apple icon (), click **Dock**, and then click **Turn
Hiding Off**. Alternatively, display the Dock,
right-click the Dock divider, and then click **Turn
Hiding Off**.

Add a Widget to the Notification Center

The Notification Center is an OS X application that you use not only to view your latest notifications, but also to display widgets. A widget is a mini-application, particularly one designed to perform a single task, such as displaying the weather, showing stock data, or working with reminders. You can customize the Notification Center to include any widgets that you find useful or informative. OS X comes with several widgets, and there are also many widgets available via the App Store.

Add a Widget to the Notification Center

1 Click **Notification Center** ().

2 Click **Today**.

OS X displays the Notification Center and its current set of widgets.

3 Click **Edit**.

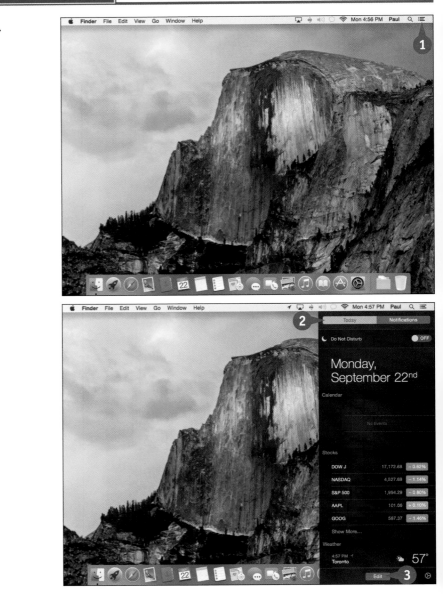

OS X displays its collection of widgets.

4 Click **Add** (⊞) beside the widget you want to add.

Ⓐ OS X adds the widget to the Notification Center.

5 Use the mouse ▶ to click and drag the widget to the position you prefer.

6 Click **Done**.

OS X updates the Notification Center.

Can I configure a widget?

In some cases, yes. For example, you can configure the Stocks widget to show just the stocks that interest you. If the widget is configurable, it displays an *i* when you position the mouse ▶ over it. Click the *i*, configure the widget, and then click **Done**.

How do I remove a widget from the Notification Center?

To remove a widget, follow steps **1** to **3** to open the widgets list for editing, and then tap the **Remove** icon (⊖) that appears to the left of the widget. OS X removes the widget and adds it to the Items list, just in case you want to use it again later. Click **Done**.

Extend the Desktop Across Multiple Displays

You can improve your productivity and efficiency by connecting a second monitor to your Mac. To work with an extra display, your Mac must have a video output port — such as a Thunderbolt port, Mini DisplayPort, or DVI port — that matches a corresponding port on the second display. If you do not have such a port, check with Apple or the display manufacturer to see if an adapter is available that enables your Mac to connect with the second display. After you connect your Mac to the display, you can extend the OS X desktop across both monitors.

Extend the Desktop Across Multiple Displays

1 Connect the second monitor to your Mac.

2 Open System Preferences.

Note: See the task "Display System Preferences," earlier in this chapter.

3 Click **Displays**.

The Displays preferences appear.

4 Click **Arrangement**.

A This window represents your Mac's main display.

B This window represents the second display.

C This white strip represents the OS X menu bar.

5 Click and drag the windows to set the relative arrangement of the two displays.

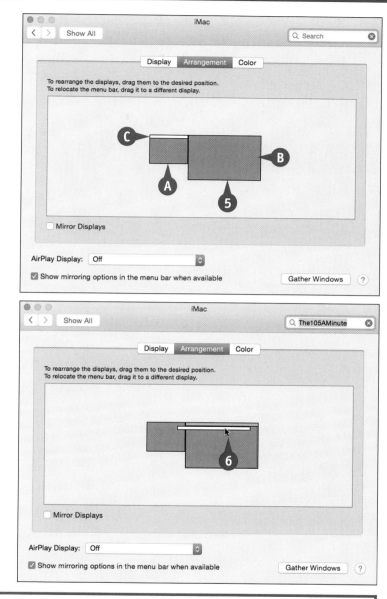

6 To move the menu bar and Dock to the second display, click and drag the menu bar and drop it on the second display.

Can I use a different desktop background in each display?

Yes. To set the desktop background on the second display, open System Preferences and click **Desktop & Screen Saver**. On the second display, you see the Secondary Desktop dialog. Use that dialog to set the desktop picture or color, as described in the task "Change the Desktop Background."

Can I just use the second display to show my main OS X desktop?

Yes. This is called *mirroring* the main display because the second display shows exactly what appears on your Mac's main monitor, including the mouse pointer. Follow steps **1** to **4** to display the Arrangement tab and then click **Mirror Displays** (☐ changes to ☑).

Customize the Share Menu

The Share menu appears in many OS X applications, including Finder, Safari, Preview, Maps, and Notes. You use the Share menu's extensions to perform actions on the application's content. For example, in Safari you can use the Sharing menu to create a bookmark; send the page URL via email, text message, or AirDrop; or share the page on Twitter, Facebook, or LinkedIn. If the Sharing menu contains extensions that you never use, you can reduce clutter on the menu by removing those items. You can also reorder the menu to put the items you use most often near the top.

Customize the Share Menu

Display the Share Menu Extensions

1 In the Dock, click the **System Preferences** icon (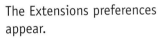).

2 In the System Preferences window, click **Extensions**.

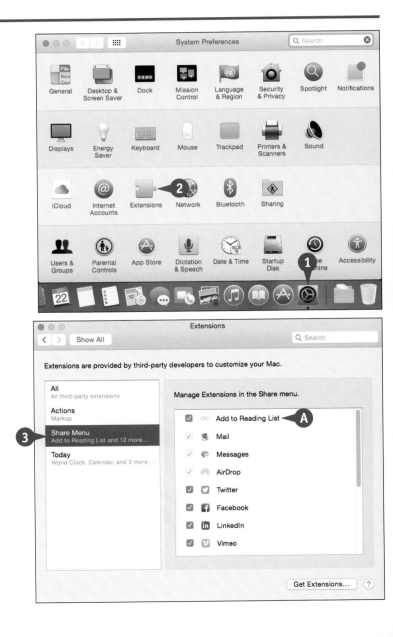

The Extensions preferences appear.

3 Click **Share Menu**.

Ⓐ OS X displays the extensions available for the Share menu.

Remove a Share Menu Extension

1 To temporarily remove an extension from the Share menu, click its check box (☑ changes to ☐).

The next time you open the Share menu, you will no longer see the extension.

Note: OS X moves the disabled extension to the bottom of the list. To enable the extension later on, scroll to the bottom of the list and click the extension's check box (☐ changes to ☑).

Move a Share Menu Extension

1 Position the mouse ▶ over the name of the icon of the extension you want to move (▶ changes to 🖑).

2 Click and drag the extension up or down to the new menu position and then release the extension.

The next time you open the Share menu, you will see the extension in its new position.

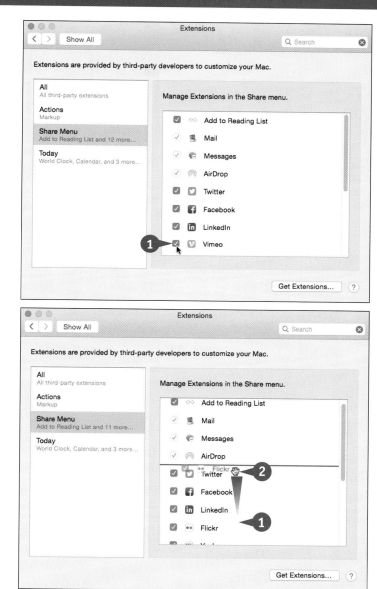

Is there a quicker method I can use to customize the Share menu?

Yes, as long as you are working in an application that includes the Share menu. In that case, click the **Share** icon (🔲) and then click **More**. OS X automatically runs System Preferences, opens the Extensions preferences, and selects the Share Menu item.

Are there more extensions available?

Yes. OS X allows third-party developers to create new extensions that you can add to the Share menu. To get these extensions, follow steps **1** to **3** to display the Share Menu extensions list and then click **Get Extensions**. OS X launches the App Store and displays the available extensions that you can download or purchase.

CHAPTER 13

Maintaining OS X

To keep OS X running smoothly, maintain top performance, and reduce the risk of computer problems, you need to perform some routine maintenance chores. This chapter shows you how to empty the Trash, delete unnecessary files, uninstall applications, back up and restore your files, recondition your notebook battery, and more.

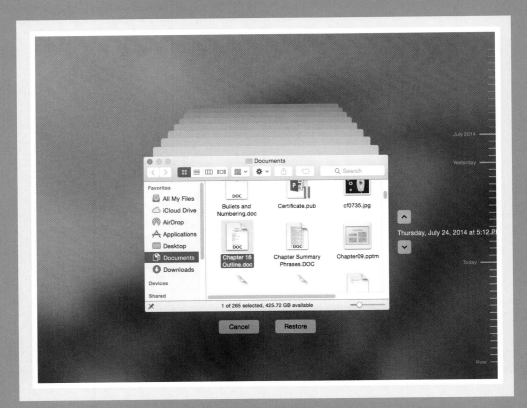

Empty the Trash

You can free up disk space on your Mac by periodically emptying the Trash. When you delete a file or folder, OS X does not immediately remove the file from your Mac's hard drive. Instead, OS X moves the file or folder to the Trash. This is useful if you accidentally delete an item, because it means you can open the Trash and restore the item. However, all those deleted files and folders take up disk space, so you need to empty the Trash periodically to regain that space. You should empty the Trash at least once a week.

Empty the Trash

1 Click the desktop.

2 Click **Finder** from the menu.

3 Click **Empty Trash**.

A You can also right-click the Trash icon (🗑) and then click **Empty Trash**.

Note: Another way to select the Empty Trash command is to press Shift + ⌘ + Delete.

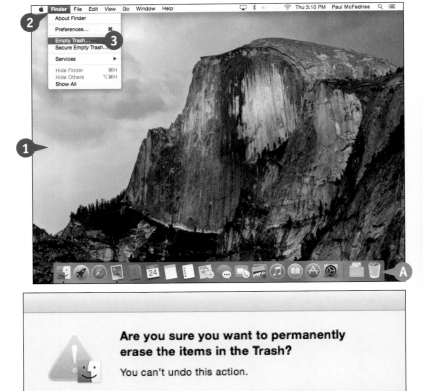

OS X asks you to confirm the deletion.

4 Click **Empty Trash**.

OS X empties the Trash (🗑 changes to 🗑).

Are you sure you want to permanently erase the items in the Trash?

You can't undo this action.

Cancel   Empty Trash **4**

Organize Your Desktop

You can make your OS X desktop easier to scan and navigate by organizing the icons. The OS X desktop automatically displays icons for objects such as your external hard drives, inserted CDs and DVDs, disk images, and attached iPods. The desktop is also a handy place to store files, file aliases, copies of documents, and more. However, the more you use your desktop as a storage area, the more the desktop can become disarrayed, making it hard to find the icon you want. You can fix this by organizing the icons.

Organize Your Desktop

1 Click the desktop.

2 Click **View**.

3 Click **Clean Up By**.

4 Click **Name**.

You can also right-click the desktop, click **Clean Up By**, and then click **Name**, or press Option+⌘+1.

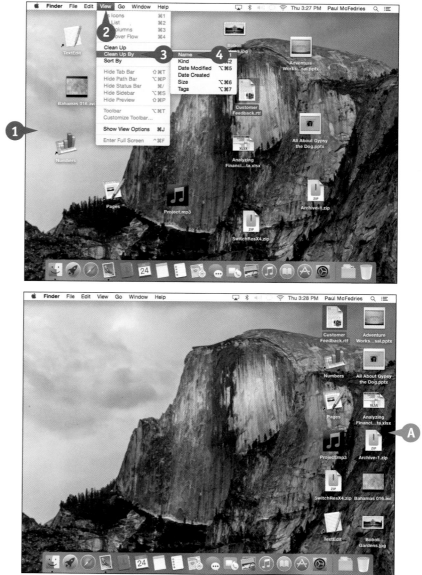

A Your Mac organizes the icons alphabetically and arranges them in columns from right to left.

Check Hard Drive Free Space

To ensure that your Mac's hard drive does not become full, you should periodically check how much free space it has left. If you run out of room on your Mac's hard drive, you will not be able to install more applications or create more documents, and your Mac's performance will suffer. To ensure that your free space does not become too low — say, less than about 50GB — you can check how much free space your hard drive has left.

You should check your Mac's hard drive free space about once a month.

Check Hard Drive Free Space

Check Free Space Using Finder

1 Click the **Finder** icon ().

2 Click **Desktop**.

Note: You can also click any folder on your Mac's hard drive.

3 In the status bar, read the available value, which tells you the amount of free space left on the hard drive.

If you do not see the status bar, press ⌘+/.

Display Free Space on the Desktop

1 Display your Mac's HD (hard drive) icon on the desktop, as described in the first Tip.

2 Click the desktop.

3 Click **View**.

4 Click **Show View Options**.

Note: You can also run the Show View Options command by pressing ⌘+J.

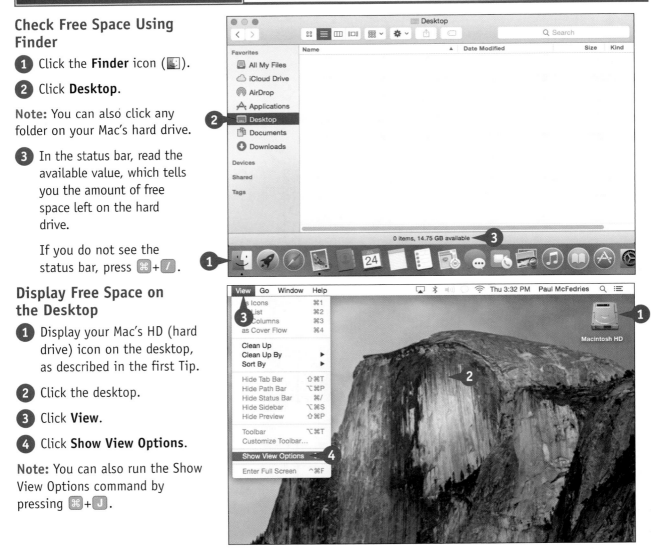

The Desktop dialog appears.

⑤ Click **Show item info**
(☐ changes to ☑).

Ⓐ Your Mac displays the amount
of free hard drive space
under the Macintosh HD icon.

⑥ Drag the **Icon size** slider
until you can read all the
icon text.

⑦ If you still cannot read all
the text, click the **Text size**
⬚ and then click a larger
size.

⑧ Click **Close** (⬛).

TIPS

My Mac's hard drive icon does not appear on the desktop. How do I display it?
If you do not see the Macintosh HD icon on your desktop, click the desktop, click **Finder** in the menu bar, and then click **Preferences**. Click the **General** tab, click **Hard disks** (☐ changes to ☑), and then click **Close** (⬛).

What should I do if my Mac's hard drive space is low?
First, empty the Trash, as described earlier in this chapter. Next, uninstall applications you no longer use, as described in the next task. If you have large documents you no longer need, either move them to an external hard drive or flash drive, or delete them and then empty the Trash.

Uninstall Unused Applications

If you have an application that you no longer use, you can free up some disk space and reduce clutter in the Applications folder by uninstalling that application. When you install an application, the program stores its files on your Mac's hard drive, and although most programs are quite small, many require hundreds of megabytes of space. Uninstalling applications you do not need frees up the disk space they use and removes their icons or folders from the Applications folder. In most cases, you must be logged on to OS X with an administrator account to uninstall applications.

Uninstall Unused Applications

1 Click the **Finder** icon (▧).

2 Click **Applications**.

3 Click and drag the application or its folder and drop it on the **Trash** icon (▢).

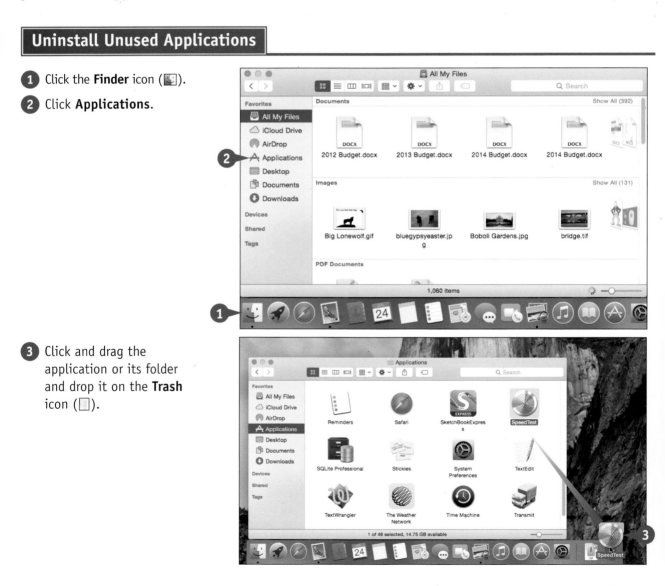

OS X prompts you for an administrator password.

④ Type the password.

⑤ Click **OK**.

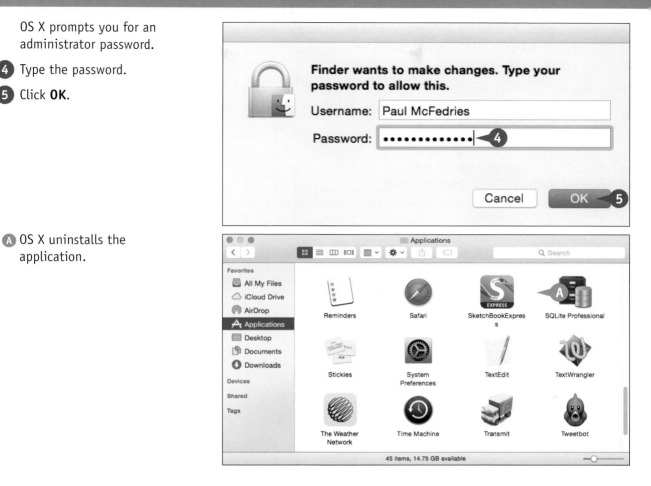

Ⓐ OS X uninstalls the application.

Is there another way to uninstall an application?

Yes, in some cases. A few Mac applications come with a separate program for uninstalling the application. Follow steps **1** and **2**. Open the application's folder, if it has one (Ⓐ). Double-click the **Uninstall** (or **Uninstaller**) icon (Ⓑ) and then follow the instructions on-screen.

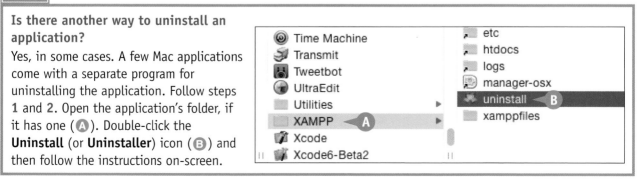

Force a Stuck Application to Close

When you are working with an application, you may find that it becomes unresponsive and you cannot interact with the application or even quit the application normally. In that case, you can use an OS X feature called Force Quit to force a stuck or unresponsive application to close, which enables you to restart the application or restart your Mac.

Unfortunately, when you force an application to quit, you lose any unsaved changes in your open documents. Therefore, you should make sure the application really is stuck before forcing it to quit. See the second Tip for more information.

Force a Stuck Application to Close

1 Click the **Apple** icon (🍎).

2 Click **Force Quit**.

The Force Quit Applications window appears.

3 Click the application you want to shut down.

4 Click **Force Quit**.

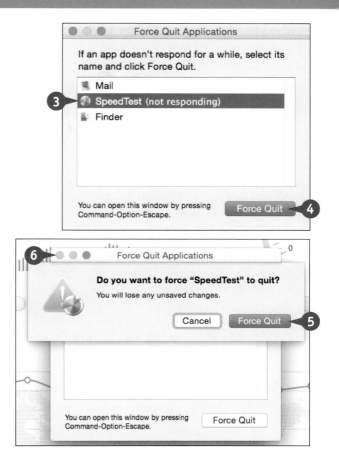

Your Mac asks you to confirm that you want to force the application to quit.

5 Click **Force Quit**.

Your Mac shuts down the application.

6 Click **Close** (▢) to close the Force Quit Applications window.

TIPS

Are there easier ways to run the Force Quit command?

Yes. From the keyboard, you can run the Force Quit command by pressing Option + ⌘ + Esc. If the application has a Dock icon, press and hold Control + Option and then click the application's Dock icon. In the menu that appears, click **Force Quit**.

If an application is not responding, does that always mean the application is stuck?

Not necessarily. Some operations — such as recalculating a large spreadsheet or rendering a 3-D image — can take a few minutes, and during that time the application can appear stuck. An application can also seem stuck if your Mac is low on memory. In this case, try quitting some of other applications to free up some memory.

Configure Time Machine Backups

One of the most crucial OS X maintenance chores is to configure your system to make regular backups of your files. Macs are reliable machines, but they can crash, and all hard drives eventually die, so at some point your data will be at risk. To avoid losing that data forever, you need to configure Time Machine to perform regular backups.

To use Time Machine, your Mac requires a second hard drive. This can be a second internal drive on a Mac mini, but on most Macs the easiest course is to connect an external hard drive.

Configure Time Machine Backups

1 Connect an external USB, Thunderbolt, or FireWire hard drive to your Mac.

If OS X asks if you want to use the hard drive as your backup disk, click **Use as Backup Disk** and then skip the rest of these steps.

2 Click the **System Preferences** icon (⚙).

3 Click **Time Machine**.

The Time Machine preferences appear.

4 Click **Select Backup Disk**.

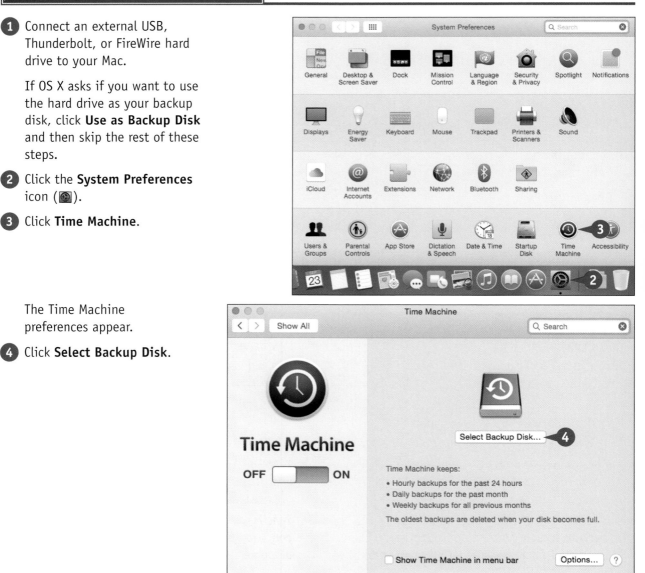

Time Machine displays a list of available backup devices.

5 Click the external hard drive.

6 Click **Use Disk**.

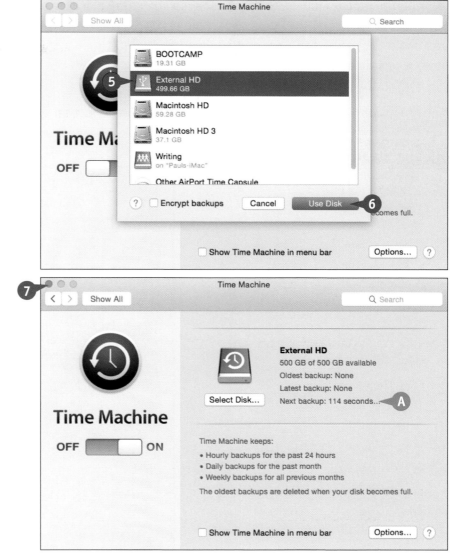

A Time Machine enables backups and prepares to run the first backup automatically in 2 minutes.

7 Click **Close** (◻).

TIP

How do Time Machine backups work?

Time Machine makes backing up your Mac easy because backups are handled automatically as follows:

- The initial backup occurs 2 minutes after you configure Time Machine for the first time. This backup includes your entire Mac.

- Another backup runs every hour. These hourly backups include files and folders you have changed or created since the most recent hourly backup.

- Time Machine runs a daily backup that includes only those files and folders that you have changed or created since the most recent daily backup.

- Time Machine runs a weekly backup that includes only those files and folders that you have changed or created since the most recent weekly backup.

Restore an Earlier Version of a File

If you improperly edit or accidentally overwrite a file, some apps enable you to revert to an earlier version of the file. Why would you want to revert to an earlier version of a file? One reason is that you might improperly edit the file by deleting or changing important data. In some cases you may be able to restore that data by going back to a previous version of the file. Similarly, if you overwrite the file with a different file, you can fix the problem by restoring an earlier version of the file.

Restore an Earlier Version of a File

① Open the file you want to restore.

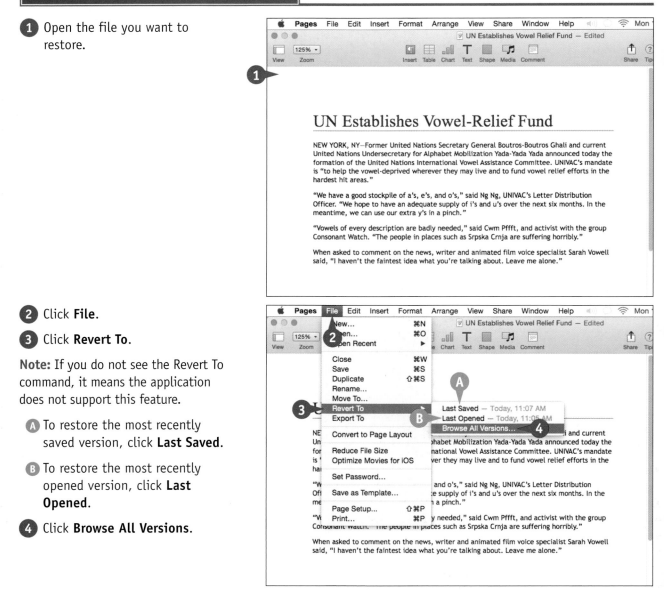

② Click **File**.

③ Click **Revert To**.

Note: If you do not see the Revert To command, it means the application does not support this feature.

Ⓐ To restore the most recently saved version, click **Last Saved**.

Ⓑ To restore the most recently opened version, click **Last Opened**.

④ Click **Browse All Versions**.

The restore interface appears.

Ⓒ This window represents the current version of the file.

Ⓓ Each of these windows represents an earlier version of the file.

Ⓔ This area tells you when the displayed version of the file was saved.

Ⓕ You can use this timeline to navigate the earlier versions.

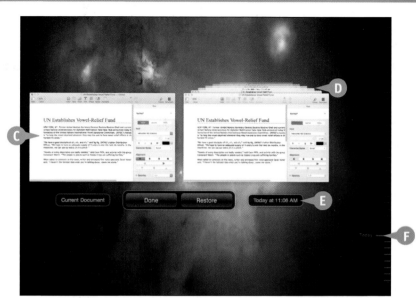

⑤ Navigate to the date that contains the version of the file you want to restore.

Note: See the Tip to learn how to navigate the Time Machine backups.

⑥ Click **Restore**.

OS X reverts the file to the earlier version.

TIPS

How do I navigate the previous versions?

There are two methods you can use:

• Use the timeline on the right side of the window to click a specific version.

• Click the title bars of the version windows.

Can I restore a previous version without overwriting the current version of the file?

Yes, you can restore a copy of the file. This is useful if the current version has data you want to preserve, or if you want to compare the current version with the earlier version. Follow steps **1** to **5** to navigate to the version of the file that you want to restore. Press and hold Option and then click **Restore a Copy**.

Restore Files Using Time Machine

If you have configured OS X to make regular Time Machine backups, you can use those backups to restore a lost file. If you accidentally delete a file, you can quickly restore it by opening the Trash folder. However, that does not help you if you have emptied the Trash folder. Similarly, if the program or OS X crashes, a file may become corrupted.

Because Time Machine makes hourly, daily, and weekly backups, it stores older copies of your data. You can use these backups to restore any file that you accidentally delete or that has become corrupted.

Restore Files Using Time Machine

1. Click the **Finder** icon ().

2. Open the folder you want to restore, or the folder that contains the file you want to restore.

Ⓐ To restore your entire hard drive, choose **Macintosh HD** in the sidebar.

Note: Restore your entire hard drive only if your original hard drive crashed and you have had it repaired or replaced.

3. Click **Spotlight** ().

4. Type **time machine**.

5. Double-click **Time Machine**.

The Time Machine interface appears.

Ⓑ Each window represents a backed-up version of the folder.

Ⓒ This area tells you when the displayed version of the folder was backed up.

Ⓓ You can use this timeline to navigate the backed-up versions.

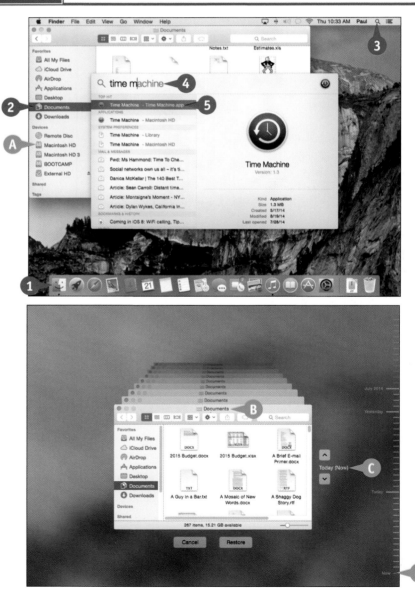

278

6 Navigate to the date that contains the backed-up version of the folder or file.

Note: See the Tip to learn how to navigate the Time Machine backups.

7 If you are restoring a file, click the file.

8 Click **Restore**.

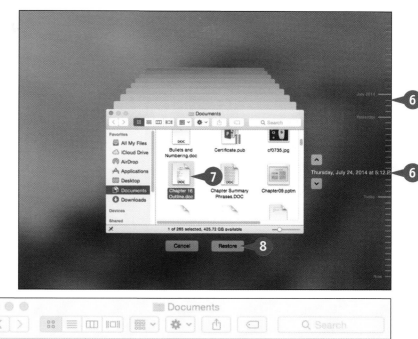

If another version of the folder or file already exists, Time Machine asks if you want to keep it or replace it.

9 Click **Replace**.

Time Machine restores the folder or file.

Note: Time Machine can also restore data from apps such as Mail and Contacts. Run the app and then launch Time Machine.

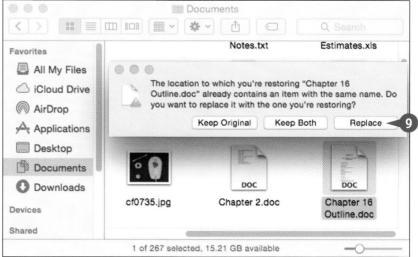

TIP

How do I navigate the backups in the Time Machine interface?

Here are the most useful techniques:

- Click the top arrow to jump to the earliest version; click the bottom arrow to return to the most recent version.
- Press and hold ⌘ and click the arrows to navigate through the backups one version at a time.
- Use the timeline to click a specific version.
- Click the version windows.

Recondition Your Mac Notebook Battery

To get the most performance out of your Mac notebook's battery, you need to recondition the battery by cycling it. *Cycling* a battery means letting it completely discharge and then fully recharging it again. Most Mac notebook batteries slowly lose their charging capacity over time. For example, if you use your Mac notebook on batteries for 4 hours today, later on you can run the computer for only 3 hours on a full charge. You cannot stop this process, but you can delay it significantly by cycling the battery once a month or so.

Recondition Your Mac Notebook Battery

Display the Battery Status Percentage

1. Click the **Battery status** icon (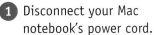).

2. Click **Show Percentage**.

   Your Mac shows the percentage of available battery power remaining.

Cycle the Battery

1. Disconnect your Mac notebook's power cord.

Ⓐ The Battery Status icon changes from ▱ to ▰.

2 Operate your Mac notebook normally by running applications, working with documents, and so on.

3 As you work, keep your eye on the Battery Status percentage.

When the Battery Status reaches 4%, the meter turns red, and when the status reaches 2%, OS X warns you that the system will soon go into sleep mode.

4 Click **Close**.

5 Reattach the power cord.

Your Mac restarts and the Battery Status icon changes from 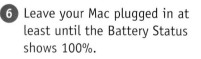 to 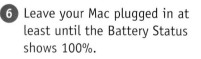.

6 Leave your Mac plugged in at least until the Battery Status shows 100%.

TIP

I do not see the battery status in my menu bar. How do I display it?
Click the **System Preferences** icon (⊚) in the Dock to open System Preferences and then click the **Energy Saver** icon. In the Energy Saver window, click **Show battery status in the menu bar** (☐ changes to ☑).

Restart Your Mac

If a hardware device is having a problem with some system files, it often helps to restart your Mac. By rebooting the computer, you reload the entire system, which is often enough to solve many computer problems.

For a problem device that does not have its own power switch, restarting your Mac might not resolve the problem because the device remains powered up the whole time. You can *power cycle* — shut down and then restart — such devices as a group by power cycling your Mac.

Restart Your Mac

Restart Your Mac

1 Click the **Apple** icon (■).

2 Click **Restart**.

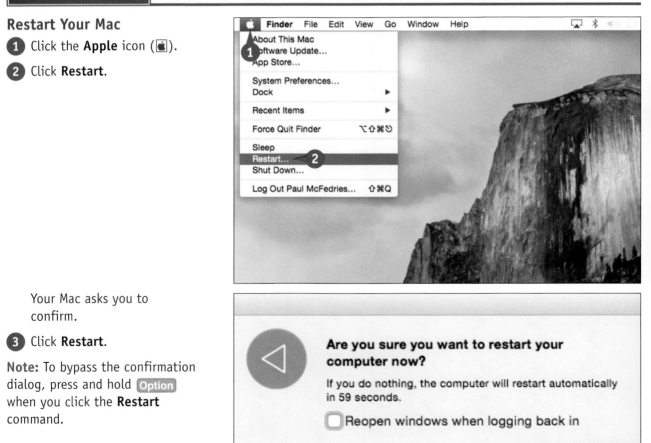

Your Mac asks you to confirm.

3 Click **Restart**.

Note: To bypass the confirmation dialog, press and hold Option when you click the **Restart** command.

Power Cycle Your Mac

1 Click the **Apple** icon ().

2 Click **Shut Down**.

Your Mac asks you to confirm.

Note: To bypass the confirmation dialog, press and hold Option when you click **Shut Down**.

3 Click **Shut Down**.

4 Wait for 30 seconds to give all devices time to spin down.

5 Turn your Mac back on.

TIP

What other basic troubleshooting techniques can I use?

- Make sure that each device is turned on, that cable connections are secure, and that insertable devices (such as USB devices) are properly inserted.

- If a device is battery powered, replace the batteries.

- If a device has an on/off switch, power cycle the device by turning it off, waiting a few seconds for it to stop spinning, and then turning it back on again.

- Close all running programs.

- Log out of your Mac — click the **Apple** icon (); click **Log Out** *User*, where *User* is your Mac username; and then click **Log Out** — and then log back in again.

CHAPTER 14

Working with iCloud

You can get a free iCloud account, which is a web-based service that gives you email, an address book, and a calendar. You can also use iCloud to automatically synchronize data between iCloud and your Mac (as well as your iPhone, iPad, or iPod touch).

Create an Apple ID

To use iCloud, you need to create a free Apple ID, which you use to sign in to iCloud on the web and to synchronize your Mac and other devices. An Apple ID is an email address. You can use an existing email address for your Apple ID, or you can sign up for a new iCloud email address, which uses the icloud.com domain name. If you use an existing email address, you are required to verify via email that the address is legitimate.

Create an Apple ID

① Click the **System Preferences** icon (⊞) in the Dock.

The System Preferences window appears.

② Click **iCloud**.

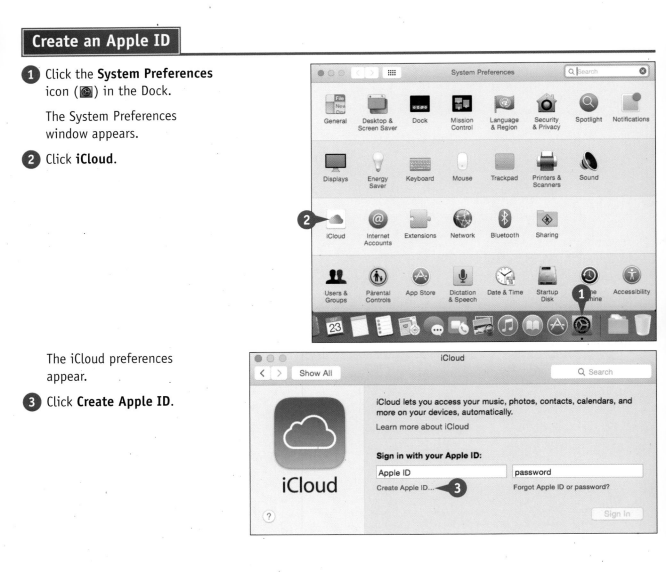

The iCloud preferences appear.

③ Click **Create Apple ID**.

The Create an Apple ID dialog appears.

④ Click and use the **Location** 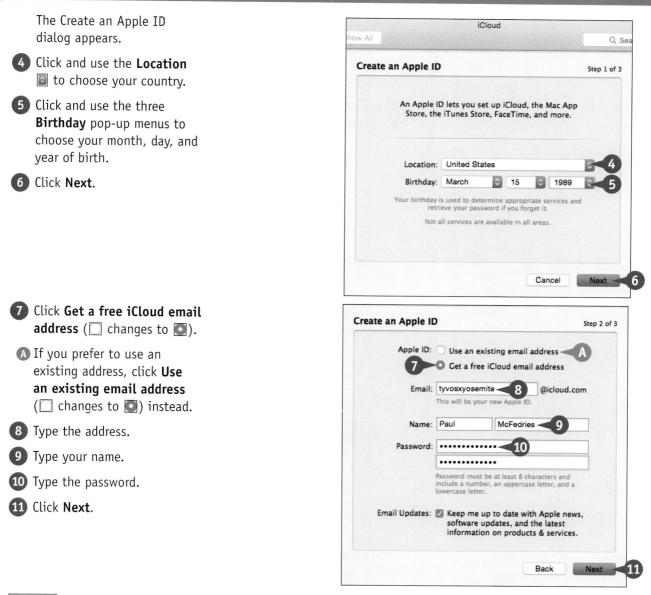 to choose your country.

⑤ Click and use the three **Birthday** pop-up menus to choose your month, day, and year of birth.

⑥ Click **Next**.

⑦ Click **Get a free iCloud email address** (☐ changes to ◉).

Ⓐ If you prefer to use an existing address, click **Use an existing email address** (☐ changes to ◉) instead.

⑧ Type the address.

⑨ Type your name.

⑩ Type the password.

⑪ Click **Next**.

TIP

If I do not want to create a new iCloud address, can I use any email address?

Yes, as long as the address belongs to you. Also, you need to be able to retrieve and read messages that are sent to that address, because this is part of the verification process. To learn how to verify an existing address that you entered in step **8**, see the Tip at the end of the task "Create an Apple ID."

continued ▶

Create an Apple ID (continued)

As part of the sign-up process, you specify which iCloud services to use. First, you decide whether you want to synchronize data such as contacts, calendars, and bookmarks with iCloud. If you are not sure, you can turn this feature off for now and decide later (see the task "Set Up iCloud Synchronization"). Second, you decide whether you want to use Find My Mac, which enables you to use iCloud to locate your lost or stolen Mac. Again, if you are not sure what to do, you can decide later (see the task "Locate and Lock a Lost Mac, iPod, iPhone, or iPad").

Create an Apple ID (continued)

12 For each security question, click to select a question and then type an answer.

13 If you want to supply Apple with an emergency email address, type it in the Rescue Email box.

14 Click **Next**.

Create an Apple ID   Step 3 of 3

Security Questions: What is the first name of your best frie — **12**

Apple

What was the model of your first car?

Alphonso di Credenza

What is the name of your favorite spo

Charlestown Chiefs

These security questions are used to verify your identity when you make changes to your account.

Rescue Email: myotheraddress@myisp.com — **13**

Add an email address used to confirm your identity or reset a forgotten password. This email address will only be used for security purposes.

Back   Next **14**

15 Click **I have read and agree to the iCloud Terms and Conditions** (☐ changes to ☑).

16 Click **Continue**.

Accept the iCloud Terms and Conditions to use iCloud.

iCloud Terms and Conditions

Welcome to iCloud

THIS LEGAL AGREEMENT BETWEEN YOU AND APPLE GOVERNS YOUR USE OF THE iCLOUD PRODUCT, SOFTWARE, SERVICES, AND WEBSITES (COLLECTIVELY REFERRED TO AS THE "SERVICE"). IT IS IMPORTANT THAT YOU READ AND UNDERSTAND THE FOLLOWING TERMS. BY CLICKING "AGREE," YOU ARE AGREEING THAT THESE TERMS WILL APPLY IF YOU CHOOSE TO ACCESS OR USE THE SERVICE.

Apple is the provider of the Service, which permits you to utilize certain Internet services, including storing your personal content (such as contacts, calendars, photos, notes, reminders, documents, app data, and iCloud email) and making it accessible on your compatible devices and computers, and certain location based services, only under the terms and conditions set forth in this Agreement. As soon as you enable iCloud, your content will be automatically sent to and stored by Apple, so you can later access that content or have content wirelessly pushed to your other iCloud-enabled devices or computers. "Apple" as used herein means:

• Apple Inc., located at 1 Infinite Loop, Cupertino, California, for users in North, Central, and South America (excluding Canada), as well as United States territories and

A copy of these Terms and Conditions is available at http://www.apple.com/legal/icloud/ww/

15 ☑ I have read and agree to the iCloud Terms and Conditions.

Cancel   Continue **16**

OS X prompts you to choose which iCloud services you want to use.

17 If you do not want to sync your data to iCloud, click **Use iCloud for mail, contacts, calendars, reminders, notes, and Safari** (☑ changes to ☐).

18 If you do not want to use iCloud to locate your Mac, click **Use Find My Mac** (☑ changes to ☐).

19 Click **Next**.

If you elected to use Find My Mac, OS X asks you to confirm.

20 Click **Allow**.

OS X sets up your iCloud account on your Mac.

Note: If you have trouble enabling Find My Mac, see the Tip in the task "Locate and Lock a Lost Mac, iPod, iPhone, or iPad."

TIP

What happens after I create my Apple ID from an existing address?
After you agree to the terms of service, Apple sends an email message to the address you typed in step **8**. When that message arrives, open it and click the verification link. In the web page that appears, type your Apple ID (that is, the email address from step **8**), type your password, and then click **Verify Address**. Return to the iCloud preferences, click **Next**, and then follow steps **15** to **20**.

Sign In to iCloud

Before you can use the features associated with your iCloud account, you must sign in to the service. iCloud is a web-based service, so you access it using a web browser. Most modern browsers should work fine with iCloud, but Apple recommends that you use at least Safari 6, Firefox 16, Internet Explorer 9, or Chrome 23.

You can also sign in to iCloud using a Mac, and for that you must be using OS X Lion 10.7.5 or later. You can also access iCloud using a Windows PC, and in this case the PC must be running Windows 8, Windows 7, or Windows Vista with Service Pack 2 or later.

Sign In to iCloud

1 In your web browser, type **www.icloud.com.**

2 Press **Return**.

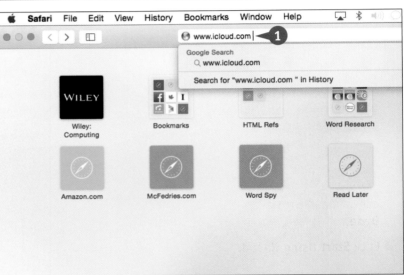

The iCloud Login page appears.

3 Use the Apple ID text box to type your Apple ID.

4 Use the Password text box to type the password for your Apple ID.

Ⓐ If you want iCloud to sign you in automatically in the future, click **Keep me signed in** (□ changes to ☑).

⑤ Click **Sign In** (→).

The first time you sign in, iCloud prompts you to configure some settings.

⑥ Click **Add Photo**, drop a photo on the dialog that appears, and then click **Done**.

⑦ Click **Start Using iCloud**.

Can I sign in from my Mac?

Yes. Click the **System Preferences** icon (⌖) in the Dock (or click and then click **System Preferences**) and then click **iCloud**. Type your Apple ID and password and then click **Sign In**.

How do I sign out from iCloud?

When you are done working with your iCloud account, if you prefer not to remain signed in to your account, click the **Sign Out** link beside your account name in the upper right corner of the iCloud page.

Set Up iCloud Synchronization

You can ensure that your Mac and your iCloud account have the same data by synchronizing the two. The main items you will want to synchronize are Mail email accounts, contacts, calendars, reminders, and notes. However, there are many other types of data you may want to synchronize to iCloud, including Safari bookmarks, photos, and documents. If you have a second Mac, a Windows PC, or an iPhone, iPad, or iPod touch, you can also synchronize it with the same iCloud account, which ensures that your Mac and the device use the same data.

Set Up iCloud Synchronization

1 Click the **Apple** icon (![apple]).

2 Click **System Preferences**.

Note: You can also open System Preferences by clicking its icon (![icon]) on the Dock.

The System Preferences window appears.

3 Click **iCloud**.

292

The iCloud preferences appear.

④ Click the check box beside a type of data you want to sync (☐ changes to ☑).

Ⓐ OS X sets up the sync.

⑤ Repeat step 4 for each type of data you want to sync.

⑥ If you do not want to sync a type of data, click its check box (☑ changes to ☐).

OS X asks if you want to keep or delete the iCloud data that you are no longer syncing.

⑦ Click here to keep the data on your Mac.

Ⓑ If you do not want to keep the data, click **Delete from Mac**.

Your Mac synchronizes the data with your iCloud account.

What happens if I modify an appointment, contact, bookmark, or other data in iCloud?
The synchronization process works both ways. That is, all the Mac data you selected to synchronize is sent to your iCloud account. However, the data on your iCloud account is also sent to your Mac. This means that if you modify, add, or delete data on your iCloud account, those changes are also reflected in your Mac data.

Set Up iCloud Keychain

You can make it easier to navigate secure websites by setting up iCloud Keychain. A *keychain* is a master list of usernames and passwords that a system stores for easy access by an authorized user. iCloud Keychain is a special type of keychain that stores website passwords auto-generated by Safari, as described in the next task, "Generate a Website Password." This means that you do not have to remember these passwords because Safari can automatically retrieve them from your iCloud account.

Set Up iCloud Keychain

1 Open System Preferences.

2 Click **iCloud**.

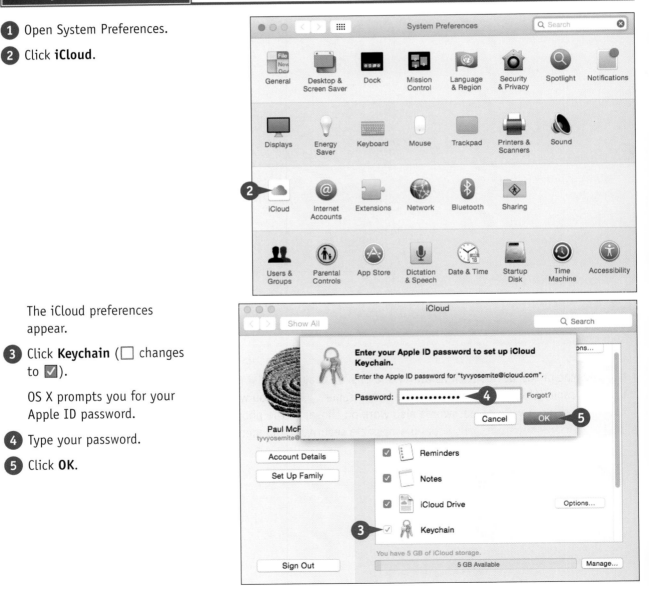

The iCloud preferences appear.

3 Click **Keychain** (☐ changes to ☑).

OS X prompts you for your Apple ID password.

4 Type your password.

5 Click **OK**.

OS X prompts you to enter an iCloud security code.

6 Type a four-digit security code.

7 Click **Next**.

OS X prompts you to confirm the iCloud security code.

8 Repeat steps **6** and **7** to confirm the security code.

OS X prompts you to enter a phone number that can receive SMS (text) messages.

9 Type the phone number.

10 Click **Done**.

OS X activates iCloud Keychain.

Create an iCloud Security Code.

Your iCloud Security Code can be used to set up iCloud Keychain on a new device.

Enter a four-digit numeric security code.

Advanced...   Cancel   Next

Enter a phone number that can receive SMS messages:

Country: +1 (United States)

Number: (317) 555-1234

This number will be used to verify your identity when using your iCloud Security Code. This can be your own number, or the number of someone you trust.

Cancel   Done

TIPS

Can I only use iCloud Keychain on my Mac?

No, *any* Mac or iOS device such as an iPhone or iPad that uses the same iCloud account has access to the same keychain, so your website passwords also work on those devices. On the downside, this sets up a possible security problem should you lose your iPhone or iPad. Therefore, be sure to configure your device with a passcode lock to prevent unauthorized access to your iCloud Keychain.

How do I change my security code or verification phone number?

If you want to use a different security code, or if the phone number you use for verification has changed, you should update these important security features as soon as possible. Display the iCloud preferences and then click the **Options** button beside Keychain.

Generate a Website Password

You can make it easier and faster to navigate many websites by using Safari to generate, and iCloud to store, passwords for those sites that require you to log in. Many websites require you to set up an account, which means you must log in with a username and password. Good security practices dictate using a unique and hard-to-guess password for each site, but this requires memorizing a large number of passwords. To enhance security and ease web navigation, you can use Safari to automatically generate for each site a unique and secure password stored safely with your iCloud account.

Generate a Website Password

Generate a Website Password

1 Turn on iCloud Keychain.

Note: See the previous task, "Set Up iCloud Keychain," to learn how to activate iCloud Keychain.

2 In Safari, navigate to a web page that requires a new password.

3 Click inside the password field.

Ⓐ Safari displays its suggested password.

4 Click the password.

Ⓑ iCloud enters the password. iCloud also enters the password in the confirmation field, if one exists.

5 Fill in the rest of the website form data as required.

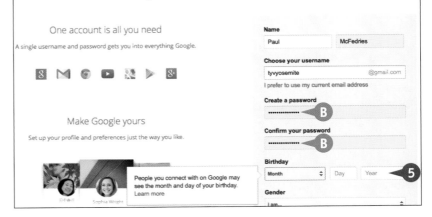

Use a Generated Website Password

1 In Safari, navigate to a web page that requires you to log in using a previously generated password.

2 Begin typing the username.

C Safari displays the full username.

3 Click **Fill password from "*website*,"** where *website* is the name of the site.

D Safari fills in the website username and password.

TIP

How do I get access to website passwords on another device?
You must activate iCloud Keychain on the other device and then authorize the other device to use the keychain. When you activate iCloud Keychain — see the previous task — iCloud gives you two ways to proceed with the authorization:

If a device that has previously been authorized to use your iCloud Keychain is available, click **Request Approval**. On the other device, click **Allow**.

If a device that has previously been authorized to use your iCloud Keychain is not available, click **Use Code**, type your four-digit iCloud security code, click **Next**, and then enter the verification code that iCloud sends via text message.

Send and Receive iCloud Mail

You can use the iCloud Mail feature to work with your iCloud email account online. Using either your Mac or any computer or device with web access, you can access iCloud using a web browser and then perform your email tasks. These include checking for incoming messages, replying to messages you receive, forwarding a received message, and composing and sending a new message. You can also configure iCloud Mail to send blind courtesy copies and to automatically send vacation messages.

Send and Receive iCloud Mail

Display iCloud Mail

1. Sign in to your iCloud account.

Note: See the task "Sign In to iCloud" earlier in this chapter.

2. If you are using another section of iCloud, click **iCloud** (not shown).

3. Click **Mail** (🖂).

Get Incoming Messages

1. Click **Get Mail** (🔄).

A. iCloud Mail checks for incoming messages, and if there are any, displays them in the Inbox folder.

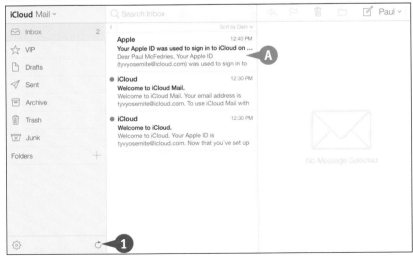

Reply to a Message

1. Click the message.

2. Click **Reply, Reply All, Forward** (⬅).

3. Click **Reply**.

4. In the message window that appears (not shown), type your message and then click **Send**.

Send a New Message

1. Click **Compose new message** (✎).

   The New Message window appears.

2. Click the To field and type the recipient's email address.

3. Click the Subject field and type the subject of the message.

4. Type your message.

5. Click **Send**.

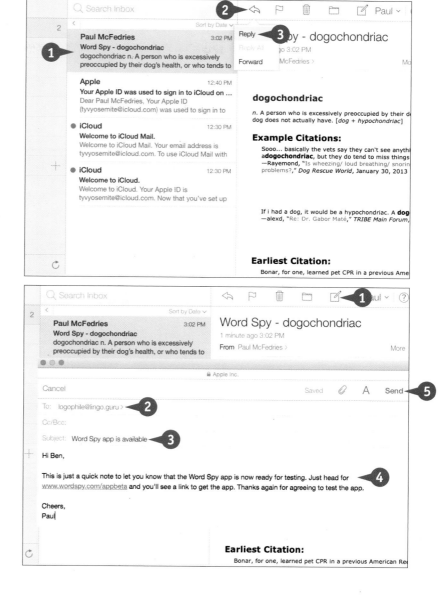

TIP

Can I use iCloud to send a message to a person without other recipients knowing?
Yes, you can send that person a blind courtesy copy (Bcc), which means that he or she receives a copy of the message, but the other message recipients do not see that person's name or address in the recipient fields. To activate this feature, open iCloud Mail, start a new message, and then click the Cc/Bcc: field.

Work with iCloud Contacts

Y ou can use iCloud to store information about your friends, family, colleagues, and clients. Using the Contacts app, you can store data such as the person's name, company name, phone numbers, email address, and street address.

The Contacts app also enables you to write notes about a contact, store extra data such as the person's job title and birthday, and assign a picture to a contact. If you already have contacts in your Mac's Contacts app, you can synchronize them with iCloud. See the task "Set Up iCloud Synchronization" earlier in this chapter.

Work with iCloud Contacts

Display iCloud Contacts

1 Click **iCloud**.

2 Click **Contacts** (▣).

Create a Contact

1 Click **Create a new contact** (⊞).

2 Click **New Contact**

3 Type the person's first name and last name.

4 Type the person's company's name.

5 Click here and then click a phone number category.

6 Type the phone number.

7 Click an email category.

8 Type the person's email address.

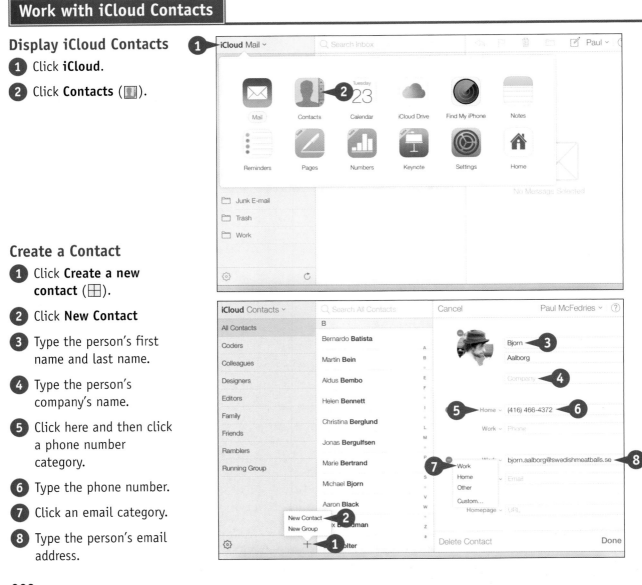

9 Click **Add new address** (not shown).

10 Click a street address category.

11 Use the text boxes in this section to type the person's street address.

12 Click **Done**.

iCloud saves the contact.

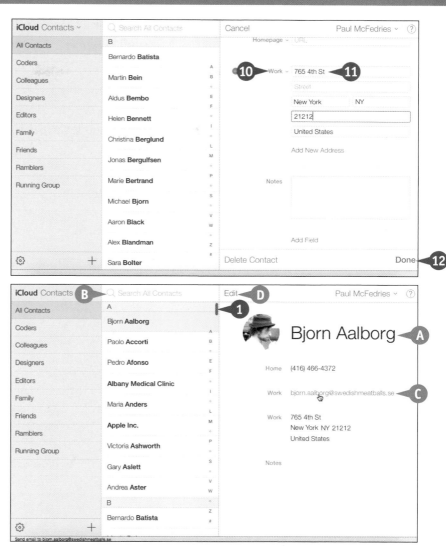

Display a Contact

1 Use the scroll bar to locate the contact.

2 Click the contact.

Ⓐ iCloud displays the contact's details.

Ⓑ You can also type part of the contact's name in the Search box.

Ⓒ To email the contact, click the address.

Ⓓ To make changes to the contact, click **Edit**.

To remove the contact, click **Edit** and then click **Delete Contact**.

TIPS

How do I add a photo for a contact?
Click the contact, click **Edit**, double-click the photo placeholder, and then drag a photo to the dialog that appears. Alternatively, click **Choose Photo**, click the photo you want to use, and then click **Choose**. Click **Done**. Note that you can use only GIF, JPEG, or PNG files that are no larger than 1MB.

Is there any way to store data such as the person's birthday or job title?
Yes. To add a field to an existing contact, click the contact and then click **Edit**. Click **Add Field**, click the field you want, and then enter the field data.

Manage Your Schedule with iCloud

You can use iCloud to manage your schedule. Using the Calendar application, you can add events (appointments and all-day activities) and reminders. For events, you can specify the date and time they occur, the event name and location, and notes related to the event.

You can also use the Calendar application to display your schedule by day, by week, or by month. If you already have events in your OS X Calendar application, you can synchronize them with iCloud. See the task "Set Up iCloud Synchronization" earlier in this chapter.

Manage Your Schedule with iCloud

Display iCloud Calendar

1. Click **iCloud**.

2. Click **Calendar** (⧉).

Navigate Calendar

1. Click **Month**.

2. Click **Next Month** (▷) or **Previous Month** (◁) to select the month you want.

3. Click the date.

Ⓐ To see just that date, click **Day**.

Ⓑ To see the date in the context of its week, click **Week**.

Ⓒ To return to today's date, click **Go to today**.

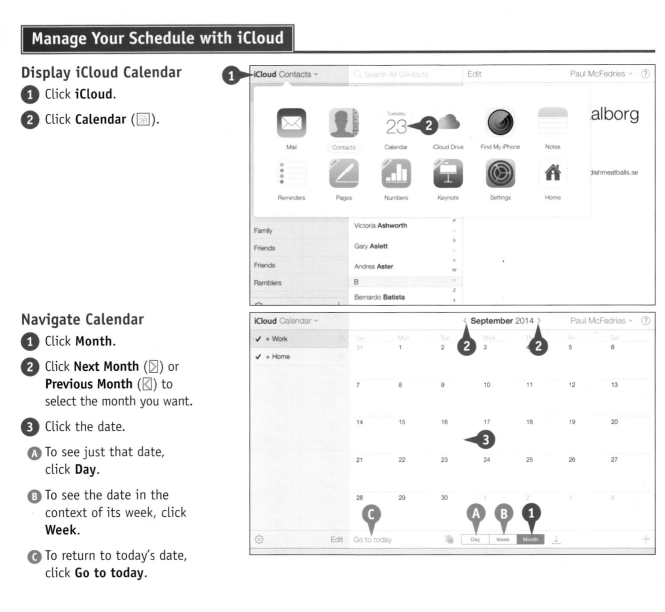

Create an Event

1 Navigate to the date when the event occurs.

2 Click the calendar you want to use.

3 Click **Week**.

4 Position the mouse ▶ at the time when the event starts.

5 Click and drag the mouse ▶ down to the time when the event ends.

Ⓓ Calendar adds the event.

6 Type the event name.

7 Type the event location.

Ⓔ If the event lasts all day, click **all-day** (☐ changes to ☑).

8 Adjust the start time, if necessary.

9 Adjust the end time, if necessary.

10 Fill in the other event details as needed.

11 Click **OK**.

Note: To edit the event, double-click it.

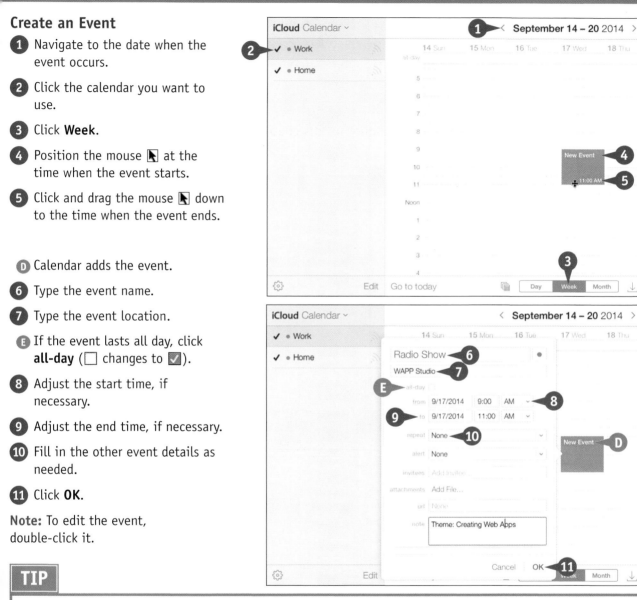

TIP

How do I create a reminder?

Click **iCloud** and then click **Reminders** (☐) to open the iCloud Reminders window. Click the list you want to use for the new reminder. Click **New Item** and then type the reminder name (Ⓐ). If you also want to add extra data such as the reminder date or notes, click **Details**, use the Details dialog to fill in the reminder details as needed, and then click **Done**.

Set Up Family Sharing

Not being able to see what other members of your family are sharing on iCloud has long been a major drawback of the service because the only way to work around it was to share an account. Now, however, iCloud offers a feature called Family Sharing, which lets up to six family members share each other's content, including photos, calendars, and reminders. And if purchases are made through the App Store, iTunes Store, or iBookstore using a single credit card, then each family member also gets access to purchased apps, songs, movies, TV shows, and e-books.

Set Up Family Sharing

Note: These steps assume you want to be the Family Sharing organizer, which means you are responsible for maintaining Family Sharing.

1 Click the **System Preferences** icon (🖥️) in the Dock (not shown).

2 Click **iCloud** (not shown).

The iCloud preferences appear.

3 Click **Set Up Family**.

The Family Sharing preferences appear.

4 Click **Continue**.

iCloud asks if you want to be the organizer.

5 Click **Continue**.

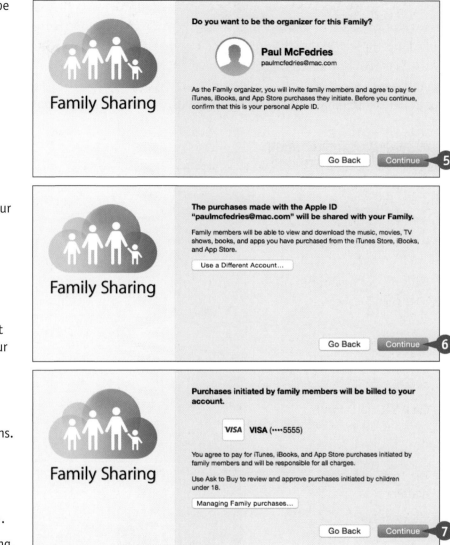

iCloud lets you know that purchases made through your account will be shared with your family.

6 Click **Continue**.

iCloud displays the payment method associated with your account.

7 Click **Continue**.

iCloud displays the Family Sharing terms and conditions.

8 Click to agree to the terms (☐ changes to ☑) (not shown).

9 Click **Continue** (not shown).

iCloud sets up Family Sharing.

TIP

How do I add family members?

When you complete the Family Sharing setup, iCloud displays the Manage Family Sharing dialog. You can also display this dialog at any time by clicking **Manage Family** in the iCloud preferences. Click **Add Family Member** (⊞), enter the person's name or email address, and then click **Continue**. Click **Ask this family member to enter the password** (☐ changes to ◉) and then type the password for that person's iCloud account. If you do not know the password, click **Send *Name* an invitation**, instead (where *Name* is the family member's name). Click **Continue**.

Locate and Lock a Lost Mac, iPod, iPhone, or iPad

You can use iCloud to locate a lost or stolen Mac, iPod touch, iPhone, or iPad. Depending on how you use your Mac, iPod touch, iPhone, or iPad, you can end up with many details of your life residing on the device. That is generally a good thing, but if you happen to lose your device, you have also lost those details, plus you have created a large privacy problem because anyone can now see your data. You can locate your device and even remotely lock the device using an iCloud feature called Find My iPhone, which also works for Macs, iPod touches, and iPads.

Locate and Lock a Lost Mac, iPod, iPhone, or iPad

1 Click **iCloud**.

2 Click **Find My iPhone** (⊙).

Note: If iCloud asks you to sign in to your account, type your password and click **Sign In**.

3 Click **All Devices**.

4 Click the device you want to locate.

Ⓐ iCloud displays the device location on a map.

5 Click **Lost Mode**.

The Lost Mode dialog appears.

6 Click a four-digit lock code.

7 Enter the lock code again to confirm (not shown).

iCloud prompts you to enter a phone number where you can be contacted.

8 Type the phone number.

9 Click **Next**.

iCloud prompts you to enter a message to display on the device.

10 Type your message.

11 Click **Done**.

iCloud locks the device and sends the message, which then appears on the device screen.

TIP

I tried to enable Find My Mac, but OS X would not allow it. How can I enable Find My Mac?
You first need to enable location services. To do this, click **System Preferences** (■) in the Dock. Click **Security & Privacy**, click the lock icon (🔒), type your OS X administrator password, and then click **OK** (🔒 changes to 🔓). Click **Privacy**, click **Location Services**, and then click **Enable Location Services** (☐ changes to ☑).

CHAPTER 15

Networking with OS X

If you have multiple computers in your home or office, you can set up these computers as a network to share information and equipment. This chapter gives an overview of networking concepts and shows you how to connect to a network, how to work with the other computers on your network, and how to share your Mac's resources with other network users.

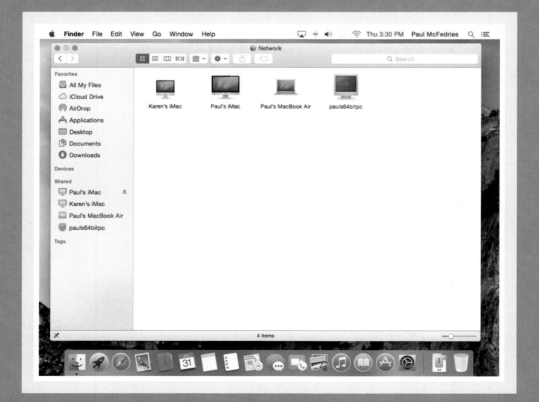

Understanding Networking

A *network* is a collection of computers and other devices that are connected. You can create a network using cable hookups, wireless hookups, or a combination of the two. In both cases, you need special networking equipment to make the connections.

A network gives you a number of advantages. For example, once you have two or more computers connected on a network, those computers can share documents, photos, and other files. You can also use a network to share equipment, such as printers and optical drives.

Shared Resources

Share Files

Networked computers are connected to each other, and so they can exchange files with each other along the connection. This enables people to share information and to collaborate on projects. OS X includes built-in security, so that you can control which files you share with other people.

Share Equipment

Computers connected over a network can share some types of equipment. For example, one computer can share its printer, which enables other network users to send their documents to that printer. Networked computers can also share hard drives, optical drives, and document scanners.

310

Network Cable

A *network cable* is a special cable designed for exchanging information. One end of the cable plugs into the Mac's network port, if it has one. The other end plugs into a network connection point, which is usually the network's router (discussed next), but it could also be a switch, hub, or even another Mac. Information, shared files, and other network data travel through the network cables.

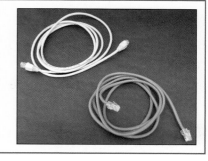

Router

A *router* is a central connection point for all the computers on the wired portion of the network. For each computer, you run a network cable from the Mac's network port to a port in the router. When network data travels from computer A to computer B, it first goes out through computer A's network port, along its network cable, and into the router. Then the router passes the data along computer B's network cable and into its network port.

Wireless Connections

A *wireless network* is a collection of two or more computers that communicate with each other using radio signals instead of cable. The most common wireless technology is Wi-Fi (rhymes with hi-fi) or 802.11. Each of the four main types (802.11ac, 802.11b, 802.11g, and 802.11n) has its own range and speed limits. The other common wireless technology is Bluetooth, which enables devices to communicate directly with each other.

Wireless Access Point

A *wireless access point* (WAP) is a device that receives and transmits signals from wireless computers to form a wireless network. Many WAPs also accept wired connections, which enables both wired and wireless computers to form a network. If your network has a broadband modem, you can connect the modem to a type of WAP called a *wireless gateway,* which includes a built-in router that extends Internet access to all the computers on the network.

Connect a Bluetooth Device

You can make wireless connections to devices such as mice, keyboards, headsets, and cell phones by using the Bluetooth networking technology. The networking tasks that you learn about in the rest of this chapter require special equipment to connect your computers and devices. However, with Bluetooth devices, the networking is built in, so no extra equipment is needed. For Bluetooth connections to work, your Mac must support Bluetooth (all newer Macs do) and your device must be Bluetooth-enabled. Also, your Mac and the Bluetooth device must remain within about 30 feet of each other.

Connect a Bluetooth Device

Connect a Bluetooth Device without a Passkey

1 Click the **System Preferences** icon (⚙) in the Dock.

2 Click **Bluetooth**.

The Bluetooth preferences appear.

3 Click **Turn Bluetooth On**.

OS X activates Bluetooth and makes your Mac discoverable.

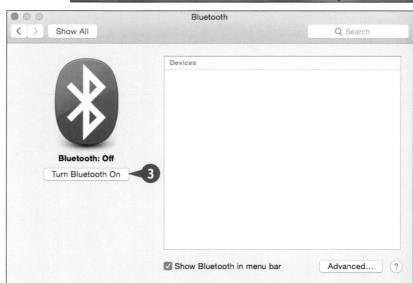

4 Perform whatever steps are necessary to make your Bluetooth device discoverable.

Note: For example, if you are connecting a Bluetooth mouse, the device often has a separate switch or button that makes the mouse discoverable, so you need to turn on that switch or press that button.

A A list of the available Bluetooth devices appears here.

5 Click **Pair** beside the Bluetooth device you want to connect.

6 Perform the steps required to pair your Mac and your device.

B Your Mac connects with the device.

TIPS

What does it mean to make a device discoverable?
This means that you configure the device to broadcast that it is available for a Bluetooth connection. Controlling the broadcast is important because you usually want to use a Bluetooth device such as a mouse or keyboard with only a single computer.

What does pairing mean?
As a security precaution, many Bluetooth devices do not connect automatically to other devices. Otherwise, a stranger with a Bluetooth device could connect to your cell phone or even your Mac. To prevent this, most Bluetooth devices require you to type a password before the connection is made. This is known as *pairing* the two devices.

continued ▶

A Bluetooth mouse and a Bluetooth headset do not require any extra pairing steps, although with a headset you must configure OS X to use it for sound output. However, pairing devices such as a Bluetooth keyboard and a Bluetooth cell phone does require an extra step. In most cases, pairing is accomplished by your Mac generating a 6- or 8-digit *passkey* that you must then type into the Bluetooth device (assuming that it has some kind of keypad). In other cases, the device comes with a default passkey that you must type into your Mac to set up the pairing.

Connect a Bluetooth Device (continued)

Connect a Bluetooth Device with a Passkey

1 Turn the device on, if required.

2 Turn on the switch that makes the device discoverable, if required.

3 Follow steps **1** and **2** from earlier in this task to display a list of available Bluetooth devices.

4 Click **Pair** beside your Bluetooth device.

The Bluetooth Setup Assistant displays a passkey.

5 Use the Bluetooth device to type the displayed passkey.

6 Press **Return**.

OS X connects to the device. If you see the Keyboard Setup Assistant, follow the on-screen instructions to set up the keyboard for use with your Mac.

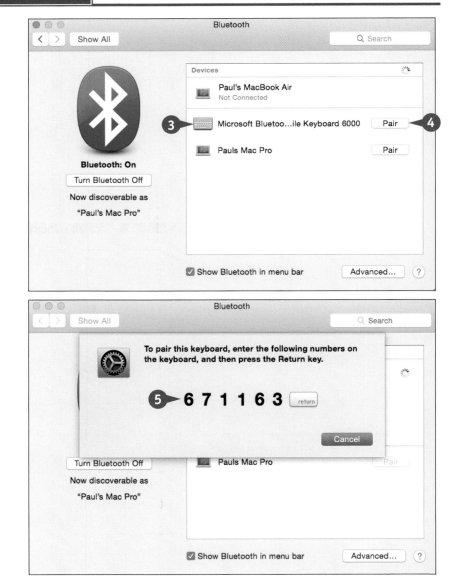

Listen to Audio Through Bluetooth Headphones

1 Click the **System Preferences** icon (⚙) in the Dock.

2 Click **Sound**.

The Sound preferences appear.

3 Click **Output**.

4 Click the Bluetooth headphones.

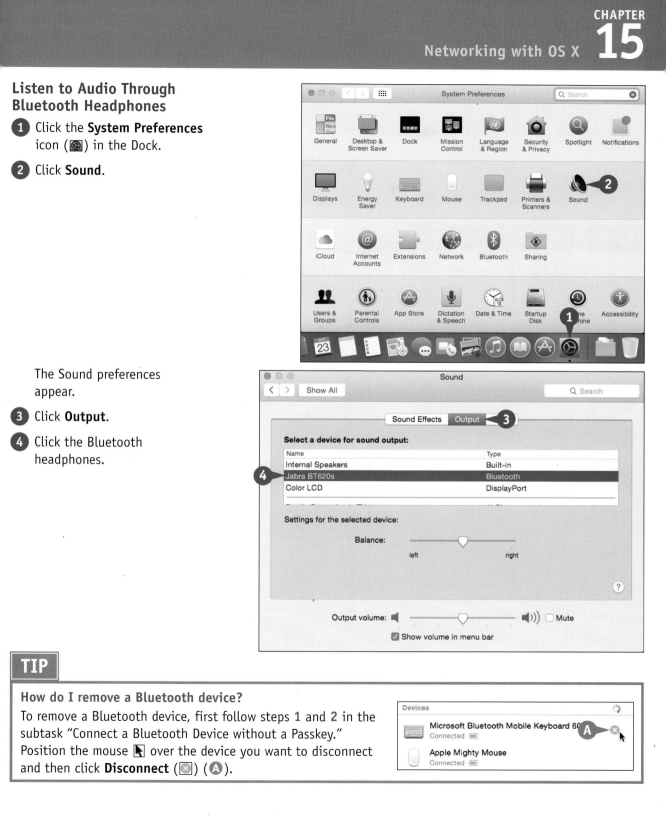

How do I remove a Bluetooth device?

To remove a Bluetooth device, first follow steps **1** and **2** in the subtask "Connect a Bluetooth Device without a Passkey." Position the mouse ▶ over the device you want to disconnect and then click **Disconnect** (⊗) (**A**).

Connect to a Wireless Network

The latest Macs have built-in wireless networking capability that you can use to connect to a wireless network within range. This could be a network in your home or a public location such as a hotel. In most cases, this also gives you access to the wireless network's Internet connection.

Most wireless networks have security turned on, which means you must know the correct password to connect to the network. However, after you connect to the network once, your Mac remembers the password and connects automatically the next time the network comes within range.

Connect to a Wireless Network

1 Click the **Wi-Fi status** icon (□) in the menu bar.

Your Mac locates the wireless networks within range of your Mac.

Ⓐ The available networks appear in the menu.

Ⓑ Networks with a lock icon (🔒) require a password to join.

2 Click the wireless network you want to join.

If the wireless network is secure, your Mac prompts you for the password.

3 Use the Password text box to type the network password.

C If the password is very long and you are sure no one can see your screen, you can click **Show password** (☐ changes to ☑) to see the actual characters instead of dots. This helps to ensure that you type the password correctly.

4 Click **Join**.

Your Mac connects to the wireless network.

D The Wi-Fi status icon changes from ☐ to 🛜 to indicate the connection.

I know a particular network is within range, but I do not see it in the list. Why not?
As a security precaution, some wireless networks do not broadcast their availability. However, you can still connect to such a network, assuming you know its name and the password. Click the **Wi-Fi status** icon (☐) and then click **Join Other Network**.

I do not see the Wi-Fi status icon on my menu bar. How do I display the icon?
Click the **System Preferences** icon (⚙) to open the System Preferences window. Click **Network**, click **Wi-Fi**, and then click **Show Wi-Fi status in menu bar** (☐ changes to ☑).

Connect to a Network Resource

To see what other network users have shared on the network, you can use the Network folder to view the other computers and then connect to them to see their shared resources. To get full access to a Mac's shared resources, you must connect with a username and password for an administrator account on that Mac. To get access to the resources that have been shared by a particular user, you must connect with that user's name and password. Note, too, that your Mac can also connect to the resources shared by Windows computers.

Connect to a Network Resource

1 Click the desktop.

2 Click **Go**.

3 Click **Network**.

Note: Another way to run the Network command is to press **Shift** + **⌘** + **K**.

The Network folder appears.

A Each icon represents a computer on your local network.

4 Double-click the computer to which you want to connect.

OS X attempts to connect to the network computer. The attempt usually either fails or OS X logs on using the Guest account.

Note: The Guest account has only limited access to the network computer.

5 Click **Connect As**.

Your Mac prompts you to connect to the network computer.

6 Click **Registered User** (☐ changes to ◉).

7 Use the Name text box to type the username of an account on the network computer.

8 Use the Password text box to type the password of the account.

9 To store the account data, click **Remember this password in my keychain** (☐ changes to ☑).

10 Click **Connect**.

Your Mac connects to the computer and shows the shared resources that you can access.

11 When you are done, click **Disconnect**.

 TIP

Is there a faster way to connect to a network computer?

Yes. In the Shared section of Finder's sidebar area, click the computer with which you want to connect (Ⓐ) and then follow steps **5** to **10** to connect as a registered user.

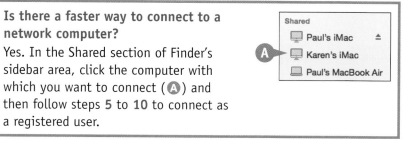

Turn On File and Printer Sharing

You can share your files with other network users. This enables those users to access your files over the network. Before you can share these resources, you must turn on your Mac's file-sharing feature. To learn how to share a particular folder, see the next task, "Share a Folder."

You can also share a printer that is connected to your Mac with other network users. This enables those users to send print jobs to your printer over the network. Before this can happen, you must turn on your Mac's printer-sharing feature; see the task "Share a Printer" later in this chapter.

Turn On File and Printer Sharing

1 Click the **Apple** icon (![Apple icon]).

2 Click **System Preferences**.

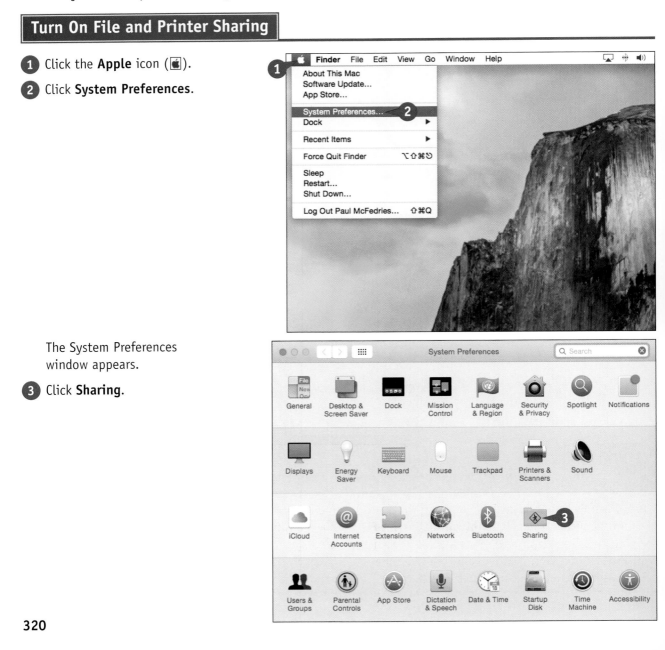

The System Preferences window appears.

3 Click **Sharing**.

The Sharing preferences appear.

4 Click **File Sharing**
(□ changes to ☑).

You can now share your folders, as described in the next task.

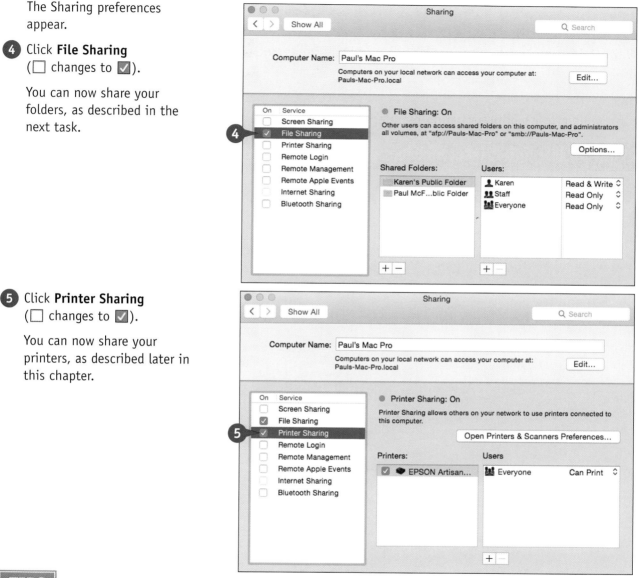

5 Click **Printer Sharing**
(□ changes to ☑).

You can now share your printers, as described later in this chapter.

TIPS

How do I look up my Mac IP address?
In System Preferences, click ◁ to return to the main window and then click **Network**. Click **Wi-Fi** if you have a wireless network connection, or click **Ethernet** if you have a wired connection. In the Status section, read the IP address value.

What is the Public folder and how do I access it?
The Public folder is a special folder for sharing files. Anyone who connects to your Mac using your username and password has full access to the Public folder. To access the folder, click the **Finder** icon (🙂), click **Go**, click **Home**, and then open the Public folder.

Share a Folder

You can share one of your folders on the network, enabling other network users to view and optionally edit the files you place in that folder. OS X automatically shares your user account's Public folder, but you can share other folders. Sharing a folder enables you to work on a file with other people without having to send them a copy of the file. OS X gives you complete control over how people access your shared folder. For example, you can allow users to make changes to the folder, or you can prevent changes.

Share a Folder

1 Open the Sharing preferences.

Note: See the previous task, "Turn On File and Printer Sharing," to learn how to display the Sharing preferences.

2 Click **File Sharing**.

Note: Be sure to click the **File Sharing** text, not the check box. This ensures that you do not accidentally uncheck the check box.

3 Under Shared Folders, click **Add** ().

An Open dialog appears.

4 Click the folder you want to share.

5 Click **Add**.

Your Mac begins sharing the folder.

Note: You can also click and drag a folder from a Finder window and drop it on the list of shared folders.

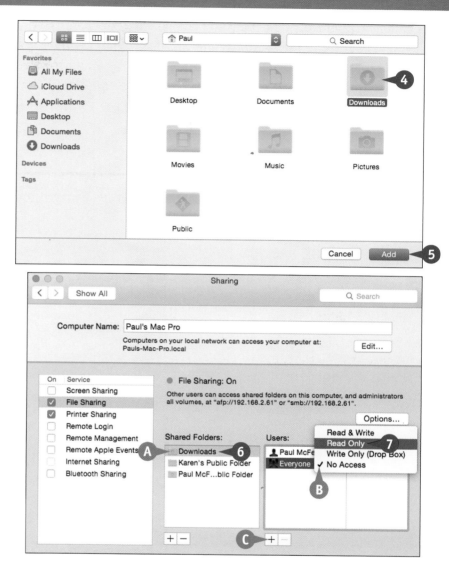

A The folder appears in the Shared Folders list.

6 Click the folder.

7 For the Everyone user, click the current permission and then click the permission you want to assign.

B The current permission is indicated with a check mark (☑).

OS X assigns the permission to the user.

C You can also click **Add** (⊞) under the Users list to add more users.

TIPS

What are the differences between the permission types?
Read & Write means users can open files, add new files, rename or delete existing files, and edit file contents. Read Only means users can only open and read files, but cannot add, delete, rename, or edit files. Write Only (Drop Box) means users can add files to the folder as a Drop Box, but cannot open the folder. No Access means users cannot see the folder.

Can I share folders with Windows users?
Yes. In the Sharing window, click **Options** and then click **Share files and folders using SMB (Windows)** (☐ changes to ☑). Click your user account (☐ changes to ☑), type your account password, click **OK**, and then click **Done**.

Share a Printer

If you have a printer connected to your Mac, you can share the printer with the network. This enables other network users to send their documents to your printer. Sharing a printer saves you money because you only have to purchase one printer for all the computers on your network. Sharing a printer also saves you time because you only have to install, configure, and maintain a single printer for everyone on your network. See the next task, "Add a Shared Printer," to learn how to configure OS X to use a shared network printer.

Share a Printer

1 Click the **Apple** icon (🍎).

2 Click **System Preferences**.

Note: You can also click the **System Preferences** icon (⚙️) in the Dock.

The System Preferences window appears.

3 Click **Sharing**.

④ Click **Printer Sharing**.

Note: Be sure to click the **Printer Sharing** text, not the check box. This ensures that you do not accidentally uncheck the check box.

⑤ Click the check box beside the printer you want to share (☐ changes to ☑).

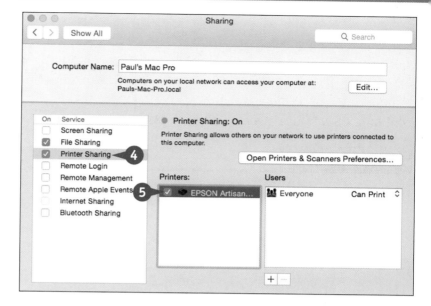

TIP

Is there another method I can use to share a printer?

Yes, you can follow these steps:

① Click the **Apple** icon (🍎).

② Click **System Preferences**.

③ Click **Printers & Scanners**.

④ Click the printer you want to share.

⑤ Click **Share this printer on the network** (☐ changes to ☑).

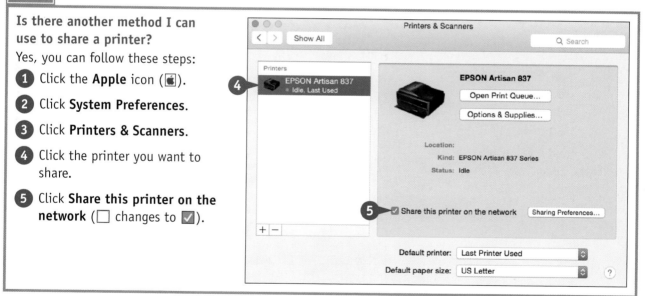

Add a Shared Printer

If another computer on your network has an attached printer that has been shared with the network, you can add that shared printer to your Mac. This enables you to send a document from your Mac to that shared printer, which means you can print your documents without having a printer attached directly to your Mac. Before you can print to a shared network printer, you must add the shared printer to OS X.

Add a Shared Printer

1 Click the **System Preferences** icon (⚙) in the Dock.

The System Preferences window appears.

2 Click **Printers & Scanners**.

3 Click **Add** (⊞).

Note: If OS X displays a list of nearby printers, click the printer you want to add and skip the rest of these steps.

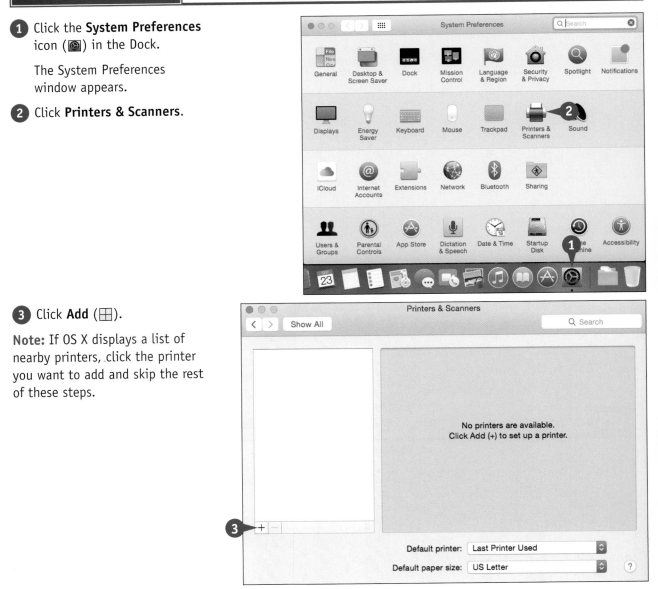

④ Click **Default**.

⑤ Click the shared printer.

Ⓐ Look for the word *Shared* in the printer description.

⑥ Click **Add**.

Note: If OS X alerts you that it must install software for the printer, click **Download & Install**.

Ⓑ OS X adds the printer.

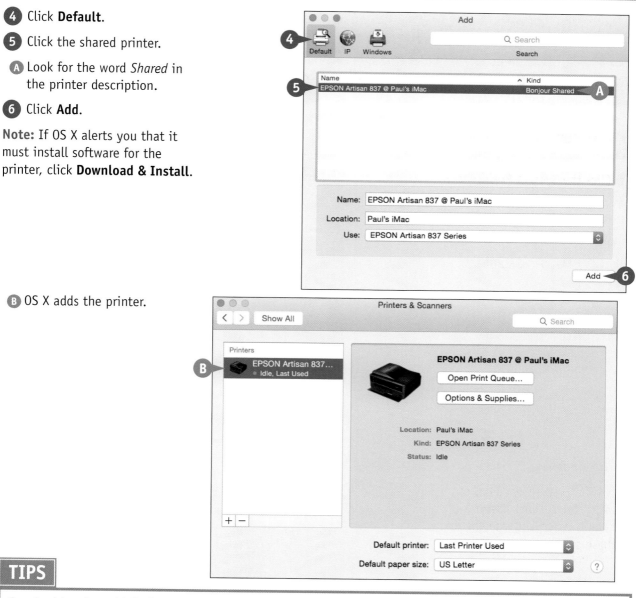

TIPS

Can I add a shared Windows printer?
Yes. Follow steps **1** to **3** and then click the **Windows** tab. Click the Windows workgroup, click the computer with the shared printer, log on to the Windows computer, and then click the shared printer you want to use. In the Print Using list, click **Add** (⊞), click **Other**, and then click the printer in the list that appears. Click **Add**.

How do I print to the shared network printer that I added?
In any application that supports printing, click **File** and then click **Print**. In the Print dialog, use the **Printer** ◳ to click **Add** (⊞) and then click the shared printer. Choose any other printing options you require and then click **Print**.

View OS X on Your TV

I f you have an Apple TV, you can use it to view your OS X screen on your TV. If you want to demonstrate something on your Mac to a group of people, it is difficult because most Mac screens are too small to see from a distance. However, if you have a TV or a projector nearby and you have an Apple TV device connected to that display, you can connect your Mac to the same wireless network and then send the OS X screen to the TV or projector. This is called AirPlay mirroring.

View OS X on Your TV

Mirror via System Preferences

1 Click the **System Preferences** icon ( ) in the Dock.

The System Preferences window appears.

2 Click **Displays**.

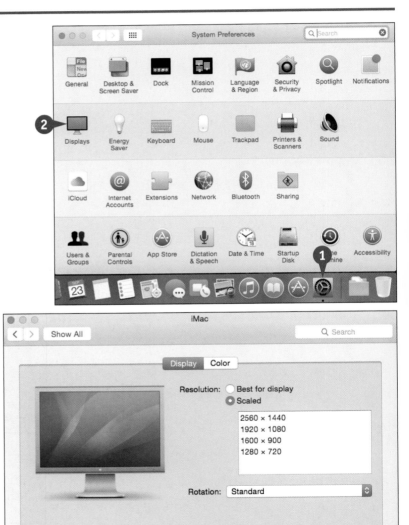

The display preferences appear.

3 Click the **AirPlay Display** and then click your Apple TV.

OS X displays your Mac's screen on your TV.

Mirror via the Menu Bar

1 Follow steps **1** and **2** to open the display preferences.

2 Click **Show mirroring options in the menu bar when available** (☐ changes to ☑).

Ⓐ OS X adds the AirPlay Mirroring icon (🔲) to the menu bar.

3 Click the **AirPlay Mirroring** icon (🔲).

4 Click your Apple TV.

OS X displays your Mac's screen on your TV (🔲 changes to 🔲).

TIPS

Is there an easy way to make my Mac's screen fit my TV screen?

Yes. If you have a high-resolution TV, the OS X screen might look a bit small on the TV. Click the **AirPlay Mirroring On** icon (🔲), and then in the Match Desktop Size To section of the AirPlay Mirroring menu, click your Apple TV.

Can I use my TV as a second monitor for the OS X desktop?

Yes. This is useful if you need extra screen real estate to display the OS X desktop and applications. Click the **AirPlay Mirroring On** icon (🔲), and then in the Use AirPlay Display To section of the AirPlay Mirroring menu, click **Extend Desktop**.

Index

Index

Index